Readers in Wonderland

The Liberating Worlds of Fantasy Fiction

From Dorothy to Harry Potter

DEBORAH O'KEEFE

continuum

NEW YORK • LONDON

2004

The Continuum International Publishing Group Inc
15 East 26 Street, New York, NY 10010

The Continuum International Publishing Group Ltd
The Tower Building, 11 York Road, London SE1 7NX

Printed in the United States of America

Library of Congress Cataloging in Publication Data

O'Keefe, Deborah.
    Readers in wonderland: the liberating worlds of fantasy fiction / Deborah O'Keefe.
        p.   cm.
    Includes bibliographical references (p.   ) and an index.
    ISBN 0-8264-1649-9 (hardcover : alk. paper)
    ISBN 0-8264-1649-7 (paperback : alk. paper)
        1. Fantasy fiction—History and criticism.   2. Fiction—20th century—History and criticism.   I. Title.
    PN3435.O39   2003
    809.3'766—dc21   2002154247

For Dan, who cheered and helped;
for my sons, Danny, Larry, and Mark;
and for my new daughters, Nell and Tina

He inquired, "Is everyone ready?
The night is uncommonly cold.
We'll start on our journey as children,
But I fear we will finish it old."

—Nancy Willard
A Visit to William Blake's Inn

CONTENTS

Preface

Children's fantasy fiction is a vast and growing field. Because there have been so many good fantasy books published in the last century, some well known and some not, I have chosen to consider a large number (more than eighty authors), rather than analyze a few books in detail. Even so, I have had to leave out dozens of wonderful books; and I have been unable to consider at all the subgenres of science fiction, horror stories, historical fantasies, and retellings of older tales. My purpose is twofold: to introduce specific admirable books—with glimpses of plot, character, texture, and theme—and to discuss ideas about individual books, types of books, and the whole field of fantasy literature. These ideas include some personal opinions stated without the backing of a lengthy analysis, but the principles on which such opinions are based should become clear. Occasionally, my own experiences are described here, to illustrate some point about the books. This is neither a memoir nor a reference book, however; it is an appreciation of the power and delight that lie in children's fantasy fiction.

I am particularly interested in what happens to readers of fantasy stories, both young and old—what they may learn, why and how they may respond. Such reading does not (or should not) preach or socialize or "improve" its audience. Yet fantasy can expand the mind and the heart, suggesting unusual choices and perspectives. Fantasy does not provide comfortable answers and solve problems. It poses questions, nudging readers toward a new openness. It is moral but not moralizing.

One technical matter should be explained. The many passages quoted from children's books appear in SMALL-CAPITAL LETTERS, to set them off clearly from the rest of my text and to suggest something of the distinct flavor of childhood reading. When I quote from other kinds of works, about children's literature or other subjects, I use a conventional format.

Many people have told me their thoughts about children's fantasy fiction: what they read in the past, what they are reading now, what they care about, and why. I am grateful for these stimulating conversations. Thanks are due to those I talked to in bookstores and libraries, especially the helpful children's room staff of the Chappaqua, New York, Library. Thanks also to good friends Marion Perret, Sherry Chappelle, and Penny Stillinger, and good editors Justus George Lawler and Evander Lomke. Most of all, I am grateful to these remarkable fantasy authors for giving me their worlds to explore.

Introduction: How to Make Sense of a World

When I was eight years old, I learned that you can fly by holding onto a balloon and that, in the right circumstances, you can have tea and cakes at a table floating in midair above the parlor carpet. These were good things to know: other books, more earthbound, were telling me instead that you can win approval by giving away your breakfast to the poor and that you can become popular if you brush your hair a lot. Realistic books (whose settings resemble worlds that did or might actually exist) engage the reader on a more literal level than fantasy: I didn't really think that I could fly with a balloon, but I did really think that brushing my hair would make me popular.

Many people consider fantasy an escape, which takes them for a while out of their dreary, frightening lives to a pleasant, impossible world like the one Mary Poppins lived in—the delight being in the unreality. This is only one piece of the truth. Reading fantasy is not so much an escape *from* something as a liberation *into* something, into openness and possibility and coherence. All fiction blatantly or subtly conveys its author's values, but with fantasy everything is hypothetical, subject to examination. Readers get perspective on their own worlds by exploring a strange fictional place and by learning how its pieces fit together. The world of fantasy fiction doesn't pretend to be a real reality, so it doesn't arouse the same expectations as most other fiction; it doesn't seem to insist that readers should behave in a certain way. The fantasy world is just there, to understand, to love—to enter.

THE STREETS WERE LINED WITH BEAUTIFUL HOUSES ALL BUILT OF GREEN MARBLE AND STUDDED EVERYWHERE WITH SPARKLING EMERALDS. EVEN THE SKY ABOVE THE CITY HAD A GREEN TINT. GREEN CANDY AND GREEN POP-CORN WERE OFFERED FOR SALE, AS WELL AS GREEN SHOES, GREEN HATS AND GREEN CLOTHES OF ALL SORTS. . . .

IN A HOLE IN THE GROUND THERE LIVED A HOBBIT. NOT A NASTY, DIRTY, WET HOLE, FILLED WITH THE ENDS OF WORMS AND AN OOZY SMELL, NOR YET A DRY, BARE, SANDY HOLE WITH NOTHING IN IT: IT WAS A HOBBIT-HOLE, AND THAT MEANS COMFORT. IT HAD A PERFECTLY ROUND DOOR LIKE A PORTHOLE, PAINTED GREEN, WITH A SHINY YELLOW BRASS KNOB IN THE EXACT MIDDLE. . . .

THE PATH HAD OPENED SUDDENLY ONTO THE EDGE OF A GREAT BLACK LAKE. PERCHED ATOP A HIGH MOUNTAIN, ITS WINDOWS SPARKLING IN THE STARRY SKY, WAS A VAST CASTLE WITH MANY TURRETS AND TOWERS. THE LITTLE BOATS MOVED OFF ALL AT ONCE, GLIDING ACROSS THE LAKE. "HEADS DOWN!" YELLED HAGRID AS THE FIRST BOATS REACHED THE CLIFF; THEY ALL BENT THEIR HEADS AND THE LITTLE BOATS CARRIED THEM THROUGH A CURTAIN OF IVY THAT HID A WIDE OPENING IN THE CLIFF FACE. . . .

Why, just now, do so many readers find it thrilling to follow Dorothy into the Emerald City of Oz (1900), Bilbo Baggins into his hobbit hole (1937), and Harry Potter into the Hogwarts School of Witchcraft and Wizardry (1997)? Today, fantasy is an enormously popular category, not a neglected stepgenre shivering in the shadows. The third edition of Ruth Lynn's *Fantasy Literature for Children and Young Adults*, which appeared in 1989, listed 3,300 books published in the United States since 1900. In 1995, the fourth edition covered 4,800 books, an increase of 45 percent in only six years. The Research Guide section mentions about 10,500 articles and books on children's fantasy, an increase of 60 percent over the third edition's listings. When the 1995 edition came out, Harry Potter did not yet exist. According to an article in the *New York Times* from November 19, 2001, a national survey reported that more than 60 percent of Americans between the ages of six and seventeen, had read at least one Harry Potter book, and 14 percent of all adults.

From Alice to Harry

It's not just that both adults and children are reading fantasy; in many cases, they are reading the very same books. The genres of adults' and children's fantasy are collapsing together: both are now reading Harry Potter and Philip Pullman, just as both have been reading J. R. R. Tolkien and C. S. Lewis for the past fifty years. We are circling back to the early custom whereby readers of all ages read the same narratives. In England in 1744, the publisher John Newbery created the first storybook explicitly for children, *A Little Pretty Pocket Book*. Before that, literate children read the same popular works as anyone—John Bunyan's *A Pilgrim's Progress* (1678) and Daniel Defoe's *Robinson Crusoe* (1719), Jonathan Swift's *Gulliver's Travels* (1726), and later, the historical adventures by Sir Walter Scott. Children also read the little chapbooks snapped up by the less privileged classes: folk tales and sensational lives of criminals.

Gradually, as the seventeenth and eighteenth centuries rejected the medieval view that children were merely small adults, a concept of distinct childhood evolved (discussed by Philippe Ariès in *Centuries of Childhood*, 1962). Children became innocent and frail and had to be protected; storybooks blossomed just for them—to improve minds, souls, and manners. The nineteenth century's morbid moral tales, saccharine family stories, and gentle fantasies were intended only for children and couldn't have appealed to any but the most sentimental adults. *(Alice's Adventures in Wonderland* was a rare exception.) Well into the twentieth century there was still many a jolly bunny and Little-Prudy-and-her-playmates sort of story, which no self-respecting child today would look at for a minute without making a scornful or obscene remark.

In the last half of the twentieth century, children came to have more uncertainty, more choices, more contact with clashing social groups; more confusing, buzzing information; and more jarring, violent, sexual images in their heads, than ever before. In many ways adults became more childish and children more like adults. As it became clear that children's experience was less constricted than formerly, that they could not be totally protected and controlled, the range of young people's books broadened. Instead of "progressing," as most children did fifty years ago, in a predictable leap from stories for middle-level children to adult romances and adventures, readers now encounter infinite gradations and can make freer individual choices. A ten-year-old in 1950 might read *Anne of Green Gables* and a few years later *Gone with the Wind*, or *Lassie Come-Home* followed later by *The Grapes of Wrath*. In 2000, there are more books not neatly classifiable for a specific age or gender. These days categories blur, subject matter is more inclusive, and narrative voices are less euphemistic and less condescending.

There are innumerable kinds of fantasy books available today, some sleazy or formulaic, but many inventive and insightful. With such great variety, generalizing is impossible, but one hypothesis seems irresistible. In nineteenth-century England and the United States, life for the middle and upper classes was in many ways simpler and more predictable than it is now, and the fantasy books written in that comparatively closed world were comparatively open. This openness revealed to readers exhilarating new perspectives. Works like *Alice* and Charles Kingsley's *Water Babies* and E. Nesbit's *The Phoenix and the Carpet* created loosely organized worlds where characters wandered through episodic adventures.

In contrast, as the second half of the twentieth century moved on, life became wildly open, unmanageable, unfathomable. Even the most sheltered children could not be protected from the tangles of the modern world. As fast travel and communication made the world accessible, for the individual it became larger in choices and images—and the fantasy books in this comparatively open world became, in important respects, comparatively closed. It's not that they are simple or tidy, but that the structures of many books now are tighter than those of the nineteenth-century fantasies. Each of those series—by Tolkien and others—that are set in a huge, challenging universe, develops a shape that is clear in spite of and because of its many parts. The task is specific; the characters come to understand the challenges they face and the rules they must follow; and the endings have a kind of closure. Nineteenth-century fantasy readers learned that the world could be broader and deeper than they thought. Fantasy readers today learn that the world can be more coherent than they thought (though perhaps just as hard to control as they expected). From the huge cosmos of Philip Pullman's *His Dark Materials* series, containing multiple parallel worlds, to the beautifully wrought small worlds of Philippa Pearce's *Tom's Midnight Garden* and Natalie Babbitt's *Tuck Everlasting*, fantasy today helps and delights readers not just by strengthening their poor small selves but by offering possible structures for the unstructurable stuff outside the self.

❧ ❧

So nonsegregated childhood has come round again; children are no longer delicate plants to be protected from rough winds but energetic, potentially unruly people who think they know everything—while not understanding much of what they know—and want to be able to do everything. "Realistic" books are particularly affected by such changes, since fantasy has always tended toward wilder, freer techniques and subjects; and it seems that the current state of realistic fiction has contributed to the increasing popularity of fantasy. In recent decades realistic fiction for young people has split into two levels: (1) reassuring, lightweight stories (often in feeble series) about simple family-and-friends problems in safe, stable communities; and (2) serious, dark stories (some of them quite wonderful) about all types of outsiders and about horrible situations of abuse, disease, death, war, crime, and madness. Both categories have attackers and defenders, some for good and some for bad reasons.

With important exceptions, realistic books became either super-ficial or unbearable. Robert Cormier, by all accounts a kind and thoughtful man, gave children powerfully written books such as *After the First Death* (1979), in which a nice young woman schoolbus driver trying to protect her tiny charges from terrorist hijackers is killed along with two children, slowly and in excruci-ating detail. It seems likely that the recent devotion to fantasy arises from a need to work through serious issues in truthful yet imaginative ways, without the superficiality of the everything's-fine sort of realistic book, and without the pull toward despair that can come from a meticulous, realistic examination of today's vast and clotted complexities. Simpler fantasy books and more chal-lenging ones can encourage readers on different levels to think more freely than usual about questions that connect to their daily experience but penetrate way beyond it and offer new perspectives on it.

When I first entered into the Internet, I naively expected that all the available information would be organized in a nice taxonomy, like what I learned in biology long ago or like the Dewey decimal system. Every fact would be logically related to everything else in a systematic hierarchy. But it's not like that: it's a huge, writhing mess—everything out there capable of being brought in here, to my small rectangular screen, in complete disorder. There's too much to take in today. The rules are too hard to discover and keep shifting; the consequences and dangers are too uncertain. But a reader who battles Voldemort with Harry Potter, fights nuclear poison with Ann in Robert O'Brien's *Z for Zachariah*, or barely survives with the Baudelaire children in Lemony Snicket's stories called *A Series of Unfortunate Events* can watch the formless take form, and even in the saddest stories may experience comfort, comprehension, and happiness. A devoted reader of fantasy books lives in a state of wild surmise.

What Fantasy Fiction Does to Us

Besides "escape reading," fantasy fans talk about wish fulfillment and identifying with brave, resourceful characters. Everyone dreams of solving the mystery, winning the prize, and capturing the villains. And every reader can become Dorothy of Oz, who saved herself in a storm at sea by climbing onto a floating chicken coop: DOROTHY FELT A SORT OF JOYOUS EXCITEMENT IN DEFYING THE STORM. "WHY, I'VE GOT A SHIP OF MY OWN!" SHE THOUGHT, MORE AMUSED THAN FRIGHTENED. Every reader can fight monsters with Harry Potter: HARRY WAS ON HIS FEET, READY. HE COULD SEE THE VAST, BLOODY EYE SOCKETS, SEE THE MOUTH STRETCHING WIDE, LINED WITH FANGS LONG AS HIS SWORD, GLITTERING, VENOMOUS. IT LUNGED BLIND-LY. HE RAISED THE SWORD IN BOTH HIS HANDS.

Every reader can share the solemn joy of Frodo and Sam, re-turning from their hideous ordeal in *The Lord of the Rings*: THEY WERE SURPRISED TO SEE KNIGHTS IN BRIGHT MAIL, WHO GREETED THEM WITH HONOUR AND BOWED BEFORE THEM. AND THEY WENT ON THROUGH THE AISLE OF TREES. ON THE FIELD A GREAT HOST WAS DRAWN UP, GLITTERING IN THE SUN. SWORDS WERE UNSHEATHED, AND HORNS AND TRUMPETS SANG, AND MEN CRIED IN MANY TONGUES, "LONG LIVE THE HALFLINGS! PRAISE THEM WITH GREAT PRAISE!" Readers respond intensely to this "great praise," which they have always longed for and feel they deserve, especially after the horrible experiences they have undergone with Frodo and Sam.

Some nervous adults worry that fantasy books may be un-healthy: Does this reading encourage children to hide from reality? Does it make them less able to solve problems? C. S. Lewis elo-quently answers this view of fantasy, in his classic essay "On Three Ways of Writing for Children" (1952):

> No literature that children could read gives them less of a false im-pression. What profess to be realistic stories for children are far more likely to deceive them. I never expected the real world to be like the fairy tales. The fantasies did not deceive me: the school sto-ries did. The dangerous fantasy is always superficially realistic. The real victim of wishful reverie does not batten on *The Tempest* or *The Worm Ouroboros*: he (or she) prefers stories about million-aires. (pp. 214–15)

Wish fulfillment, like escapism, is only a minor part of fantasy's appeal, the part that makes people love Superman.

❧ ❧

The most widely known work on the function of fantasy is Bruno Bettelheim's *The Uses of Enchantment* (1976). Bettelheim's psychoanalytical theory, which is influential though controversial, argues that reading traditional fairy tales will help children greatly in their psychological growth. The tales relieve unconscious pressures and foster a healthy ego; they show the child how to cope with contradictory feelings and make difficult choices. Certainly, as Bettelheim claims, imaginative reading contributes richly to the personal growth of a wise, integrated individual, but the main appeal of fantasy reading lies elsewhere. The Oz and Harry Potter books are not loved merely because they teach how to deal with good and bad mothers, sub- and superhuman helpers, personal wishes and fears inside the self, but because they show how to deal with weird and complicated worlds *outside.*

Readers of fantasy, both adults and children, are not so much vicarious participants as fascinated spectators. Reading these stories is a practice and example of making sense of a world—discovering interrelations of individual, community, and cosmos; past, present, and future; feeling, thought, and action; the human, the natural, and the supernatural. It's the fact that there *is* a totality, a pattern, a network of connections in a fictional world, that provides the satisfaction. Even when the total world presented is a grim one, its fullness is a revelation and a comfort. It suggests to readers that they too can find sense and pattern in a confusing world. Fantasy books don't just help readers to develop a self; they help them respond to all that is the non-self.

In an article on "Children and Fairy Stories" (1969), J. R. R. Tolkien explains that a writer of fantasy is the "subcreator" of a Secondary World, "which your mind can enter. Inside it, what he relates is 'true': it accords with the laws of that world. You therefore believe it, while you are, as it were, inside"(p. 114). You come to understand the geography and science of the Secondary World, its laws, customs, and social relations. A fantasy world usually includes things that are impossible in the real world, but it cannot proceed frivolously. It must follow its own rules consistently once they are established.

Consider the design of one of the simpler fantasy universes. *The Wonderful Wizard of Oz* is a loosely structured book, but its characters wander in a highly organized, geometrical world. The Emerald City lies at the center, surrounded by countries of blue-clothed Munchkins in the East, yellow Winkies in the West, red Quadlings in the South, and purple Gillikins in the North, all surrounded by an impassable desert that separates Oz from nonfairyland places like Kansas. Each of the four countries has its reigning witch—good witches in the North and South, wicked in the East and West. In Oz there is a delightful contrast between orderly landscape and disorderly adventures: however weird and threatening are the things that happen to Dorothy and her friends, it is clear that, in such a well laid out world, everything will come out all right.

Most readers do not remember for long the details of Peter Pan's adventures or Mary Poppins's excursions with the children, but they remember the texture of those worlds, the feel of how they work (the underground safety of Peter's den, for instance, and the network of mysterious grown-ups Jane and Michael meet in their London excursions with Mary Poppins). They forget the names of the characters in Mary Norton's *The Borrowers* but do not forget the spatial and psychological perspective, what it is like to be a tiny person living in the walls of a house.

Psychologists Jerome and Dorothy Singer recognize the value of "secondary worlds." In *The House of Make-Believe* (1990) they claim that children's make-believe play—sometimes including the creation of imaginary worlds called "paracosms"—is a crucial part of cognitive and emotional growth. And Jerome Bruner (in *Actual Minds, Possible Worlds*, 1986) distinguishes two equally important modes of human thought: logico-scientific and narrative. He argues that Jean Piaget and his followers are wrong in focusing on the child's rational, logical development and slighting the lifelong importance of narrative thought, emotion, and imagination. Piaget believes that the young child benefits somewhat from fantasy play, then outgrows it and moves on to rational activities, which are the highest goal. Bruner argues that for a child learning to deal with the world outside the self, emotional growth is as important as intellectual; becoming a rational being is not enough. Stories, particularly fantasy stories, teach people how to "subjunctivize"—how to go beyond their personal selves and the actualities of their everyday reality, and explore all kinds of human possibilities.

A child just recently introduced to a real world beyond the self finds it exciting and comforting to enter a variety of fictional worlds and figure out how they are put together. But why do so many adults also enjoy such fantasy excursions? Grown-up readers of children's fantasy have been accused of escapism, regression to an immature state. Yet an adult may be drawn to fantasy fiction because it offers not a simplified alternative to the complex ordinary world, but an equally complex, difficult, alternative world, dense with patterns to discover and solutions to work out and meanings to find.

While some fantasy fiction is interesting only to child readers and some only to adults, a huge middle ground of books attracts readers of many different ages. They can experience these worlds differently but with equal enjoyment and insight. The journey of a fifty-year-old reading *Alice's Adventures in Wonderland* or Ursula K. Le Guin's *A Wizard of Earthsea* is different from that of a ten-year-old. It can't be said that one experience is better, or truer to the book, than the other. Adults could stick to their own kinds of fantasy—despairing dystopias, technically inclined science fiction, magic realism, erotic tales with supernatural elements, horror, and so on—but many do not. Children's fantasy books can be more brilliant, less turgid and dreary, than many adult fantasy books. Perhaps good children's fantasy is irresistible because it has clarity, directness, and shapeliness; also, in many cases, very fine writing. (What it does not provide is "childish" sweetness.) Anyway, the line often blurs. Some writers, such as Ray Bradbury and Le Guin, are equally at home on younger and older shelves. Lois Lowry's *The Giver* for young readers has echoes of *1984*; Virginia Hamilton's *Justice* series is a cousin of Arthur Clarke's *Childhood's End*.

According to the philosopher Susanne Langer, symbolization is one of the basic, universal human needs; it means the expression of ideas, perhaps in talk or laughter, more elaborately in ritual, science, and art. Humankind is a form-seeking animal. Langer writes, "We unconsciously abstract a form from each sensory experience, and use this form to conceive the experience as a whole, as a 'thing'" (*Philosophy in a New Key*, 1942, p. 72); and "Art penetrates deep into personal life because in giving form to the world, it articulates human nature: sensibility, energy, passion, and mortality" (*Feeling and Form*, 1953, p. 401). A work of fiction provides a virtual world to experience, a vivid illusion of life felt and lived. Fantasy fiction, with its worlds so different from the familiar one yet so connected to familiar wishes and fears, can offer the strongest kind of illusion. People do not outgrow this need to illuminate ordinary life by visiting extraordinary universes.

A book published in 1990, subtitled "The Psychology of Optimal Experience," explains the usefulness of fantasy fiction from a different point of view. The book's misleading main title, *Flow*, sounds as if it could be promoting a state of undisciplined, free-floating, vague contentment. But Mihaly Csikszentmihalyi's purpose is quite the reverse. He explains that the richest human life involves activities of a certain structured kind that help individuals control their attention and energy, challenge their abilities, and develop their understanding and enjoyment. Such activities—puzzles and sports and games, intellectual pursuits, crafts and, certainly, arts—are pursued for their own sake rather than extrinsic rewards. They have goals, rules, structures that stretch body or mind; they require skill, concentration, and energy. Someone in this state, engaging in these activities, is strengthening the self; but at such moments, awareness of the self is diminished, and connection with what is outside the self is heightened.

Csikszentmihalyi discusses all manner of human activities: the mental games that keep an isolated prisoner from going mad, the precise moves that get a rock climber to the top, the deliberations of a mathematician. Certainly the experience of fantasy fiction is one such activity of "flow": readers find challenge and delight in discovering patterns and rules and meanings in an unfamiliar world; they lose their finite selves momentarily in the reading, and emerge with selves expanded and strengthened. All good literature does this, not just fantasy, but the strangeness of fantasy fiction increases the challenge and the fun. If character and reader face a large task in figuring out the shape and logic of the world in any fantasy story, think how enormous is the task when the character is a child, just beginning to understand the real world. It is the extreme instance of a self coming to terms with the universe of the non-self. Older, jaded readers as well as young readers can have their own journeys clarified by these stories.

Setting Forth

The most useful definition of children's fantasy is simple and untheoretical: fantasy books in which the main characters are children rather than adults. It's impossible to discuss all of fantasy literature, and good fantasy for adults is mostly the same as good fantasy for children. This book will examine only books with young characters at the center. Obviously, children read many books with adult characters (Arthur C. Clarke's, Edgar Rice Burroughs's, and others'), but there is no space to include those. (It could be said that the young hobbits are adults and thus should be excluded, but at least they're short.) Since children's and adults' fantasy spreads across a broad continuum, without sharp distinctions, there is no need to propose a rigid definition of the two.

What is fantasy, anyway? It's easy to recognize, hard to define strictly. Basically, fantasy is a type of fiction containing something impossible, contrary to the laws of nature as we know them. All fiction is, in a sense, fantasy, being stories removed from the level of everyday reality; the category of fantasy is a matter of degree. So-called realistic fiction pretends to mirror everyday reality precisely (though its picture is necessarily distorted), while fantasy flaunts its deviations from reality. For the sake of particular themes and effects, fantasy writers create the unbelievable, twist the taken-for-granted, and turn things inside out. They do this also for the sake of the game—the kind of serious, complicated, structured play activity discussed by Csikszentmihalyi in *Flow*.

Science fiction, by definition, is a subcategory within fantasy, since it is one type of fiction that includes the impossible. A science fiction book tries to make somewhat plausible its deviations from reality, by extrapolating in some way from science as it is currently known. Some scholars, liking symmetry, say that science fiction deals with the future while fantasy deals with the past. More precisely, science fiction may indeed deal with the future but fantasy, the more general category, has things to say about past, present, and future; different works point in different directions. It is true that many fantasy writers are enamored of the past and create worlds that echo or engage with the past. But not all.

The scope of this book cannot include science fiction; nor will it include horror fiction, though that is another legitimate subgenre within the category of fantasy. The horror genre appeals to a different human impulse than do fantasy books concerned with imaginary worlds (worlds seen directly or through visitors to our "real" world)—it appeals to a cruder, elemental need to stare into the abyss of our worst terrors and our violent desires. A complete review of fantasy fiction would also include historical fantasy, where a character moves from a contemporary world back into a historical era. Once that fantasy introduction is accomplished, it is simply a typical historical novel, with perhaps a concluding return to the present.

One delightful sort of fantasy—stories about animals and toys—will be treated briefly, only because these have been written and talked about extensively. The Beatrix Potter books and *Winnie-the-Pooh* and *The Wind in the Willows* and *Babar* and *Charlotte's Web* are well known and much loved. Other popular animal and toy books will be omitted for lack of space, such as Rumer Godden's Doll books, the Paddington books, the Freddy the Pig books, *The Rescuers*, *The Cricket in Times Square*, and Brian Jacques's immensely popular *Redwall* series. But many of the things said about fantasy worlds that are populated largely by humans or their counterparts can apply equally to those animal and toy fantasy worlds. Grand epic worlds where good struggles with evil appear not only in "human" books like C. S. Lewis's and Tolkien's, but also in animal books such as Richard Adams's *Watership Down*, Russell Hoban's *The Mouse and His Child*, and William Harwood's *Duncton Wood* series, six enormous, riveting books about the heroic adventures of a bunch of theologically inclined British moles. In *Readers in Wonderland*, sadly, moles and bears and rabbits must go, even the most charming or noble, to make room for humans, superhumans, subhumans, and alien quasi-humans.

❧❧ ❧❧

What *will* be considered here? Mostly fantasy books published since 1950, along with a few notable older ones. Small picture books like William Steig's *Sylvester and the Magic Pebble* and cheerful stories like Joan Aiken's *Black Hearts in Battersea*; books of magic like E. Nesbit's *The Phoenix and the Carpet* and children's series like Lloyd Alexander's Prydain books; serious tales like Lois Lowry's *The Giver* and heroic epic series like William Nicholson's *Wind on Fire* trilogy—the best fantasy fiction of each category. While a large number of books will be discussed, it would require several volumes to cover all the good ones. There's a great deal of excellent children's fantasy out there; readers need not be discouraged by bookstore shelves cluttered with the forgettable kind.

These children's fantasy books can be distinguished by the worlds they inhabit. How large or small is the particular world of a book? How seriously threatening are the challenges faced by the characters? How light or dark or ironic or funny is the tone of the story? These chapters will examine six increasingly complex categories of fantasy worlds. The most densely elaborated books are not necessarily "better" (Beatrix Potter's small, exquisite *Tale of Mrs. Tittlemouse* would be better company on a desert island than all the formulaic Brian Jacques *Redwall* books about warring mice); and they are not necessarily suited more to older readers. Generally, though, the most complex fantasy books require (and contribute toward) greater maturity in their readers. Their style, their themes, their detailed vastness must be chewed slowly and swallowed carefully.

Chapter 1 considers the simpler sorts of books, with a single plot in which a child character goes out into a strange new world, does something there, and returns home. The appeal lies in the interaction of the one child-hero, the created world big enough and not too big, and the voice of the storyteller. Chapter 2 discusses books set in worlds that are larger but still happy. Harmony is attainable here; threats are easily dissolved and balance restored. Chapter 3 looks at the many ways fantasy books play with time, space, and scale. Characters here jostle readers' rigid, everyday perspectives by traveling backward or forward in time; visiting other universes; becoming tiny or enormous; making wishes that come true.

The next chapters deal with more complex, often troubling, fantasy worlds. Chapter 4 considers a middle type—more threatening than the Oz and Mary Poppins sort of world, but less serious than the dark, heroic fantasy books. These are the more comfortable series for middle-level children. Chapter 5 examines some stories that present a problematic fantasy world in depth rather than breadth. Each explores a piece of a world: the last girl confronting the last man after nuclear destruction, for instance, or mythic lovers feuding through many generations. Finally, Chapter 6 takes on the epic, heroic fantasy series, books both deeply traditional and strikingly original. Great wars of good and evil are described here, and archetypal quests, peopled by ambiguous heroes and sturdy modern children and weird beings out of dreams and nightmares. Tolkien, Rowling, and their colleagues are found here.

❧ ❧

The process of reading fantasy fiction is well described in a *New York Times* essay (September 27, 2002) written by the novelist Katie Roiphe. She tells of the books she read during a long hospital stay when she was twelve years old.

> I broke open the books and chased the words. It was a breathless activity like running. Books gave me perspective the way religion might have for another kind of impressionable teenager. As I read, the characters multiplied in my head, each one decreasing the importance of my own situation, making it less. It was like looking down at my house from an airplane.

This vantage point—the view from on high, flying—is a motif in countless fantasy stories. Flying and looking, a reader finds that the self becomes less, as Roiphe says, but it also becomes more—understanding and freedom and integrity expand.

In Miss Mulock's classic story *The Little Lame Prince* (1874), the crippled boy floated above his tower-prison on a magic cloak and learned from his flights much about the kingdom he would rule so kindly in later years. Many a child reader has flown alongside the prince, reading with a burning intensity. Eight-year-old Georgie, in Jane Langton's *The Fledgling* (1980), was obsessed with learning to fly; an old Canada goose from Walden Pond finally taught her how. THEY WERE FLOATING, SOARING, SKIMMING LIKE SEA GULLS, LIKE HAWKS, LIKE SWALLOWS. SHE BANKED AND TURNED, LIFTING HER HEAD TO GAZE ONCE AGAIN OVER THE WHOLE BROAD LANDSCAPE FROM HORIZON TO HORIZON, FEELING THE SLEEVES OF HER JACKET FILL WITH AIR. Georgie's mother, thinking about her two girls, concluded that Georgie DOESN'T EVEN KNOW THAT SHE EXISTS. SHE'S JUST EYES AND EARS, THAT'S ALL SHE IS, JUST LOOKING AND LISTENING. SHE DOESN'T THINK TO HERSELF, "THIS IS ME, GEORGIE." INSTEAD SHE PULSES WITH THE SUNRISE AND THE RAIN AND THE GEESE FLYING OVER THE HOUSE.

WHEREAS, ELEANOR! ELEANOR IS ALL ELEANOR! AND EVERYTHING OUTSIDE ELEANOR BECOMES ELEANOR TOO. THERE ISN'T ANYTHING ELSE BUT ELEANOR IN ALL THE WORLD. These are the two kinds of people. It's clear who will develop the stronger, truer self: Eleanor, who is all self all the time, or Georgie, who pulses with the rain and the geese, who gazes over the whole broad landscape, who flies up into a fantasy world.

1

A Child Goes into the World

There's a game for little children, played at summer camps, in which one child roams around swinging her clasped hands like a trunk, while campers and counselors stand on the edges singing:

> One elephant
> Went out to play,
> On a spider's web one day.
> He had such
> Enormous fun
> That he called for another elephant to come.

The elephant taps another child with her trunk. That one starts roaming too, while the song switches to "Two elephants. . . ." Then each taps another girl, until everyone is shuffling around the floor. Then the campers have crackers and milk and go to bed. Here, in a primitive form, is the self meeting its world—exploring the intricate spider web of non-self beyond its borders. This excursion into the world is shown to be enormous fun, though it's risky for an elephant to play on a spider web.

Brief Excursions

Some fantasy books present a vast, complex world eager to over-whelm a small person in the middle of it, while others show the merest beginnings of the small person's journey outward. The most rudimentary "journey" is described in Margaret Wise Brown's well-loved picture book *Goodnight Moon* (1947), where a bunny in bed names the objects around him as he goes to sleep. His actions in the book consist of sitting up, turning so he can see a picture behind his bed, getting back into bed, and shutting his eyes. In comparison, Peter Rabbit's actions look as strenuous as the labors of Hercules: sneaking snacks from the garden, knocking down flowerpots, fleeing Mr. McGregor's murderous rage, escaping from a net, losing his clothes, then going to bed with only a dose of camomile tea for supper.

Good stories do help children psychologically as they struggle through developmental tasks to become individuals; as they balance biological, emotional, and social needs; as they come to terms with loves and hates and fears and wishes. Stories also help children, and adults too, discover the shapes of worlds outside themselves—the elephant's spider web, Peter's garden, Middle-earth, whatever—so they can map them and make sense of them and live in them.

In some stories the child actually creates an outside world, as if by magic. Dr. Seuss's first book, *And to Think That I Saw It on Mulberry Street* (1937), describes Marco's uneventful walk to and from school. Though he saw nothing to report to his father but an old horse and wagon, his imagination gradually transformed the scene into a loud, colorful parade of beasts, bands, rajahs, magicians, and confetti. Marco's father had given conflicting instructions: KEEP YOUR EYELIDS UP AND SEE WHAT YOU CAN SEE, but also STOP TELLING SUCH OUTLANDISH TALES. STOP TURNING MINNOWS INTO WHALES.

Marco's father was smug and annoying. His son ran home with this grand creation in his head: I FELT SIMPLY GREAT! FOR I HAD A STORY THAT NO ONE COULD BEAT!—BUT DAD SAID QUITE CALMLY, "JUST DRAW UP YOUR STOOL AND TELL ME THE SIGHTS ON THE WAY HOME

FROM SCHOOL. . . . WAS THERE NOTHING TO LOOK AT . . . NO PEOPLE TO GREET? DID NOTHING EXCITE YOU OR MAKE YOUR HEART BEAT?" "NOTHING," I SAID, GROWING RED AS A BEET, "BUT A PLAIN HORSE AND WAGON ON MULBERRY STREET." The demands of reality punctured Marco's exciting vision; nonetheless, Marco and the child reading his story still possess the wild parade and always will. There it is— the swirling scene, bright red, yellow, blue, and green, more interesting and real than the old horse and wagon and Marco's stuffy Dad. Marco did feel triumphant about his creative act, transcending the drab real world. Five pages of reality, at the story's beginning and end, frame twenty-five pages of imagination. That's how important are the Other worlds that the child finds to journey in. Fantasy books all present some kind of tension between primary and secondary worlds (to use Tolkien's terminology), though some show the merest glimpse of a secondary world lurking behind the primary one, and others exist totally in a secondary world with only a hint of normal reality.

One satisfying picture book is Crockett Johnson's *Harold and the Purple Crayon* (1955). The title page and beginning of the story are covered with scribbled purple lines drawn by an inquisitive-looking toddler with a crayon. The scribbles lack meaning and structure. ONE EVENING, AFTER THINKING IT OVER FOR SOME TIME, HAROLD DECIDED TO GO FOR A WALK IN THE MOONLIGHT—it's time for some meaning, some direction. Needing a moon and a path, he drew them with his crayon, and thus set out into this world even as he created it. Harold was responsible for his world but could not prevent the unexpected from happening; he could only act and react wisely. So, when he drew a dragon that frightened him and caused his hand to shake, thereby sketching the waves of a deep ocean, he escaped drowning by creating and climbing into a purple boat. AFTER HE HAD SAILED LONG ENOUGH, HAROLD MADE LAND WITHOUT MUCH TROUBLE—literally. It's harder to find home: a tired Harold drew a lot of houses before he realized his window was always located right around the moon, so he drew it like that. AND THEN HAROLD MADE HIS BED AND HE DREW (literally) UP THE COVERS. An ending simple but eloquent.

The most basic story pattern shows a human or animal child leaving home to find adventure in a puzzling world, finding it, then returning home wiser. This is the classic shape of the tales Bettelheim claims are so important to a child's development. As he says in *The Uses of Enchantment:*

> Having taken the child on a trip into a wondrous world, at the end the tale returns the child to reality, in a most reassuring manner. This teaches the child that permitting one's fantasy to take hold of oneself for a while is not detrimental, provided one does not remain permanently caught up in it. The hero returns to reality—a happy reality, but one devoid of magic. (p. 63)

Thousands of books following this pattern appeared in the last century or so, both realistic stories and fantasies. Many are dull and fatuous—hordes of bears, bunnies, and babies wandering vaguely until they finally go home and get tucked in by their mommies. But the primitive strength of this story line shines forth in the better versions, from Beatrix Potter's *Squirrel Nutkin* to *The Wizard of Oz* to *The Hobbit*, which is subtitled "There and Back Again."

Picture books by Maurice Sendak and William Steig retell the basic story with resonance and wit. In Steig's *Sylvester and the Magic Pebble* (1969), the donkey hero felt wonder and delight when he found the magic wishing pebble, fear when menaced by a lion, frustration and depression when his hasty wish turned him into a rock with no way of touching the pebble to turn back again. Sylvester the rock and his forlorn parents endured a winter of grieving—the necessary period of bleakness and waiting found in all such tales, the descent into the dark underworld—until springtime, when his parents noticed a shiny pebble that Sylvester would have loved for his collection and happened to place it on top of the rock, setting him free. Back home, they agreed to lock the wishing pebble away: "WHAT MORE COULD THEY WISH FOR?" Sylvester no longer thought that with the pebble "I CAN HAVE ANYTHING I WANT, ANYBODY CAN HAVE EVERYTHING ANYBODY WANTS!" We know from all the old tales that there is a price for everything, a consequence;

there is always a catch. Sylvester knew better now. The last picture shows him in a loving huddle on his parents' laps on a lumpy sofa, realizing that THEY HAD ALL THAT THEY WANTED.

Jane Yolen discusses this idea in *Touch Magic* (2000): "Magic has consequences. A condition of choice overlies the best stories and that is what is missing in so much of the new literature for children. Instead of that reminder of the hard work of choosing, we are each told we can marry the prince or princess. There is never the risk of a mouthful of toads" (p. 60).

❧ ❧

The richest stories do not explain everything; mysteries remain mysterious. In Steig's *The Amazing Bone* (1976), a dreamy little pig named Pearl was so enthralled by the beauty of springtime— THE WARM AIR TOUCHED HER SO TENDERLY, SHE COULD ALMOST FEEL HERSELF CHANGING INTO A FLOWER. HER LIGHT DRESS FELT LIKE PET- ALS—that a small talking bone hidden in the leaves spoke to her, agreed to be her friend and travel in her purse, and saved her from becoming the fox's dinner by shouting out the magic shrinking words. Amazed that the bone could speak languages and produce sound effects, she asked, "YOU'RE A BONE. HOW COME YOU CAN SNEEZE?" "I DON'T KNOW," THE BONE REPLIED. "I DIDN'T MAKE THE WORLD." It couldn't even explain what made it say the saving magic words, ADOONIS ISHGOOLAK KEKEBOKKIN YIBAPP. "I WISH I KNEW. THEY JUST CAME TO ME." Pearl and her bony friend humbly accepted their good luck. They didn't earn it, but they were alert and responsive enough to receive it. We learn that a loving nature is what we need in a mysterious, charming, but dangerous world. We don't need to explain everything.

Much has been written about Maurice Sendak's Max and Mickey, bold boys who master their universes. Mischievous and wild, Max (1963) sailed in his private boat, away from his bed- room punishment, to *Where the Wild Things Are* AND TAMED THEM WITH THE MAGIC TRICK OF STARING INTO ALL THEIR YELLOW EYES WITHOUT BLINKING ONCE. Then he led the wild rumpus of giant beasts until he sent them to bed and sailed back home to supper. Stubborn Mickey, in *In the Night Kitchen* (1970), FELL THROUGH

THE DARK, OUT OF HIS CLOTHES PAST THE MOON & HIS MAMA & PAPA SLEEPING TIGHT INTO THE LIGHT OF THE NIGHT KITCHEN. The bakers, who worked in the night to change things into something new and yummy, mixed him in batter to make a Mickey-cake—until he jumped from the bowl, nourished and doughy, and took over his own fate: I'M NOT THE MILK AND THE MILK'S NOT ME! I'M MICKEY! Making a squashy airplane out of dough, he flew up to the Milky Way, baptized himself swimming naked in the enormous bottle, then poured milk from his cup down to the bakers for their morning bread. Mission accomplished, he slid down the bottle and into his bed, mumbling HUM and YUM.

The classic plot patterns of these stories are appealing and comforting, but adults and children love to read them not only because Sylvester and Pearl and Max and Mickey are lovable children they identify with who solve their problems and return home proudly, in a state of greater wisdom and mastery, but because the worlds they encounter on the way are full of excitement and wonder, worth mastering. In my own childhood reading, rather than identifying with the characters or feeling events from inside, I watched and responded and tried to figure out the whole thing. While intensely caring that everything worked out right, I wanted even more to see how it all fit together, in a manner that seemed convincing. (So, for instance, I was desolate when Beth died in *Little Women*, but I wouldn't have wanted her not to.)

Sylvester's world indoors was comfortable, a snug donkey house (rocking chair, wallpaper, family photos) next to friendly chicken and pig families. The outdoors was beautiful and changeable, with shortlived flowers and eternal rocks. While Sylvester as a rock was wretched, for readers the grand cycle of seasons somewhat dims the misery—a huge starry sky, autumn, winter howling with hungry wolves. Our view is larger than Sylvester's, though we are thrilled at his recovery. The universe of this book balances a small stable family, a helpful community, and an outside world with strange rules of cause and effect that can't be argued with. Even denser than Sylvester's world is Pearl's, which contains the glory of springtime and the weirdness of the bone's magic utterances, along with the menace of the fox and his rickety house, and the busyness of bakers, streetcleaners, old gaffers in the town. Sweet Pearl in her pink dress and bonnet was exquisitely responsive to her world. She couldn't escape the fox through her own efforts, but endured bravely until saved by the bone she had discovered by being so responsive.

Like Steig's worlds, Sendak's are immensely rich in details that are startling but perfect. THAT VERY NIGHT IN MAX'S ROOM A FOREST GREW AND GREW—AND GREW UNTIL HIS CEILING HUNG WITH VINES AND THE WALLS BECAME THE WORLD ALL AROUND. Readers young and old are fascinated by the child-hero in his wolf suit who was dwarfed by trees and Wild Things but tough enough to stare them down. They love the Wild Things themselves—great hairy horned archetypal creatures that actually resemble gargoyles that tower over New College, Oxford—as much as they admire Max. And they love the whole tale, its story arc and its smallest detail; the central wild adventure and the framework of beginning and end.

Fantasy Tales and Their Readers

The pattern outside such stories reflects the pattern inside: readers immerse themselves in the journeys of characters like Max and Mickey; in doing so, they experience the same movement away from and back to daily life, and the same exciting interval between, in a brave new place. Readers' journeys are different from characters' because the whole book is the adventure. In *Playing and Reality* (1971), psychologist D. W. Winnicott discusses what he calls "transitional phenomena." As infants develop beyond a state of absorption in the "Me," toward an understanding of the "Not-Me," they are greatly helped by certain objects and activities that are neither. These reside on some intermediate ground somewhat linked to the Me, yet somewhat separate.

In their earliest form, these phenomena may be pacifiers, security blankets, or teddy bears. Later, games and playing of all kinds serve a similar purpose; later still, all the creations of the cultural world. As Winnicott says,

On the basis of playing is built the whole of man's experiential existence. We experience life in the area of transitional phenomena, in the exciting interweave of subjectivity and objective observation, and in an area that is intermediate between the inner reality of the individual and the shared reality of the world that is external to individuals. (p. 64)

Transitional phenomena, including art, science, and religion, are valuable to all people all their lives. Fantasy fiction seems to be a particularly good kind of "transitional" experience, as it exists so clearly in regions that are neither the Me nor the normal reality of the Not-Me.

The House of Make-Believe (1990), a study by Dorothy Singer and Jerome Singer that examines children's imaginative play, offers intriguing descriptions of developmental processes. As early as the peekaboo stage, when a baby delights in finding a hidden object and realizing it still exists, the act of playing helps the baby understand its place in the scheme of things: "Of special importance for pretend play is the capacity to sustain the object in thought, that is, to develop an image, cognitive map, or plan of it in its physical absence" (p. 90).

From this primitive moment on, such maps and symbolic images will serve the child well in many types of learning—physical, psychological, cognitive, and social. A transitional object like a stuffed animal is a symbolic image, while fantasy stories show the reader places and times with many parts, which cry out to be comprehended and mapped. Fantasy stories share the same spirit as games with a spatial aspect. I never liked playing jump rope, which seemed static, but I loved hopscotch, where you followed the patterned path, hopping carefully to the end and back or—in my favorite variation on the game—you hopped to the center of a snail-shaped design and back out to the edge. It's the ancient labyrinth. Equally thrilling were cobweb games played at birthday parties. A parent would set up the cobweb by twisting a string strand for each child around furniture, stair rails, and such. The intertangled strings required such care to unwind that the players reached their prizes at the end of the strings feeling sure that an adventure had been accomplished.

One interesting kind of pretend play is highlighted in *The House of Make-Believe*. There is evidence that playing with imaginary companions is both common and constructive. Children with such playmates are far from unhappy or maladjusted; in fact, some studies show them to be less fearful than other children, and more cooperative, sociable, happy, and verbal. The Singers also suggest that many adults have their own imaginary companions who provide comfort and inspiration: these are commonly known as gods and saints. According to the authors, "A significant proportion of the adult world continues to hold an active belief in invisible spirits" (p. 90). From this viewpoint, Jesus is a comforting imaginary companion.

So children and adults alike who engage in symbolic play and imaginative storytelling navigate more comfortably in the transitional land between Self and Other. Disputing Piaget's view, Dorothy and Jerome Singer insist that "our impulse for make-believe and pretending, for role-enactment and fantasy, scarcely fades away at all" (p. 90).

The Question behind the Quest

While sharing traditional themes and incidents, each good fantasy book has its own shape, a unique purpose and path. In Sendak's small, haunting *Outside Over There* (1981), young Ida's journey was one of atonement for her carelessness and self-absorption, which allowed goblins to kidnap her baby sister while she gazed out the window playing her wonder horn. Going to search for her, Ida found the cave where the stolen baby was hidden and discovered that under their hoods the goblins were babies too, wild and naked and sticky with bits of the eggshells they recently broke out of. This time, she played her horn purposefully: SHE CHARMED THEM WITH A CAPTIVATING TUNE. . . . A FRENZIED JIG, A HORNPIPE THAT MAKES SAILORS WILD BENEATH THE OCEAN MOON, until the dancing babies fell into confusion. Ida seized her sister and carried her home to their Mama in the arbor—a rescue mission bringing the kidnapped sister out of baby anarchy back to the loving harmony of the family.

Nancy Willard's *Sailing to Cythera* (1974) is a story of mastery; Anatole's journey is a joyous celebration. Anatole found adventures by chance, like a knight riding about in search of deeds to do. With great aplomb (and with his cat Plumpet), he met problems and solved them boldly; he was rewarded with the wonders and delights of magical places. In the house of the sun, for instance, a banquet grew out of Anatole's tiny advertising booklet: WANDS OF COWSLIP BREAD, PLATTERS OF CANDIED VIOLETS AND MARZIPAN MARIGOLDS, GREAT TUREENS OF DAFFODIL SOUP AND CROCKS OF ROSE-PETAL JAM. HE ATE TWO LOAVES OF BREAD AND THREE PLATES OF VIOLETS, AND THEN HE LAUGHED.

On a trip to the christening for Plumpet's aunt's ninth and last life, the guests would have been stranded forever on the heavenly meadow where the party took place, because the train engineer went missing—except that young Anatole took over the train and led them bravely home. "DO YOU MEAN WE CAN'T GET OUT OF HERE?" DEMANDED THE RACCOON. THEN ANATOLE RAISED HIS HAND. "I KNOW SOMETHING ABOUT TRAINS. I BELIEVE I COULD DRIVE IT IF THE SQUIRREL WOULD HELP ME." ANATOLE OPENED THE THROTTLE AND PLUMPET PULLED THE WHISTLE CORD. SLOWLY THE TRAIN BEGAN TO MOVE THROUGH THE ENORMOUS TREE, OUT OF THE CITY. There is always the cost, though, in a successful adventure. When the train reached the river, Anatole had to pay the old man whose one hundred white lions could form a raft to carry the train across. So he lost his grandfather's watch, his sneakers, and his favorite T-shirt; but he got himself and his comrades home.

Besides the cost, there's always the rules. In Lewis Carroll's *Alice's Adventures in Wonderland* (1865), the rules were weird and constantly shifting, as the world fell into chaos. That's one reason many children dislike the book. In other stories, though, magic rules provide a reassuring structure: the lands of adventure are wide, but beyond certain limits you cannot go, or bad things will happen. In *Sailing to Cythera*, you must catch the midnight train or stay forever in the paradise of Morgentown. On the train, Plumpet the cat ate three roast mice politely given her by some owls, but that was allowed within the social code. "LOVELY PLUMP LITTLE THINGS," SHE SAID, LICKING HER CHIN. "I HOPE YOU'RE NOT THINKING OF EATING THE OWLS," EXCLAIMED ANATOLE. "CERTAINLY NOT," SAID PLUMPET, SHOCKED. "IT'S AGAINST THE RULES HERE. WHERE WOULD WE ALL BE IF WE TRIED TO EAT EACH OTHER UP?"

When Anatole wanted to help his friend, the amnesiac soldier who had lost thirty years of his life, he knew he must follow instructions carefully, accept helpful advice gratefully, but also overcome obstacles bravely, by himself. "SO YOU WISH TO TURN BACK THE SUN," CALLED THE OLD MAN. "IF ANYONE CAN FIND THE SUN'S HOUSE IT'S THIS BOY HERE. BUT THE WAY IS LONG AND VERY DIFFICULT." "VERY DIFFICULT?" ASKED ANATOLE, WHO LOVED A GOOD ADVENTURE IF IT WAS NOT TOO DANGEROUS. "OF COURSE," SAID THE OLD MAN, "BUT THERE ARE ALWAYS PEOPLE WHO WANT TO MAKE THE JOURNEY BECAUSE THERE ARE ALWAYS PEOPLE WHO WANT TO BE MAGICIANS."

"CAN THE SUN MAKE ME INTO A MAGICIAN?" THE OLD MAN SHOOK HIS HEAD. "THE SUN WON'T, BUT THE JOURNEY WILL. IT'S THE JOURNEYS WE MAKE FOR OTHERS THAT GIVE US THE POWER TO CHANGE OURSELVES. THE HARDEST PART IS GETTING HOME AGAIN, FOR YOU CAN'T GO HOME THE WAY YOU LEFT IT. NOBODY CAN GIVE YOU THE MAGIC TO TAKE YOU HOME. YOU HAVE TO FIND THAT MAGIC ON YOUR OWN."

Balancing obedience and independence, Anatole worked his way through good, dangerous adventures, found his own way home, and made terrific friends—like the dreadful Blimlim beast, who moved into the dark space under Anatole's bed to keep away frightening bad things, and the wise soldier who told him, "WHEN I WAS A KID, I USED TO PICK POCKETS IN REVERSE. INSTEAD OF TAKING THINGS OUT, I PUT THINGS IN. A GUMDROP HERE. A CANDY CANE THERE." Anatole came home still modest, but triumphant.

Norton Juster's classic *The Phantom Tollbooth* (1961) is a tale of enlightenment. Milo started out bored and dismal. Through his journey, he came to appreciate the world at home—words and numbers, sights and sounds, became exciting and new. Milo's task, after he drove his toy car through the magic tollbooth in his bedroom, was clear but impossible: to rescue the princesses Sweet Rhyme and Pure Reason, whose imprisonment had caused destruction and chaos all over The Lands Beyond. Because that world was in terrible shape, its rules were harmful ones, such as Ordinance 574381-W: "IN THE DOLDRUMS, LAUGHTER IS FROWNED UPON AND SMILING IS PERMITTED ONLY ON ALTERNATE THURSDAYS. VIOLATORS SHALL BE DEALT WITH MOST HARSHLY."

Some of his adventures were happy, like the exotic visit to the Word Market in Dictionopolis ("GET YOUR FRESH-PICKED IFS, ANDS, AND BUTS." "HEY-YAA, HEY-YAA, NICE RIPE WHERES AND WHENS.") Synonym Buns and Just Desserts were delicious, though Half-Baked Ideas were hard to digest, such as "THE EARTH IS FLAT" and "EVERYTHING HAPPENS FOR THE BEST." Gradually Milo realized he must do more than enjoy himself—he must save this troubled land. First, he restored sounds to a silent valley by tricking the depressed Soundkeeper, who had locked them up. (The valley needed all its sounds, even the grating noises of THAT AWFUL DYNNE.) After visiting places like the dangerous island of Conclusions, reached by Jumping, Milo was strong enough to attack the Mountains of Ignorance, where Rhyme and Reason were captive. Outwitting the terrible Senses Taker (who tried to seize your Sense of Duty, of Proportion, of Purpose, and of Humor) and the worst demons of all—the Hopping Hindsight, the Gross Exaggeration, and the Threadbare Excuse—he escaped with the princesses, restored the city of Wisdom, and was declared a Hero of the Realm. Back home, the Tollbooth disappeared, and Milo could no longer visit The Lands Beyond. But he didn't mind; he had acquired wisdom and purpose in his travels and saw his own world through new eyes. He now knew about the beauty of good words, sounds, and numbers, the danger of bad logic, and the inexorability of cause and effect. Milo's world, once empty, had become rich and full.

Quest tales like these, at least the good ones, seem both unique and universal, embodying familiar motifs that could be called Freudian or Jungian. Sendak's Ida, Willard's Anatole, Juster's Milo, and other such journeying children follow well-worn fantasy paths that were first walked by fairy-tale people—Snow White and Hansel and Rumpelstiltskin and the rest. The specificity and richness of detail in each world make it unique, along with the style and tone in which that world is presented. A passage from *Sailing to Cythera* can't be mistaken for a passage from *The Phantom*

Tollbooth: it's possible to recognize not just people and places and other pieces as belonging to a particular fictional world, but the very air that hovers over that world, which is the mood and viewpoint of its author.

The Voice of the Storyteller

If you suspect that exciting action is all that counts in fantasy fiction—if you have any doubts that a unifying narrative voice is essential—just consider a kind of "book" that has no voice at all: the choose-your-own-plot genre popular in the 1970s and 1980s, in which a reader selects from various plot options and jumps around among stilted, conventional little sections. (The Dungeons and Dragons game is a live-action relative of these books, and video games are a sophisticated descendant.)

To look at one example, the Lone Wolf "Role Playing Adventure" books by Joe Dever start with "Game Rules for You, the Reader," who must choose from random numbers that assign you special skills and equipment; you must also follow rules for Combat, adding or subtracting points for Endurance and Combat Skill as you follow the adventure. At the start of Book 1, *Flight from the Dark* (1984), you are the sole survivor of an attack by evil Darklords on the Warrior Knight monastery at Kai; you must travel to the city of the King and warn him. So you conduct your journey by choosing from sequences of dreary passages. For instance, 208: THE GHOULISH CREATURES THRUST THEIR SPEARS AT YOU AND ATTACK. IF YOU WIN, YOU CAN RUN TO THE SAFETY OF THE FARMHOUSE BY TURNING TO 148. OR YOU CAN RETURN TO THE WOODS. TURN TO 320. . . .

Or 339: YOU QUICKLY SIDESTEP JUST AS A LONG DAGGER SHATTERS THE GLASS TOP OF THE COUNTER. A SWARTHY YOUTH IS ATTACKING YOU AND YOU MUST FIGHT HIM. IF YOU KILL HIM WITHIN 4 ROUNDS OF COMBAT, TURN TO 94. IF YOU ARE STILL FIGHTING AFTER 4 ROUNDS, TURN TO 203. If you make unlucky choices, you will come upon something like this: 292: THE LAST THING THAT YOU EXPERIENCE OF THIS LIFE IS THE FEELING OF BEING SUCKED INTO THE VOID OF DARKNESS. NO TRACE

OF YOU REMAINS IN THIS WORLD. YOU HAVE BECOME A SLAVE OF AN AN-
CIENT EVIL. YOUR ADVENTURE ENDS HERE. Perhaps there is a puzzle aspect to these proceedings that might
appeal to some young (or older?) readers, but of a rudimentary
kind. These "adventures" are clichéd clumps of fantasy-type
language—ghoulish creatures, swarthy youth, ancient evil, that
sort of thing. (The map accompanying these books is very Tolkien-
oid, with imitative place names like Durenor and The Rymerift.)
In this sort of book, which can't be called a "world," there is no
sign of a storyteller, to understand, create, describe, or interpret.
No Mind is behind it all, wondering or worrying or judging or la-
menting or having fun, or loving its creations.

Turning from this odd type of narrative, it's a relief to meet the
storyteller behind a real story. Sometimes, even in twentieth-
century books, the narrator speaks directly to readers, stating an
opinion or sharing a joke or nudging them to respond to the characters in some particular way. In A. A. Milne's *Winnie-the-Pooh*
(1926), the "I" who tells the stories—a patronizing but affection-
ate voice—makes it clear he is smarter than anyone else. The
Winnie-the-Pooh reader is the next smartest and understands what
is going on; Christopher Robin is the next smartest, well above the
animal characters, most of whom are pretty dim. (For instance,
Christopher Robin sat in a tree watching while Pooh and Piglet
went round and round it, getting more and more frightened at
their own footprints in the snow.)

More often, a storyteller is revealed indirectly, through a turn of
mind and a turn of phrase, a perspective and personality that in-
form the whole book. Nancy Willard, in *Sailing to Cythera*, does
not address her readers directly, but we hear her particular voice
in passages like this: "NO TRAINS RUN ON GRAND AVENUE," SAID ANA-
TOLE. "ALL THINGS COME TO THOSE WHO WAIT," SAID PLUMPET, AND SHE
SAT DOWN ON A BENCH THAT WAS NOT THERE UNTIL SHE LOOKED FOR
IT. A MAN HURRIED PAST THEM, PUSHING A BAGGAGE CART, AND THEN A
TRAIN WHISTLE SOUNDED, FAR BEYOND THE GARDEN. THE FLOWERS
CLOSED THEIR PETALS AND DREAMED OF A TRAIN PLATFORM, ON WHICH
ANATOLE NOW FOUND HIMSELF STANDING, MUCH TO HIS SURPRISE,
WATCHING THE TRAIN RUSH CLOSER AND CLOSER. The voice of this

storyteller is complicated and simple, homey and magical, friendly and observant. The narrator within a story is not identical to the author, of course, but is a deliberately chosen speaker, speaking for the author in this specific context.

The Phantom Tollbooth's storytelling voice is just as compelling as that of *Sailing to Cythera*, and totally different. Norton Juster's narrator, like Nancy Willard's, does not comment or nudge, but he conveys his delight in the book's clever games, ideas, and surprises. His personality appears in the aptness of his names and puns, and the neatness of his paradoxes and sentence structures. After introducing Milo as surrounded by a cloud of glumness and convinced that life is dull and predictable—WHEREVER HE WAS HE WISHED HE WERE SOMEWHERE ELSE, AND WHEN HE GOT THERE HE WONDERED WHY HE'D BOTHERED—the storyteller brings into Milo's room the mysterious object that starts the adventure that changes Milo's mood forever: WHO COULD POSSIBLY HAVE LEFT SUCH AN ENORMOUS PACKAGE AND SUCH A STRANGE ONE? FOR, WHILE IT WAS NOT QUITE SQUARE, IT WAS DEFINITELY NOT ROUND, AND FOR ITS SIZE IT WAS LARGER THAN ALMOST ANY OTHER BIG PACKAGE OF SMALLER DIMENSION THAT HE'D EVER SEEN.

The excitement in a book like *The Phantom Tollbooth* lies not in characters' actions and emotions but in clever ideas, shown in fresh perspectives that provide little explosions of insight. Here is how the Terrible Trivium speaks: DEMON OF PETTY TASKS AND WORTHLESS JOBS, OGRE OF WASTED EFFORT, AND MONSTER OF HABIT: "NOW DO COME STAY WITH ME. WE'LL HAVE SO MUCH FUN TOGETHER. THERE ARE THINGS TO FILL AND THINGS TO EMPTY, THINGS TO TAKE AWAY AND THINGS TO BRING BACK, THINGS TO PICK UP AND THINGS TO PUT DOWN, AND BESIDES ALL THAT WE HAVE PENCILS TO SHARPEN, HOLES TO DIG, NAILS TO STRAIGHTEN, STAMPS TO LICK, AND EVER SO MUCH MORE."

As Michele Landsberg points out (1987) in *Reading for the Love of It* (p. 160),

Style is not a detachable frill that "fancier" writers tack on like a ruffle on a dress. Style *is* the writer; it is not possible to differentiate the manner of expression from what the author notices, what she values, how she reacts to it, what she thinks is important to mention, the emotional weight and colour of her own experiences.

Consider some strong, individual styles that couldn't be more different, though they are all used to tell stories about the weird travels of a little boy: if Nancy Willard's style is cheerfully lyrical and Norton Juster's is witty, Roald Dahl's in *Charlie and the Chocolate Factory* (1964) is wickedly exaggerated, almost sadistic; Antoine de Saint-Exupéry's in *The Little Prince* (1943) is soulful; Natalie Babbitt's in *The Search for Delicious* (1969) is informal and intimate but also traditional, like the style of an old tale.

People feel strongly about Roald Dahl's children's books. Some consider him the King of Bad Taste. They are disgusted at his disgusting descriptions of ugly characters and his gleeful punishment of bad characters. In *James and the Giant Peach* (1961), AUNT SPONGE WAS ENORMOUSLY FAT AND VERY SHORT. SHE HAD SMALL PIGGY EYES, A SUNKEN MOUTH, AND ONE OF THOSE WHITE FLABBY FACES THAT LOOKED EXACTLY AS THOUGH IT HAD BEEN BOILED. SHE WAS LIKE A GREAT WHITE SOGGY OVERBOILED CABBAGE. AUNT SPIKER, ON THE OTHER HAND, WAS LEAN AND TALL AND BONY. SHE HAD A SCREECHING VOICE AND LONG WET NARROW LIPS, AND WHENEVER SHE GOT ANGRY OR EXCITED, LITTLE FLECKS OF SPIT WOULD COME SHOOTING OUT OF HER MOUTH AS SHE TALKED. AND THERE THEY SAT, THESE TWO GHASTLY HAGS. The cruel aunts came to a hideous end, run over by the magical giant peach: AUNT SPONGE AND AUNT SPIKER LAY IRONED OUT UPON THE GRASS AS FLAT AND THIN AND LIFELESS AS A COUPLE OF PAPER DOLLS CUT OUT OF A PICTURE BOOK. In *Charlie and the Chocolate Factory*, while polite Charlie Bucket won the whole factory, the other four children were punished for their greed, stupidity, and disobedience: Augustus had all his fat squeezed out in the factory pipes, Violet was turned permanently purple, Veruca and her parents were embedded with slime from going down the garbage chute, and Mike was overstretched on the gum-stretching machine.

Chocolate Factory becomes tedious in the flatness of its cartoon characters and the smirking meanness of its punishments. But the sadism is distanced and unreal, the sort of thing children understand and love. Angry six-year-olds may tell their mothers, "I hate you so much I'm going to grind you up into hamburger and cut your ears off," and enjoy reading about such events in Roald Dahl books. Children adore bad taste. Maybe Dahl's approach is liberating for them, but maybe it's infantilizing: maybe the greatest authors are subtler and don't write like angry six-year-olds.

Many readers feel that the pathos of the starving Bucket family in *Chocolate Factory*, and the book's liveliness, are not enough to counteract its nastiness. Some of his other books are more appealing, with a less hateful flavor. *James and the Giant Peach*, once the aunts have been squashed, turns into a spirited account of the hero's soaring flight over the ocean to New York on the sweet, fleshy peach, a flight away from fear and passivity, toward resourcefulness and friendship. The most successful Dahl book may be *The BFG* (1982), where the author's gleeful obsession with brutality, confined to the nine "venomsome" giants with names like Fleshlumper, Childchewer, and Meatdripper, is more than balanced by the kindness of the delightful smaller giant—the Big Friendly Giant—a vegetarian who talked funny. Sophie, the hero, was a clever, bespectacled orphan, and the Queen of England was a charmingly down-to-earth deus ex machina. Together with the BFG, they saved England's children from the bad giants.

Somehow, in *The BFG*, Dahl's narrating voice comes together beautifully, speaking sometimes with affection, sometimes with indignation, always with a wild, playful delight in language. When Sophie said, "There's no such thing!" about the BFG's vile-tasting snozzcumber vegetable, the BFG replied: "YESTERDAY, WE WAS NOT BELIEVING IN GIANTS, WAS WE? JUST BECAUSE WE HAPPEN NOT TO HAVE ACTUALLY *SEEN* SOMETHING WITH OUR TWO LITTLE WINKLES, WE THINK IT IS NOT EXISTING. I IS NOT A VERY KNOW-ALL GIANT MYSELF, BUT IT SEEMS TO ME THAT YOU IS AN ABSOLUTELY KNOW-NOTHING HUMAN BEAN. YOUR BRAIN IS FULL OF ROTTEN-WOOL." When enraged, he would shout, "SAVE OUR SOLOS! DELIVER US FROM WEASELS!" He was plain-spoken but softhearted: After Sophie escaped one of the bad giants, THE BFG PICKED HER UP AND HELD HER TENDERLY IN THE PALM OF HIS HAND. "OH, I IS SO HAPPY TO BE FINDING YOU ALL IN ONE LUMP!" HE SAID. Such an eloquent, melodramatic giant had to turn into a writer; eventually, the Queen of England built him a house next to her castle at Windsor, where he lived peaceably near Sophie and prepared his memoirs.

How to Frighten a Child

Should we worry about scary or sad material in children's books? Probably not, if the children are reading good books where threatening and frightening stuff is part of a coherent, meaningful fictional world. On the other hand, if they are reading violent trash, the violence is even more noxious than the trashiness. Discussing the huge, toothy, clawed monsters in his *Where the Wild Things Are* (quoted by Nat Hentoff in *Only Connect*, 1969, p. 330), Maurice Sendak says,

> I have yet to hear of a child who was frightened by the book. Adults who are troubled by it forget that Max is having a fine time. He's in control. And by getting his anger at his mother discharged against the wild things he's able to come back to the real world at peace with himself. . . . The book doesn't say that life is constant anxiety. It simply says that life has anxiety in it.

C. S. Lewis (in *Only Connect*) makes a useful distinction:

> Those who say that children must not be frightened may mean (1) that we must not do anything likely to give the child those haunting, disabling, pathological fears against which ordinary courage is helpless. Or (2) that we must try to keep out of his mind the knowledge that he is born into a world of death, violence, wounds, adventure, heroism and cowardice, good and evil.

He supports the first position, but obviously not the second.

> I think it possible that by confining your child to blameless stories in which nothing at all alarming ever happens, you would fail to banish the terrors, and would succeed in banishing all that can ennoble them or make them endurable. (pp. 216–17)

I recently asked one of my sons if he remembers being scared of anything in fantasy books as a child. He answered no, not at all; he was much more scared of reality. The books made more sense. Even if you believe in sheltering a child from frightening books, it's impossible to guess what will scare a particular child. I know a generally fearless woman who is frightened of birds. She says it started with a childhood illustration—the one of Icarus tumbling out of the sky with his great fluffy wings outstretched. This picture, from a collection of myths, seemed pretty and unfrightening to me as a child, even though I was generally timorous. Anthony Storr, an English psychiatrist, describes (in *Only Connect*) a mother reading to her child:

"All day long the boy stood at the window. And, as he stood, soldiers came and laid hands on him, and led him up to the cask, where a big fire was blazing, and the horrid black pitch boiling and bubbling over the sides. He looked and shuddered, but there was no escape. Suddenly, some men were seen running, crying as they went that a large ship was making straight for the city. The king declared he would not have the boy burned before its arrival." At this point, the five-year-old girl burst into tears. Her mother put down Andrew Lang's *Brown Fairy Book* and hastened to comfort her. "Don't cry. The boy was quite all right. He didn't get thrown into the cask of pitch." "But I *wanted* him to be thrown into the cask of pitch," sobbed the little girl. (p. 91)

Apparently it helps children and does not traumatize them when they confront fears and violent emotions in fiction, indirectly; but adult attempts to explain rationally to children that such fears and emotions are normal can be enormously upsetting. Externalizing inner processes through play and fantasy gives a child mastery rather than terror. So, presumably, children would be cheered by reading Sophie's conversation with the BFG about the habits of his cousins, the bad giants. Their frisson of fear would soon fizzle, because the description is so silly and picturesque.
"HOW DO THEY CATCH THE HUMANS THEY EAT?" SOPHIE ASKED.
"THEY IS USUALLY JUST STICKING AN ARM IN THROUGH THE BEDROOM WINDOW AND SNITCHING THEM FROM THEIR BEDS," THE BFG SAID.

"HOW ELSE DO THEY CATCH THEM?" SOPHIE ASKED. "SOMETIMES," THE BFG SAID, "THEY IS SWIMMELING IN FROM THE SEA LIKE FISHIES WITH ONLY THEIR HEADS SHOWING ABOVE THE WATER, AND THEN OUT COMES A BIG HAIRY HAND AND GRABBLES SOMEONE OFF THE BEACH." "CHIL-DREN AS WELL?" "OFTEN CHIDDLERS," THE BFG SAID. "LITTLE CHIDDLERS WHO IS BUILDING SANDCASTLES ON THE BEACH. THAT IS WHO THE SWIM-MELING ONES ARE AFTER. LITTLE CHIDDLERS IS NOT SO TOUGH TO EAT AS OLD GRANDMAMMA, SO SAYS THE CHILDCHEWING GIANT." Watching the realistic movie *Jaws* could give a child terrible fears of the beach, the disabling kind C. S. Lewis warns should be avoided; but reading this scene from *The BFG* would, most likely, only elicit nervous giggles.

๏๛ ๛๏

Besides evil and violence and anger, children's books deal with sadness and loss. When C. S. Lewis listed aspects of life that a child must learn about, he included wounds and death. Many well-meaning books have been written about absent fathers, dying pets, senile grandmothers, in the hope that children might benefit from an earnest realistic treatment of such situations. Here again, a good fantasy story may offer a wider view, perhaps including won-der, and reconciliation or transcendence. Some fantasy books are matter-of-fact about sad events, as when Babar's mother got shot by a hunter. Charlotte's death, alone in her web at the fairground, is the saddest thing many children have met so far in their lives, but it is tempered by the burst of renewed life next spring, back home in the barn, when her baby spiders emerged from the egg sac to comfort Wilbur.

The author who calls himself Lemony Snicket has created a very clever phenomenon in *A Series of Unfortunate Events* (from 1999). The events described are indeed grotesquely horrible: the three Baudelaire orphans rushed from one disaster to another (in one book after another), tormented by witless adults, bad luck, bad food, and the cruel Count Olaf who was after their fortune. A child reader might despair at these events—except for the strong characters and the storyteller. Violet, Klaus, and Sunny were re-sourceful and resilient, smart enough to get out of predicaments, at least temporarily. Violet invented gadgets that enabled the children to escape, Klaus did research in obscure books, and Sunny the toddler helped by biting things. There is no triumph for these children, but at least there's hope. The storyteller mitigates the horrible events by his enveloping, cushiony presence: constantly explaining and commenting and defining words—above all, constantly expressing sympathy—he distances the bad events and reassures the reader that he will always be around even though the Baudelaires will always lose any kind adults they run into.

AS FERVENTLY AS THE BAUDELAIRE ORPHANS WISHED THEIR CIRCUMSTANCES WERE DIFFERENT, I WISH THAT I COULD SOMEHOW CHANGE THE CIRCUMSTANCES OF THIS STORY FOR YOU. EVEN AS I SIT HERE, SAFE AS CAN BE AND SO VERY FAR FROM COUNT OLAF, I CAN SCARCELY BEAR TO WRITE ANOTHER WORD.

While the children's feelings seem real, the events are too ridiculous to seem really real: "DOES THIS MEAN THAT THERE'S A POISONOUS SNAKE LOOSE IN THIS HOUSE?" MR POE ASKED. "NO, NO," DR LUCAFONT SAID. "THE MAMBA DU MAL IS SAFE IN ITS CAGE. IT MUST HAVE GOTTEN OUT, BITTEN DR MONTGOMERY, AND LOCKED ITSELF UP AGAIN."

Lemony Snicket's style is old-fashioned; the books themselves are pretty, little hard covers with ornate endpapers: the total effect is charming, funny, and comforting, even when Violet was locked in a tower by Count Olaf in *The Bad Beginning* or when their perfect guardian was slain among his exotic snakes in *The Reptile Room*. WHEN BRUCE HAD USED THE WORD "BRILLIANT" ABOUT UNCLE MONTY, HE MEANT "HAVING A REPUTATION FOR CLEVERNESS OR INTELLIGENCE." BUT WHEN THE CHILDREN USED THE WORD—AND WHEN THEY THOUGHT OF IT NOW, STARING AT THE REPTILE ROOM GLOWING IN THE MOONLIGHT—IT MEANT MORE THAN THAT. IT MEANT THAT EVEN IN THE BLEAK CIRCUMSTANCES OF THEIR CURRENT SITUATION, EVEN THROUGHOUT THE SERIES OF UNFORTUNATE EVENTS THAT WOULD HAPPEN TO THEM FOR THE REST OF THEIR LIVES, UNCLE MONTY AND HIS KINDNESS WOULD SHINE IN THEIR MEMORIES.

❧ ❧

Another way to present and interpret sad events, besides distancing them with a chatty narrator, is to bring them closer by making the narrator into an actual character. In Saint-Exupéry's *The Little Prince*, the storyteller is one of the two main characters, an aviator who survived a crash in the Sahara Desert, where he met a mysterious little boy. The middle part of the little prince's journey is narrated by the aviator objectively; he described the boy's visits to the tiny planets of a king, a conceited man, a tippler, a businessman, and others. Most of the book, however, beginning and end, consists of the aviator's opinions and emotions. He drew moral messages, from the little prince's encounters, about the stupid behavior of grown-ups. He told about the little prince's love for the beautiful flower he left back on his own tiny planet, and he eloquently expressed his own love for the lonely little boy. The style is ironic in the satirical parts ("AND WHAT DO YOU DO WITH FIVE-HUN-DRED MILLIONS OF STARS?" the little prince asked the businessman; "NOTHING. I OWN THEM. I AM CONCERNED WITH MATTERS OF CONSE-QUENCE"); it's sentimental in the poetic parts ("OH, LITTLE PRINCE! BIT BY BIT I CAME TO UNDERSTAND THE SECRETS OF YOUR SAD LITTLE LIFE.")

This book is lovely of its kind: whether you respond to it is a matter of taste. For me, the aviator is overwrought, too arch and gushy, and the ending is lugubrious, with the little prince arranging for the poisonous golden snake to bite him, thus sending him back to his planet and his beautiful rose. He explained to the aviator, "MY STAR WILL BE JUST ONE OF THE STARS, FOR YOU. AND SO YOU WILL LOVE TO WATCH ALL THE STARS IN THE HEAVENS. THEY WILL ALL BE YOUR FRIENDS. . . . TONIGHT—YOU KNOW . . . DO NOT COME. I SHALL LOOK AS IF I WERE SUFFERING. I SHALL LOOK A LITTLE AS IF I WERE DYING."

The more effective aspect of the book is not quite so heavy-handed: it is the recurring theme of hidden truth and beauty. The aviator explained that grown-ups were obtuse because they saw only a picture of a hat when a child had actually drawn a boa constrictor digesting a hidden, swallowed elephant. The boy announced that he could find a hidden well in the desert, and he did: "WHAT MAKES THE DESERT BEAUTIFUL," SAID THE LITTLE PRINCE, "IS THAT SOMEWHERE IT HIDES A WELL." The aviator remembered living as a child in an old house where a hidden treasure, never found, brought enchantment to the inhabitants. At one point the fox told the little prince: "IT IS ONLY WITH THE HEART THAT ONE CAN SEE RIGHTLY; WHAT IS ESSENTIAL IS INVISIBLE TO THE EYE"—which makes this theme explicit—and the aviator said to himself, looking at the sleeping little prince, "WHAT I SEE HERE IS NOTHING BUT A SHELL. WHAT IS MOST IMPORTANT IS INVISIBLE. . . ." The theme is most powerful when it is buried in the action of the story, revealing the meaning of the story only indirectly.

๛ ๛

No one type of storytelling voice is generally better than another; the storyteller simply needs to be right for the particular story. Natalie Babbitt, one of the best of today's writers for children, tells her stories in a style both delicate and sensible. Her narrator, unobtrusive but comfortably in control, knows what the story means, knows how it all fits together, and knows who's right and who's wrong.

The original oral fairy tales like "Rapunzel" and "Hansel and Gretel" were fluid, shifting things, changing in tone and form and detail as they spread to different times and countries. It was not until the early years of children's literature that authors like Charles Perrault in the seventeenth century and Hans Christian Andersen in the nineteenth started to produce something more structured than the old tales, what's now called the literary fairy tale—a story that is deliberately unified in shape and theme and narrative voice. Today's children's fantasies, with their authors firmly in charge, are descendants of those literary fairy tales.

Natalie Babbitt's *The Search for Delicious* (1969), for instance, carefully weaves together a prologue telling how the kingdom was created long ago and a simple story of a boy's journey to find who he is, along with an account of the brief civil war started by the king's nasty brother-in-law. The storyteller does not call attention to herself or speak to the reader directly, but her style and tone of voice tell you a lot about her, what and how she thinks. Here is the first paragraph:

THERE WAS A TIME ONCE WHEN THE EARTH WAS STILL VERY YOUNG, A TIME SOME CALL THE OLDEST DAYS. THIS WAS LONG BEFORE THERE

WERE ANY PEOPLE ABOUT TO DIG PARTS OF IT UP AND CUT PARTS OF IT
OFF. PEOPLE CAME ALONG MUCH LATER, BUILDING THEIR TOWNS AND
CASTLES (WHICH NEARLY ALWAYS FELL DOWN AFTER A WHILE) AND
PLAGUING EACH OTHER WITH QUARRELS AND SUPPER PARTIES. THE CREA-
TURES WHO LIVED ON THE EARTH IN THAT EARLY TIME STAYED EACH IN
HIS OWN PLACE AND KEPT IT BEAUTIFUL. THERE WERE DWARFS IN THE
MOUNTAINS, WOLDWELLERS IN THE FORESTS, MERMAIDS IN THE LAKES,
AND, OF COURSE, WINDS IN THE AIR. In five sentences Babbitt tells
about the past and present of this land and gives hints about its
future; she reveals something about the relations among the natu-
ral world, the people, and the other creatures who lived there.

Soon she introduces the mermaid child Ardis, who lost her key
that opened the stone house in the lake that controlled the spring,
and Ardis wept for her doll made of stones and ferns, which was
stuck inside the closed stone door. Centuries later, quarrels broke
out at court because the prime minister was writing a dictionary
and no one could agree on the definition for *delicious*—apples?
fried fish? beer? pudding? Twelve-year-old Gaylen, the prime minister's adopted son, was sent out on a fine horse to settle the question, by taking a poll in the kingdom's four towns. In his journey,
Gaylen, like all such youthful travelers, encountered helpers and
obstacles and villains. Hemlock, the queen's evil brother, had been
plotting a coup and now took advantage of the "delicious" issue
to stir up trouble: he rode ahead and proclaimed falsely that the
king planned to forbid certain foods.

While the citizens rioted and Hemlock dammed the lake, causing a horrible drought, Gaylen fell into despair but finally saved
the kingdom from dying of thirst: he recognized the lost key and
returned it to Ardis, who recovered her doll, and he persuaded her
to destroy Hemlock's dam. THE KING RAISED HIS HEAD AND LOOKED
ABOUT HIM. THEN HE SMILED AND HELD UP HIS HAND. "DRINK!" HE
SHOUTED. "IT'S ALL OVER, BY HARRY!" AND ALL OF A SUDDEN EVERY-
BODY WAS IN THE WATER, SPLASHING AND LAUGHING AND SLIPPING ON
THE ROCKS, DRENCHED INSTANTLY FROM HEAD TO FOOT. "DELICIOUS!"
A MAN CALLED TO HIS NEIGHBORS. And everyone agreed that "DELI-
CIOUS IS A DRINK OF COOL WATER WHEN YOU'RE VERY, VERY THIRSTY."
The story is nicely rounded; it is filled with familiar, resonant

elements from other tales, yet it creates a fresh new world where individual characters have their own voices; it is told in a style that is clean but subtle, down-to-earth but poetic. It's thoughtful and it's funny. That is what a fantasy story can do.

⋙ ⋘

For many children, the most delightful activity, better than a familiar ritual at home or a rousing team game, is the out-and-back-again excursion. The pieces of the trip are exciting—trapeze acts and cotton candy at the circus, snakes and campfires on a hike, dinosaur bones on a school field trip. Even more satisfying is the overall shape of the day: anticipation, fulfillment, exhaustion. There is no reason I should remember with great nostalgia the bus rides, many decades ago, back to Camp Runoia after our annual outing to the rocks and the lobster pound at Pemaquid Point. Inclined to carsickness, I hated the oily smell and the jiggling bus, and I disliked the endless drone of "A hundred bottles of beer on the wall" sung by dozens of manic little girls. But I was happy. The communal journey was completing itself as dusk fell, and soon we would run through the mosquitos back to the scratchy blankets of our cabin beds.

The experience of reading a fantasy book is a similar excursion: not always fun, but an interesting trip out of oneself in the company of a friendly adult, who explains things, and a bunch of other people, some likeable and some not. It's a field trip, to a neutral, new, transitional place, after which you know a little bit more about yourself and about what is out there. This involves moving outward; at the same time, it involves taking something from out there into yourself.

In *Touch Magic,* Jane Yolen describes the way children absorb wonder and wisdom from their world:

> Just as the child is born with a literal hole in its head, where the bones slowly close underneath the fragile shield of skin, so the child is born with a figurative hole in its heart. Slowly this, too, is filled up. What slips in before it anneals shapes the man or woman into which that child will grow. (p. 25)

Yolen also describes the opposite process—what happens when a child won't ingest imagination—in a quotation from the folklorists Iona and Peter Opie: "A child who does not feel wonder is but an inlet for apple pie" (p. 79).

Before their hearts harden and nothing more can slip inside, children need to take in as many mysteries as they can, and they need to go outwards on as many journeys as possible. They can visit the Wild Things with Max, they can evade Count Olaf with the Baudelaire children, and they can fly with James on his giant peach: "OH, ISN'T IT BEAUTIFUL!" THEY CRIED. "WHAT A MARVELOUS FEELING!" UP AND UP THEY WENT, HIGH ABOVE THE HIGHEST CLOUDS, THE PEACH SWAYING GENTLY FROM SIDE TO SIDE AS IT FLOATED ALONG.

2

Lighter Worlds:
Living in Harmony and Balance

Today, much fantasy fiction reflects reality by describing serious struggles: good versus evil, freedom versus slavery, sanity versus madness. Darkness looms very large. It is easy to overlook happy stories. Nothing is more exhilarating, though, for both children and adults, than a fantasy world where problems dissolve; where you fly on a peppermint stick, sail in an umbrella, talk with a chicken, or cook for a dragon. Opposites are reconciled, losses are balanced by gains. These books are celebrations, of the individual and the community and the intertwining of the two: Mozart rather than Beethoven.

The theologian Harvey Cox (*The Feast of Fools*, 1969) points out how much humankind needs both festivity (celebration) and fantasy (envisioning alternative kinds of life), whether in a religious or a secular context. These activities connect human beings to their past and future: "No other creature relives the legends of his forefathers, blows out candles on a birthday cake, or dresses up and pretends he is someone else" (p. 11). Although the proportion of grim, serious fantasy books now is higher than it used to be, the late twentieth century produced a good number of happy fantasies that sizzle with energy and shine with joy. They describe the intersection where a child's still-developing self joins smoothly with the community outside itself.

Heroes Who Don't Go Home

There's another pattern besides the home-away-and-back-again plot of stories like *The Phantom Tollbooth*; here the characters (often young adults rather than children) go off into the world and do *not* come back. Thus initiated, they find new lives, maybe help to create or protect a community. The greatgrandparents of this genre are the Owl and the Pussycat (by Edward Lear, 1871), who sailed away for a whole year and a day but ended up happily wed, with new friends (Pig, who provided the ring, and Turkey, who married them), in a new land. THEY DINED ON MINCE, AND SLICES OF QUINCE, / WHICH THEY ATE WITH A RUNCIBLE SPOON; / AND HAND IN HAND, ON THE EDGE OF THE SAND, / THEY DANCED BY THE LIGHT OF THE MOON. These are dancing stories.

Some of them have irrepressible, swashbuckling, wandering heroes. My favorites of this picaresque type include one old book and one newer: Lindsay's Australian tale *The Magic Pudding* (1918) and Steig's *Dominic* (1972). Norman Lindsay, a writer little known in the United States but popular in British lands, chronicled the adventures of Bunyip Bluegum, a gentlemanly koala bear who set off to see the world and fell in with the scruffy sailor Bill Barnacle and his friend Sam, a penguin. Their other companion was the Puddin', a surly magical object given to shouting rude remarks. The Puddin' had a remarkable talent, explained Bill: "THE MORE YOU EATS THE MORE YOU GETS. ME AN' SAM HAS BEEN EATIN' AWAY AT THIS PUDDIN' FOR YEARS, AND THERE'S NOT A MARK ON HIM." He could be steak and kidney pudding or apple dumpling, plum duff, or boiled jam roll. IF YOU WANTED A CHANGE OF FOOD FROM THE PUDDIN', ALL YOU HAD TO DO WAS TO WHISTLE TWICE AND TURN THE BASIN ROUND.

Blueyip Bluegum was invited to join this hearty though pugnacious bunch. "MY PROPOSAL TO YOU IS—BECOME A MEMBER OF THE NOBLE SOCIETY OF PUDDIN'-OWNERS. THE DUTIES OF THE SOCIETY,"

WENT ON BILL, "ARE LIGHT. THE MEMBERS ARE REQUIRED TO WANDER ALONG THE ROADS, INDULGIN' IN CONVERSATION, SONG AND STORY, EATIN' AT REGULAR INTERVALS AT THE PUDDIN'." This happy band, not surprisingly, had its enemies. A pair of Puddin' thieves, Wombat and Possum, tried to seize the Puddin' by force and by trickery, and several times they had him in their clutches. But the true owners won out. Eventually they stopped wandering and settled in a snug tree house. ON WINTER NIGHTS THERE IS ALWAYS PUDDIN' AND HOT COFFEE FOR SUPPER, AND MANY'S THE GOOD GO-IN I'VE HAD UP THERE, A-SITTING ROUND THE FIRE. As Bill said in his "Breakfast Ballad,"

> IF THERE'S ANYTHIN' BETTER THAN CAMP FIRELIGHT,
> IT'S BRIGHT SUNSHINE ON WAKIN'.
> IF THERE'S ANYTHIN' BETTER THAN PUDDIN' AT NIGHT,
> IT'S PUDDIN' WHEN DAY IS BREAKIN'.

Life's riches are inexhaustible, if you're cheerful and tough and if you watch out for Puddin' thieves.

❧ ❧

William Steig's Dominic, a plain but robust hound, traveled the world alone like a knight, seeking adventure and rescuing those in need. Dominic was bold, eloquent, and generous. His splendid talents included fighting and gymnastics, dancing and piccolo playing. True, he congratulated himself too smugly on these talents, and he wasn't always too smart, but gradually his character deepened.

Early on, he thought the world as flawless as he was himself: "WHAT A WONDERFUL WORLD! HOW PERFECT!" HAD IT BEEN UP TO HIM WHEN THINGS WERE FIRST MADE, HE WOULDN'T HAVE MADE THEM A WHIT DIFFERENT. EVERY LEAF WAS IN ITS PROPER PLACE. THE SKY WAS PROPERLY BLUE. But when Bartholomew Badger died, the rich pig who was his friend and benefactor, Dominic realized that THE BEAUTY AND THE SADNESS BELONGED TOGETHER SOMEHOW, THOUGH THEY WERE NOT THE SAME AT ALL. His travels brought him closer to the heart of the universe, as when he discovered that MICE WERE HAVING A MOONLIGHT REVEL IN A CLEARING SURROUNDED BY TALL GRASS AND THEY HAD STRUNG THEIR PRISMATIC LANTERNS BETWEEN

STALKS OF TIMOTHY. DOMINIC, ENCHANTED, WATCHED THE PROCEED-INGS FROM THE TOP OF A ROCK. THERE WAS DELICATE, STATELY MOUSE MUSIC PRODUCED BY TINY ZITHERS, LUTES, AND TAMBOURINES. His re-action showed him to be a creature of both civilization and nature: first, he played his elegant piccolo softly, along with the mice, and then, unable to restrain himself, HE RAISED HIS HEAD AND, STRAINING TOWARD INFINITY, HOWLED OUT THE BURDEN OF HIS LOVE AND LONG-ING IN SOUNDS MORE MEANINGFUL THAN WORDS.

After giving away the fortune in jewels left him by Mr. Badger and destroying the villainous Doomsday gang, Dominic moved on to new adventures. In a magic garden he discovered the beautiful sleeping dog princess he was destined to wake and set out again, with her, into the world. Dominic's life was a celebration of the unity of nature. Why else would Steig give his animal characters the names of other animals? The goose was Mrs. Fox, the turtle Mr. Wallaby, the mouse Mr. Lyon, and so on. At the wild boars' wedding, when it was time for toasting, A RABBIT SHOUTED, "I NOW PROCLAIM THE ETERNAL BROTHERHOOD OF THE ENTIRE ANIMAL KINGDOM!"

Even the forest trees joined in the brotherhood. While Dominic was sleeping in the woods and about to be attacked by the Dooms-day Gang, the trees frightened the villains away by bending over and calling out "For shame!" CONVINCED THAT NATURE ITSELF COULD NO LONGER ABIDE THEIR DESTRUCTIVE, CRIMINAL WAYS, THEY EACH SLUNK ABOUT SEPARATELY, MAKING EFFORTS TO REFORM AND GET INTO NATURE'S GOOD GRACES AGAIN, AS EVERY WANTON ONE OF THEM HAD BEEN IN HIS ORIGINAL CHILDHOOD. DOMINIC, IN AWE AND GRATI-TUDE, KNELT AND MADE OBEISANCE TO THE TREES. Steig's tone is as delicate as the mouse music: he sees that Dominic is at once pomp-ous and carefree, ridiculous and touching. Thoroughly doglike, Dominic is also totally human.

&* *&

The wandering-hero stories most popular a half century ago were the Oz books. Yes, at the end of L. Frank Baum's *The Wonderful Wizard of Oz* (1900) Dorothy stopped wandering and went home to Kansas; but the later Oz books (which I liked as much as *The*

Wizard or more) contain unstructured journeys rather than neat, circular plots. The whole series has a delightful drifting air about it, to the point of incoherence. It's a coherent kind of incoherence: the stories' casual structure indicates that things *are* casual—not causal. One need not analyze past or future, and cannot make precise plans or control events; one can only pursue goals with energy and courage, seizing chances as they appear.

Each of the Oz books describes several loosely connected journeys. In *The Wizard of Oz*, the companions followed the yellow brick road from the Eastern land of the Munchkins to the Emerald City, only to find that the Wizard would not grant their wishes unless they traveled to the Western land of the Winkies and destroyed the Wicked Witch, which they did, only to return to the Emerald City and find that Dorothy must travel to the Southern land of the Quadlings to ask the Good Witch how to get home to Kansas. In each book there is a great deal of to-ing and fro-ing, and around each corner there is some new wonder or horror. Most of these are isolated encounters, with no relation to what comes before or after. In *The Emerald City* (1910), for instance, the travelers visited Bunbury, where the citizens were baked goods, and later Bunnybury, where the citizens were highly civilized rabbits.

In the better Oz books, an exciting sense of freedom arises from this lack of tight cause-and-effect plotting. Like Lindsay's Puddin' owners and Steig's Dominic, Dorothy and her friends know that the universe is big and open and life is a surprise. These books are drenched in an American (also Australian) spirit of possibility and fluidity, not the hierarchical, dense air found in many English children's books. Things are so fluid, in fact, that transformations are common (in *Ozma*, all the good characters except Dorothy and the hen were turned into statues and bric-a-brac) and even genders change from time to time (young Ozma was turned into a boy by a sorceress and for years didn't know who she really was). The task faced by Oz people and Oz readers is not, as it is in many other fantasies, understanding the shape of an intricately designed plot, but rather following a linear pattern and coping with one piece at a time. The pieces, exciting or charming, don't have to add up to a whole.

Oz problems are simple in being not complex, and also simple in being easy to solve. Sheer luck often saved the travelers, or friendly helpers appeared at just the right time, or the threat turned out to be feebler than it seemed at first. Dorothy didn't know she would melt the Wicked Witch by throwing water at her, and Billina the chicken accidentally overheard the Nome King telling how Ozma and the others could be released from their enchanted forms as bric-a-brac. Dozens of helpers like the Scarecrow, Glinda the Good, Shaggy Man, and the Queen of the Mice used their special talents to protect the vulnerable child characters from real harm. People would get lost for a while or wet or hungry or menaced by wolves, but things always improved. Many episodes quickly provide a sigh of relief after the briefest shiver of fear.

So the Oz books are full of, not exactly mastery, but always hope, a breezy confidence that ignores complexity. Just as appealing as the author's cheerful voice are the moments of delight scattered through the stories like raisins in a bland porridge. I don't remember much from my childhood reading in Oz about who went where and why and with whom; but I have always remembered Dorothy, shipwrecked in a strange land, standing on tiptoe to pick her lunch off a tree. It was covered with SQUARE PAPER BOXES, WHICH GREW IN CLUSTERS ON ALL THE LIMBS, AND UPON THE BIGGEST AND RIPEST BOXES THE WORD "LUNCH" COULD BE READ. THERE WERE LUNCH-BOX BLOSSOMS ON SOME OF THE BRANCHES, AND ON OTHERS TINY LITTLE LUNCH-BOXES THAT WERE AS YET QUITE GREEN. THE LEAVES OF THIS TREE WERE ALL PAPER NAPKINS, AND IT PRESENTED A VERY PLEASING APPEARANCE TO THE HUNGRY LITTLE GIRL. The ripe box she chose proved to contain, NICELY WRAPPED IN WHITE PAPERS, A HAM SANDWICH, A PIECE OF SPONGE-CAKE, A PICKLE, A SLICE OF NEW CHEESE AND AN APPLE. EACH THING HAD A SEPARATE STEM, AND SO HAD TO BE PICKED OFF THE SIDE OF THE BOX. The best detail was that each piece of food in the box grew on its own stem. Magic in Baum's stories is mysterious but ordinary, earthy rather than otherworldly.

In among long stretches of undistinguished writing you find such juicy episodes, and resonant motifs pop up from time to time, for instance, The Head. Heads in Oz are something you cannot take for granted; bad things can happen to them, as this world is dangerously as well as gloriously open. Characters worried a lot about how well their brains were functioning. The Scarecrow's head, for example, was sturdier than his straw-filled body but needed occasional repainting of the features, while Jack Pumpkin-head's head was constantly at risk of rotting and had to be periodi-cally replaced. In *The Road to Oz* (1909), Button Bright had his head transformed into a fox head by a sinister stranger, and Shaggy Man received a donkey head. They had to wear these nasty transformations until they could bathe in the Truth Pond, which restored their true heads.

The most horrible heads appeared in *The Emerald City of Oz*: The Whimsies, violent, evil spirits whose heads were the size of doorknobs, WERE SO ASHAMED OF THEIR PERSONAL APPEARANCE AND LACK OF COMMONSENSE THAT THEY WORE BIG HEADS, MADE OF PASTE-BOARD, WHICH THEY FASTENED OVER THEIR OWN LITTLE HEADS. ON THESE PASTEBOARD HEADS THEY SEWED SHEEP'S WOOL FOR HAIR, AND THE WOOL WAS COLORED MANY TINTS—PINK, GREEN AND LAVENDER BEING THE FAVORITE COLORS. On the fake heads they painted gro-tesque, ferocious features. THEY FOOLISHLY IMAGINED THAT NO ONE WOULD SUSPECT THE LITTLE HEADS THAT WERE INSIDE THE IMITATION ONES. The Scoodlers were equally horrid: when the travelers asked, "WHAT DO YOU WANT US FOR?" "SOUP!" THEY ALL SHOUTED, AS IF WITH ONE VOICE. The Scoodlers used their own hideous heads as weap-ons by throwing them at enemies and then retrieving them.

Even more sinister was Princess Langwidere in *Ozma of Oz* (1906), who wore a different head every day. WHEN THE PRINCESS GOT OUT OF HER CRYSTAL BED IN THE MORNING SHE WENT TO HER CABI-NET, OPENED ONE OF THE VELVET-LINED CUPBOARDS, AND TOOK THE HEAD IT CONTAINED FROM ITS GOLDEN SHELF. THEN, BY THE AID OF THE MIRROR SHE PUT ON THE HEAD—AS NEAT AND STRAIGHT AS COULD BE— AND AFTERWARD CALLED HER MAIDS TO ROBE HER FOR THE DAY. THE THIRTY HEADS WERE IN GREAT VARIETY, NO TWO FORMED ALIKE BUT ALL BEING OF EXCEEDING LOVELINESS. She didn't much like No. 26, though, and when Dorothy happened by the palace, Langwidere remarked, "YOU HAVE A CERTAIN STYLE OF PRETTINESS THAT IS DIFFER-ENT FROM THAT OF ANY OF MY THIRTY HEADS. SO I BELIEVE I'LL TAKE

YOUR HEAD AND GIVE YOU NO. 26 FOR IT." "WELL, I B'LIEVE YOU WON'T!" EXCLAIMED DOROTHY, even though it got her locked in the tower. The memorable images in Oz stories make some point about human behavior, usually a point that is unoriginal but satisfyingly relevant. Characters tell each other and themselves to be brave and try hard and use the talents they have and make the best of a bad situation. While Oz people don't develop or grow, they care about being themselves, avoiding vanity, and tolerating all kinds of other creatures. "PARDON ME IF I SEEM INQUISITIVE—ARE YOU NOT ALL RATHER—AHEM!—RATHER UNUSUAL?" ASKED THE WOGGLE-BUG. "NOT MORE SO THAN YOURSELF," ANSWERED THE SCARECROW. "EVERYTHING IN LIFE IS UNUSUAL UNTIL YOU GET ACCUSTOMED TO IT."

Tolerance is a constant theme, as when Billina the hen defended her taste for eating live bugs by insisting that it's more attractive than Dorothy's taste for dead animals. When Aunt Em criticized the Fuddles (people made from puzzle pieces, who would scatter themselves when frightened and need to be reassembled), one of the Fuddles answered with dignity: "MADAM, YOU HAVE PERHAPS NO-TICED THAT EVERY PERSON HAS SOME PECULIARITY. MINE IS TO SCATTER MYSELF. WHAT YOUR OWN PECULIARITY IS I WILL NOT VENTURE TO SAY; BUT I SHALL NEVER FIND FAULT WITH YOU, WHATEVER YOU DO." As Jane Yolen points out in *Touch Magic*, "A child who can love the oddi-ties of a fantasy book cannot possibly be xenophobic as an adult. What is a different color, a different culture, a different tongue for a child who has already mastered Elvish, or respected Puddleg-lums?" (p. 54).

All characters of goodwill were treated well in Oz, regardless of humble origin or peculiar appearance. Princess Ozma, the ruler of this democratic land, was especially careful when people from a modest level of society came before her. The rough hobo Shaggy Man and Dorothy's poor farmer aunt and uncle were stunned to be received with courtesy and given splendid apartments in the palace. Tactfully, Ozma ordered for the Shaggy Man clothes that would respect his identity: After bathing, he found in his new closet an elegant suit. HIS COAT WAS OF ROSE-COLORED VELVET, TRIMMED WITH SHAGS AND BOBTAILS, WITH GOLDEN SHAGS AROUND THE EDGES. HIS VEST WAS A SHAGGY SATIN OF A DELICATE CREAM COLOR.

SHAGGY SLIPPERS OF ROSE LEATHER WITH RUBY BUCKLES COMPLETED HIS COSTUME. HE SIGHED WITH CONTENTMENT TO REALIZE THAT HE COULD NOW BE FINELY DRESSED AND STILL BE THE SHAGGY MAN.

Fifty years after Dorothy was born in Kansas, a sister hero appeared in Sweden, even bolder and stronger. Astrid Lindgren's Pippi Longstocking (1950) could pick up her horse and put him on the porch; she beat up the strong man in the circus; she decided after one day that school was boring and never went back. Pippi's world was as wild and as celebratory as Dorothy's. The benign influence of Oz has oozed everywhere.

Celebrating the Community

It may be easier for a reader to enter a harmonious fictional world when its inhabitants are animals. Even when the characters behave more like people than like their animal selves, they are not really human, so readers can more easily ignore the sad discrepancy between people's behavior in real life and the behavior of characters in the cheerful sorts of fantasy. We are liberated from our normal assumptions and can believe, for instance, in the delightful Gallic society created by Babar the elephant.

In *The Story of Babar* (1933), the naked little elephant ran away after his mother was shot by a hunter and found himself in the city. A kind Old Lady took him in and gave him handsome clothes, a motor-car, and an education. Babar tasted the delights of the department store, the elevator, the patisserie. Now he was ready to go back to the jungle, bringing civilization with him. The old king had just succumbed to the poison of a bad mushroom, so the elephant tribe declared Babar their new king. In *Babar the King* (1935), his plans came to fruition: the elephants built a new city, using supplies delivered by a long line of dromedaries. King Babar MARKS WITH SIGN-BOARDS WHERE THE STREETS AND HOUSES SHOULD GO. HE ORDERS SOME TO CUT DOWN TREES, SOME TO MOVE STONES. THE OLD LADY IS PLAYING THE PHONOGRAPH FOR THEM AND BABAR PLAYS ON HIS TRUMPET; HE IS FOND OF MUSIC. ALL THE ELEPHANTS ARE AS

HAPPY AS HE IS. THEY DRIVE NAILS, DRAW LOGS, DIG, FETCH AND CARRY, OPENING THEIR BIG EARS WIDE AS THEY WORK. The resulting city is perfection, a French version of Southern California: three straight rows of ten charming round houses each, facing the lake, and slightly larger houses for King and Queen and for the Old Lady. Grassy strips and symmetrically placed palm trees separated houses and rows. Behind them stood an impressive building containing the Bureau of Industry, Library, Workshops, and School. Nearby was an even more impressive building labeled *Amusement Hall, Musique, Circus, Theatre, Movies, Danse.* Babar gave each citizen a gift: DRESSES, PAINT BOXES, DRUMS, FISHING TACKLE, OSTRICH FEATHERS, TENNIS RACKETS AND MANY OTHER THINGS.

What more could an elephant want, or a lover of fantasy? The rest of the book describes happy citizens working, cooking, going to school, and playing music. There was a parade to celebrate the founding of Celesteville, also a gathering in the Amusement Park, which resembles the Tuileries, with palm trees and classical statuary of noble elephants. IN THE GARDENS THE ELEPHANTS SAUN-TER AROUND DRESSED MAGNIFICENTLY. THE CHILDREN HAVE SUNG THEIR SONG, BABAR HAS KISSED EACH ONE. THE CAKES WERE DELICIOUS! WHAT A WONDERFUL DAY! Alas, two accidents happened after the parade. A snake bit the Old Lady, and General Cornelius was in-jured when his house caught fire. Babar worried about misfortune coming to his people, but the patients recovered and everyone was optimistic. "LET'S WORK HARD AND CHEERFULLY AND WE'LL CONTINUE TO BE HAPPY." Babar's world is an ideal balance of work and play, individual and community, solidity and lyricism—very pretty, and very funny.

Ɉʒ Ɉʒ

It's ironic that the monarchy in *Babar* is a free and egalitarian sys-tem, while the society of animals in *Winnie-the-Pooh* (by A. A. Milne, 1926), which has no government, is rife with hierarchy and snobbery. Outsiders like Tigger are viewed with suspicion; Rab-bit's friends-and-relations are too lowly to have names; the Forest people are mostly self-centered. The characters' flaws are seen as lovable eccentricities, though—Rabbit's bossiness, Owl's intellectual phoniness, Piglet's meekness, Tigger's bounciness, Pooh's greediness, and Eeyore's gloom. FOR A LONG TIME THEY LOOKED AT THE RIVER BENEATH THEM, SAYING NOTHING. "TIGGER IS ALL RIGHT REALLY," SAID PIGLET LAZILY. "OF COURSE HE IS," SAID CHRISTOPHER ROBIN. "EVERYBODY IS REALLY," SAID POOH. "THAT'S WHAT I THINK," SAID POOH. Differences were unimportant, in the Forest.

An uneasy note entered the Pooh stories: Christopher Robin's friends began to wonder what he was doing in the mornings and why his spelling was improving, and finally they realized he was going away. He explained to Pooh, "I'M NOT GOING TO DO NOTHING ANY MORE. THEY DON'T LET YOU." But the Forest people have had such fine and numerous adventures together that the final note of loss is buried under the larger sense that this is an eternal, fresh world where you set out every day not knowing if you will find the North Pole or catch a Heffalump or write a poem. POOH AND PIG-LET WALKED HOME THOUGHTFULLY TOGETHER IN THE GOLDEN EVE-NING. "WHEN YOU WAKE UP IN THE MORNING, POOH," SAID PIGLET AT LAST, "WHAT'S THE FIRST THING YOU SAY TO YOURSELF?" "WHAT'S FOR BREAKFAST?" SAID POOH. "WHAT DO YOU SAY, PIGLET?" "I SAY, I WONDER WHAT'S GOING TO HAPPEN EXCITING TODAY?" SAID PIGLET. POOH NOD-DED THOUGHTFULLY. "IT'S THE SAME THING," HE SAID.

Other animal utopias have that same sense of a timeless world where conflict is a small, secondary part of life. In Kenneth Gra-hame's The Wind in the Willows (1908), the rich and conceited Mr. Toad went so far—stealing cars, brawling, bragging, breaking out of jail—that his neighbors, the animals of the riverbank, con-ducted an intervention and forced him to reform. Toad was the only discontented, greedy animal in the neighborhood; the oth-ers—Mole, Rat, Badger, and Otter—gloried in their homes and their friendships, and in the cycles of nature. Who doesn't remem-ber Mole revisiting his old shabby home under the snow with Rat, and the boys' choir of field-mice singing Christmas carols? Or Rat's riverside picnic with Mole? COLD CHICKEN, COLDTONGUE COLDHAMCOLDBEEFPICKLEDGHERKINSSALADFRENCHROLLSCRESSSAND WIDGESPOTTEDMEATGINGERBEERLEMONADESODAWATER. (Celebration always means food, and food means celebration.) The river bank animals knew that alien societies existed outside their territory—

the Wild Wood contained bad animals, and the Wide World beyond contained creatures even stranger, human beings. Within their own circle, though, the animals lived in harmony with each other and with the turning world.

In *The Impulse of Fantasy Fiction* (1983), C. N. Manlove describes fantasy as concerned with "the sense of individuality that comes from making things strange and luminous with independent life. At the core of the genre is a delight in being" (p. ix). In celebrating things as they are or might be, fantasy stories represent different worldviews; but they all are "full of the feeling that creation itself is of value; the great enemy of fantasy is nonentity. What is delighted in fantasy is often not only the worlds themselves and what they contain, but the creation, the making of them" (p. xii).

In addition to celebrating its world, a happy fantasy—even a simple, "childish" one—can show how a community works. Although Walter R. Brooks's *Freddy the Pig* books (1940s) are written for younger children, they include detailed, clever, but not pedantic accounts of how a democratic society operates, its values and institutions. In one book, the farm animals figured out how to run a bank; in another one, Jinx the cat was tried for murder of a crow on circumstantial evidence and acquitted through the logical reasoning of his counsel; in another, the animals elected a mayor. The books embody not a civics lesson but the spirit of a community in action.

E. B. White's *Charlotte's Web* (1952), one of the best-loved fantasy tales, contains much fear and sorrow: in the beginning, when the farmer decided to kill Wilbur, the weakest pig in the litter; in the middle, when Wilbur learned about the bloodthirsty habits of his friend the spider and when he was scheduled for slaughtering; and at the end, when Charlotte died alone in her web. These frightening facts of barnyard life were tolerable because they existed within a warm, triumphant natural cycle. LIFE IN THE BARN WAS VERY GOOD, THOUGHT WILBUR, THIS WARM DELICIOUS CELLAR WITH THE GARRULOUS GEESE, THE CHANGING SEASONS, THE HEAT OF THE SUN, THE PASSAGE OF SWALLOWS, THE NEARNESS OF RATS, THE SAMENESS OF SHEEP, THE LOVE OF SPIDERS, THE SMELL OF MANURE, AND THE GLORY OF EVERYTHING. Within this comfortable daily universe there were even a few higher, triumphant moments: Wilbur won a special prize at the county fair, because Charlotte had shown everyone his wonderful qualities by weaving words ("TERRIFIC," "SOME PIG," "RADIANT") in her web.

The Moominfamily stories, by the Finnish author Tove Jansson (from 1948), also absorb terrible events into the pleasant texture of everyday life. The odd adventures of these blobby Moomin creatures included the time their house was flooded. They were forced to retreat upstairs and break a hole in the floor to get at the supplies below. MOOMINPAPPA FOUND SAWING HIS OWN FLOOR TO PIECES JUST A LITTLE DREADFUL, BUT AT THE SAME TIME HIGHLY SATISFYING. A FEW MINUTES LATER MOOMINMAMMA FOR THE FIRST TIME SAW HER KITCHEN FROM THE CEILING. ENCHANTED, SHE LOOKED DOWN TO A DIMLY LIT, LIGHT-GREEN AQUARIUM. ALL THE CHAIRS AND THE TABLE WERE FLOATING AROUND NEAR THE CEILING. "DEAR ME, HOW FUNNY," SAID MOOMINMAMMA AND BURST OUT LAUGHING. IT FELT VERY REFRESHING TO SEE ONE'S KITCHEN LIKE THAT.

The lovely rural universe of Beatrix Potter acknowledges the dark side of existence. Peter Rabbit's father was put in a pie by Mr. McGregor. Tom Kitten (in *The Roly-Poly Pudding*, 1908) was captured by two enormous rats, ROLLED UP IN A BUNDLE, AND TIED WITH STRING IN VERY HARD KNOTS, while the rats discussed the proper ingredients for a KITTEN DUMPLING ROLY-POLY PUDDING FOR DINNER. In *The Tale of Mr. Tod* (1912), Peter and Benjamin Bunny followed the badger and the fox to the foul lair where their kidnapped cousins were hidden. THERE WERE MANY UNPLEASANT THINGS LYING ABOUT, THAT HAD MUCH BETTER HAVE BEEN BURIED; RABBIT BONES AND SKULLS, AND CHICKENS' LEGS AND OTHER HORRORS. IT WAS A SHOCKING PLACE, AND VERY DARK. Jemima Puddle-Duck let herself be beguiled by a gentlemanly fox and almost became his dinner.

Other Beatrix Potter stories present lighter themes, about parties and housecleaning and dollhouses and kittens with dirty clothes. Her universe can include dreadful things without being overwhelmed by them. The horror of these things is faced calmly, and mitigated by the beauty of her detailed illustrations, by the close-up, small-person's perspective from which they are drawn, and by the small, tidy shape and size of the books, along with the large amount of soothing white margin on each page. Most of all, evil in Potter's world is contained and almost (but not quite) canceled out by the crisp precision of her style and humor. The perfection of her foxgloves is ultimately stronger than the nastiness of her foxes; her kindly, domestic cats and mice outlast her villains. Even though a few of their relatives get put in a pie, Beatrix Potter's creatures are philosophical, content.

Since 1950

Those books were very important to mid-twentieth-century children—*Babar, Pooh, The Tale of Mrs. Tittlemouse, Oz, Wind in the Willows.* Scenes of parties and snug gatherings showed that everything would turn out all right. Even sour Eeyore would be included, and even Toad would behave well—issues of great concern to well-behaved readers. Decades later, the triumphal Banquet at Toad Hall and Christopher Robin's party where Pooh was honored and given a Special Pencil Case, which shut with a click, may remain as real to readers as memories of actual picnics and bonfire parties.

Since that seemingly tranquil time, when the United States and its allies had just routed the villains and tidied up the world, the world has become increasingly untidy. Good fantasy books of the celebratory, hopeful type have still been written, but they are less cozy, more restless and wide-ranging in their adventures. And most of them present worlds that are recognizably human (though fantastic), instead of the more remote animal idylls of the earlier stories. The books of Joan Aiken and Carol Kendall, and more recently Eva Ibbotson and Patricia Wrede, describe young characters who develop their own lively selves while working strenuously to create or protect a community. These stories achieve a triumphant balance between the individual and the group.

❧❧ ❧❧

The best-known books of Joan Aiken take place in an imaginary nineteenth-century England infested by wolves and ruled by Stuart kings, currently James III. (Hanoverians had never succeeded in ousting the Stuarts, though they still plotted to do so.) The realm was unsettled and volatile, the opposite of Babar's placid kingdom. In *The Wolves of Willoughby Chase* (1962), child characters used resourcefulness and energy to rearrange pieces of the old, crumbling world into a new, better one. Awful things happened to Bonnie, daughter of the rich, generous Sir Willoughby, and her poor cousin Sylvia; but the things are too grotesquely awful and too funny to be frightening to a reader. When timorous Sylvia traveled from London to stay at Willoughby Hall and wolves attacked the train, a gentleman in her compartment reassured her by saying, "THEY DON'T OFTEN EAT A PASSENGER, I PROMISE YOU." A HEAVY BODY THUDDED SUDDENLY AGAINST THE WINDOW, AND SHE HAD A MOMENTARY VIEW OF A POINTED GRAY HEAD, RED SLAVERING JAWS, AND PALE EYES GLEAMING WITH FEROCITY. The wolf crashed through into the compartment, but the gentleman SEIZED ONE OF THE SHATTERED PIECES OF GLASS AND STABBED THE BEAST. IT FELL DEAD. "TUSH," SAID SYLVIA'S COMPANION, BREATHING HEAVILY. "UNEXPECTED—MOST."

While Bonnie's parents were away on a voyage, Miss Slighcarp, the governess, fired the servants, forged Sir Willoughby's signature to a new will, and took to wearing Lady Green's ballgowns. She starved Bonnie and Sylvia, locked them in a dark cupboard, then sent them to an orphan school run by her accomplice, where pupils had numbers instead of names. Mrs. Brisket made money out of her pupils' hard labor: WHEN THE SHEETS HAD BEEN PAINFULLY SCRUBBED AND RINSED THREE TIMES BY HANDS THAT WERE RED AND SORE FROM THE HARSH SOAP AND ICY WATER, EMMA SHOWED SYLVIA HOW TO USE THE WRINGER. "NEVER TOUCH IT. ONE GIRL LOST HER FINGERS IN IT." People were impossibly bad or impossibly good. Simon, a loyal shepherd lad from Willoughby Chase, followed the girls to the school, helped them escape, then smuggled them to London in his donkey cart full of geese and feathers to find Sir Willoughby's lawyer. Kindly adults helped them, but the children's own resourcefulness and persistence caused the happy outcome, in which lawyers and constables popped out of secret tunnels in Willoughby Chase to capture Miss Slighcarp and her associates, who had sold the contents of the mansion and turned it into a Select Seminary.

There is a common pattern in this book and others by Aiken: some spunky children make their way through a society that doesn't work and along the way pick up other people to join them in seeking their goals, always including some devoted lower-class adults and some kindred-spirit mentors and some helpful officials. Together they create a new community, including people of different ages and social strata. In *The Wolves*, Bonnie's parents—who were thought to be drowned—reappeared and restored Willoughby; poor, ladylike Aunt Jane was given the Dower House on the estate to run as a delightful school for the orphan pupils; and Simon the shepherd boy was adopted by Sir Willoughby. The ruffians were beautifully punished. So traditional society survived in greatly improved form.

Black Hearts in Battersea (1964) follows the same plot pattern, where children shake up and improve the corrupt status quo, but its story is even more antic. Simon, now an art student, befriended Dido Twite, an irrepressible London urchin. Dido and Simon uncovered a Hanoverian plot to blow up the Duke and Duchess of Battersea along with King James III. Aiken happily uses the whole repertoire of melodrama: children switched at birth (Simon turned out to be the duke's heir), victims of shipwreck washed up on the island of the old nurse who knew the secret, and so forth. Sophie, Simon's old friend from the orphan home who was maid to the duchess, repeatedly saved her employers from assassination by dextrously using the duchess's enormous tapestry embroidery, which the old lady had been working on for years. When their opera box was set on fire, for instance, Sophie hung the tapestry over the railing and persuaded them to slide down it to safety. When wolves cornered them in an abandoned hut, Sophie nailed it up to block the door. And when the whole party sailed to London in an enormous balloon to expose the Hanoverian conspiracy, Sophie flung Her Grace's tapestry over the puncture caused by an enemy bullet. The aristocracy, though flawed, was as indestructible as the duchess's tapestry. Predictably, Sophie turned out to be the duke's daughter and Simon's sister.

You can tell an Aiken story by its fast, ridiculous action and loopy style; Aiken writes like a granddaughter of Charles Dickens, cousin of Edward Gorey, and aunt of Lemony Snicket. There is always some kind of lush archaic jargon, sailors' talk in *Nightbirds in Nantucket,* aristocrats' chat and London lowlife language in *Battersea.* "WE COULD SNIBBLE UP NOW, THERE'S ONLY A COUPLE OF COVES ON PEEP-GO." SHE ORDERED HIM NOT TO SQUAT THERE GAPING LIKE A JOBBERKNOLL. "I MIGHT AS WELL PRIG SOME PECK WHILE THE GOING'S GOOD." The breezy talk works well in these tall tales about a dangerous world where courage, intelligence, and goodwill could forge a new community out of old materials.

❧ ❧

In Carol Kendall's books, society does not need to be created: the Minnipins did that eight centuries earlier, when their forefathers, fleeing enemies, discovered the beautiful Land Between the Mountains and built twelve villages along the river. What this conservative society did need was greater tolerance for the differences among its citizens. Life was pleasant but rigidly traditional in Slipper-on-the-Water, the village in which *The Gammage Cup* (1959) takes place. People there did what was expected; they wore brown and green clothes and lived in cottages with green doors, all except a few free spirits: Gummy composed poems, while Curley Green made pictures and painted her door scarlet; Walter the Earl studied old parchments and dug for treasures, to learn about the past of his people; Muggles, the jolly soul who ran the museum, wore an orange sash and asked improper questions. (Incidentally, a Pennsylvania children's writer named Nancy Stauffer, accusing J. K. Rowling of stealing from her book, cited her own use of the word *Muggles*—which means dull, unmagical people in the Harry Potter books—as evidence, but her suit was thrown out. It's possible that one or both of these authors unconsciously remembered the name from *The Gammage Cup*, written about forty years earlier. Kendall's character Muggles is rebellious and quite the opposite of dull.)

When the outraged townspeople exiled these harmless eccentrics, they built a refuge in the nearby mountains and happened to discover that the mushroom people, evil enemies of the Minnipins, were heading through a tunnel to attack the Land Between the Mountains. Using their brains and their unique skills, and also the ancient weapons and armor unearthed by Walter the Earl, the exiled citizens saved their land from the mushroom people. Slipper-on-the-Water declared them heroes and in their honor took to wearing bright clothing and painting village doors wild colors. The relation of the individual to the group was restored to a proper balance, people were free to be creative, and everyone lived happily in this snug, hobbit-like land. A sequel describes another set of lively Minnipins proving their heroism, by venturing out of the Land Between the Mountains and dealing with weird new creatures and experiences.

Kendall writes charmingly; the exciting events move briskly; the robust characters are appealing. We cheer for shy Muggles: she gradually turned into a strong, clever leader. Some of her wise *Maxims*, collected after the heroic events, appear at the beginnings of chapters: WHEN SOMETHING HAPPENS, SOMETHING ELSE ALWAYS HAPPENS. . . . IF YOU DON'T LOOK FOR TROUBLE, HOW CAN YOU KNOW IT'S THERE? . . . THE BEST THING TO DO WITH A BAD SMELL IS TO GET RID OF IT.

❧ ❧

The special islands of Eva Ibbotson's books are sequestered from the real world like Kendall's land of the Minnipins, but their populations are full of odd creatures, not homogeneous at all. In both *The Secret of Platform 13* (1994) and *Island of the Aunts* (1999), good characters, to solve the problems of their own small islands, had to interact with complicated larger worlds that threatened their harmonious lives. Platform 13 in London's King's Cross Railway Station was the location of a gump: each country had its own gump, a mound on the earth with A HIDDEN DOOR WHICH OPENED EVERY SO OFTEN TO REVEAL A TUNNEL WHICH LED TO A COMPLETELY DIFFERENT WORLD. This gump, which opened for nine days every nine years, allowing people and magical creatures to pass back and forth, led to a secret cove from which ships sailed to the Island.

All kinds lived there: SENSIBLE PEOPLE WHO UNDERSTOOD THAT EVERYONE DID NOT HAVE TO HAVE EXACTLY TWO ARMS AND LEGS, BUT MIGHT BE DIFFERENT IN SHAPE AND IN THE WAY THEY THOUGHT. SO THEY LIVED PEACEFULLY WITH OGRES WHO HAD ONE EYE, OR DRAGONS. THEY UNDERSTOOD THAT ELLERWOMEN HAD HOLLOW BACKS AND HATED TO BE LOOKED AT ON A SATURDAY AND THAT IF TROLLS WANTED TO WEAR THEIR BEARDS SO LONG THAT THEY STEPPED ON THEM EVERY TIME THEY WALKED, THEN THAT WAS ENTIRELY THEIR OWN AFFAIR. The royal family were just right for this reasonable place: NOT GREEDY, NOT COVERED IN JEWELS, BUT BRAVE AND FAIR. THE ROOMS OF THE PALACE WERE SIMPLE AND COOL; THE WINDOWS WERE KEPT OPEN SO THAT BIRDS COULD FLY IN AND OUT. INTELLIGENT DOGS LAY SLEEPING BY THE HEARTH; BOWLS OF FRESH FRUIT AND FRAGRANT FLOWERS STOOD ON THE TABLES—AND ANYONE WHO HAD NOWHERE TO GO FOUND SANCTUARY THERE. Then the Queen's baby was kidnapped.

The islanders had to wait nine years to try and recover him, as the gump closed after the careless nursemaids brought news that the baby had been seized in London. Finally, a scraggly rescue party could be sent from the Island to the home of Mrs. Trottle, the hideous, rich kidnapper who had wanted a baby and was used to getting what she wanted. The rescuers were A WHEEZING OLD WIZARD, A SLIGHTLY BATTY FEY, AND A ONE-EYED GIANT WHO LIVED IN THE MOUNTAINS MAKING CHEESE; also a nice, sensible girl hag named Odge. Meeting a bright young boy at the Trottle mansion, they assumed he was the lost heir but were dismayed to find he was just Ben, the kitchen boy. The Trottle child was Raymond, a horrid screaming child in yellow silk pajamas. Hearing about the splendid Island—GREEN FIELDS WITH WILDFLOWERS AND GROVES OF ANCIENT TREES, SEALS AND BUZZARDS AND RABBITS AND CRABS—Raymond merely whined, "IS THERE A PIER WITH SLOT MACHINES AND AN AMUSEMENT ARCADE?" The rescuers, though heartbroken at the prince's dreadfulness, struggled bravely against Mrs. Trottle and her henchmen to bring him home, where, of course, it was revealed that hardworking Ben was the true heir. The Island was once again a paradise for all: the lovely and the unlovely, together.

Island of the Aunts is an unusual book, an environmental fantasy with a sense of humor. Once again Ibbotson points out how greedy and decadent our society tends to be. THE TAPS WERE GOLD AND SO WERE THE SHOWER FITTINGS, AND ON SHELVES ALL ROUND WERE CUT-GLASS BOTTLES FULL OF WONDERFUL THINGS: COLORED CRYSTALS AND GLITTERING HAIR SPRAYS AND CREAMS FOR MAKING THE BODY FIRM, AND MORE CREAMS FOR MAKING IT SOFT ONCE IT WAS FIRM, AND MORE CREAMS STILL FOR MAKING IT NOT JUST SOFT AND FIRM BUT ALSO PINK. As usual, her people are either sensible and loving or else wicked and materialistic.

On an abandoned island formerly used for secret army tests and thus not recorded on any map, three spinster sisters who had founded a refuge for creatures in need (selkies, stranded jellyfish, eels with skin diseases, mermaids caught in oil slicks) began to worry what would happen when they died. Who would tend the stoorworm, a gigantic worm PALE AND GLISTENING AND UTTERLY STRANGE, given to discussing philosophical questions like, "WHY DON'T WE THINK WITH OUR STOMACHS?" OR "WHY ARE WE BACK TO FRONT IN THE MIRROR BUT NOT UPSIDE DOWN?"

The solution involved posing as Aunts from a London child care agency, kidnapping some nice but unhappy children, and bringing them to the island to test whether they would be good custodians of the future. Two of the resulting children were perfect: Minette, whose divorced parents fought over having to care for her, and Fabio, whose Brazilian mother let his late father's parents bring him up as an English gentleman. (They detested their "foreign" grandson but were distraught when he vanished, because he was their property.) The third child, a nightmare boy like Raymond in *Platform 13*, was brought to the island by accident. Lambert Sprott, hating the place and its creatures while the other children were learning to love and take care of them, got through to his father on his cell phone; Mr. Sprott then set off in his yacht to track down the hidden island, planning to seize the exotic creatures and make money off them. He would charge TWO HUNDRED POUNDS FOR HELICOPTER RIDES TO THE ISLAND OF FREAKS. THE PRETTY MERMAID WAS WORTH A FORTUNE. AS FOR THAT CREEPY WORM, HE COULD JUST SEE THE VISITORS CLUTCHING EACH OTHER AND SCREAMING. IT WOULD BE A CROSS BETWEEN A ZOO, A CARNIVAL, AND DISNEYLAND.

The Sprott gang captured everyone and flung them in his boat, but it was rammed by the gigantic, enraged Kraken, the magnificent Soul of the Sea, who would swim round and round the world's oceans healing the damage caused by humans. As he swam, he hummed the magical Great Hum, which made people behave, throwing back excess fish, leaving their oil-drilling stations, and stowing their rubbish elsewhere. The island people were rescued, but Minette and Fabio had to go back to their families, who didn't mind because the publicity brought them money. The children didn't mind either, because the Aunts made wills leaving the island to Minette and Fabio. The hilarious, healing island would survive. Eva Ibbotson is one of the most inventive and good-natured of fantasy writers. You never know what will happen next, or what startling creature will pop up.

❧ ❧

Patricia Wrede's *Enchanted Forest* series plays with fairy tale conventions. In *Dealing with Dragons* (1990), a princess whose family was upset that she couldn't do anything right complained, "I DID EXACTLY WHAT THEY TOLD ME, AND THE BEGGAR-WOMAN WAS A FAIRY IN DISGUISE, BUT INSTEAD OF SAYING THAT WHENEVER I SPOKE DIAMONDS AND ROSES WOULD DROP FROM MY MOUTH, SHE SAID THAT SINCE I WAS SO KIND, I WOULD NEVER HAVE ANY PROBLEMS WITH MY TEETH." A giant complained he was tired of meeting quotas for ravaging, pillaging, and marauding. One of Wrede's major themes is the distress characters feel at society's rigid roles and expectations.

The most eloquent rebel was Cimorene, a princess so disgusted at the wimpy behavior demanded of her that she ran away and volunteered to work for one of the dragons. This was a shocking affront to convention, because normally a family arranged that a dragon would capture a marriageable princess and keep her a while, so that a knight could rescue and wed her. Cimorene enjoyed her work for the comfortable dragon Kazul, cooking and cataloguing messy piles of treasure; other princesses sat around whining instead of doing anything useful in the dragon caves. When knights came knocking to challenge the dragon and win Cimorene's hand, she sent them packing. To one crestfallen knight she said, "I'D RATHER NOT BE RESCUED, THANK YOU JUST THE SAME. AND EVEN IF I WANTED TO, YOU'RE GOING AT IT ALL WRONG. SHOUTING, 'COME OUT AND FIGHT' THE WAY YOU DID. NO SELF-RESPECTING DRAGON IS GOING TO ANSWER TO A CHALLENGE LIKE THAT. 'STAND FORTH AND DO BATTLE' IS THE USUAL CHALLENGE." Cimorene was smart and efficient, also fearless. When an enraged twelve-foot-tall jinn shouted, "TIS MY WILL THAT THOU SHALL DIE BY MY HAND. THOU HAST BUT TO CHOOSE THE MANNER OF THY DEATH"—"OLD AGE," CIMORENE SAID PROMPTLY. Adventuring through the Mountains of Morning and the Enchanted Forest, she exposed a plot by evil wizards and unmasked a traitor dragon. Kazul became the new King of Dragons, and Cimorene was promoted to King's Cook and Librarian.

The second book, *Searching for Dragons* (1990), enters the Enchanted Forest, an unnerving place. PEOPLE THERE WERE ALWAYS GETTING CHANGED INTO FLOWERS OR TREES OR ANIMALS OR ROCKS, OR DOING SOMETHING CARELESS AND HAVING THEIR HEADS TURNED BACK-WARD, OR BEING CARRIED OFF BY OGRES OR TROLLS. It was a benign place, though, for those of goodwill. Young King Mendanbar was an engaging fellow, not too proud to help with the plumbing. While calling on the dragons, he used his magic sword to fix a stopped-up sink for Cimorene. These two attractive young people wandered about solving problems and then got married. In the third book in the series, *Calling on Dragons* (1993), Cimorene became the only pregnant hero I know of in children's fantasy fiction, wielding the magic sword, whooshing about the land on transport spells, and melting wizards with buckets of soapy water.

Wrede, like Baum in the later Oz books, runs out of ideas for clever magic incidents and starts repeating herself. Too many of her characters have predictable tics of speech or behavior; too many jokes go on too long. At her best she offers informal, forth-right characters in a tricky magical world. The most interesting aspects of her stories are spatial: for instance, the details of life in the dragons' elaborate network of caves. And in Mendanbar's castle, THERE WERE CORRIDORS THAT LOOPED AND CURLED AND TWISTED, ROOMS THAT LED INTO OTHER ROOMS, AND EVEN ROOMS THAT HAD

BEEN BUILT INSIDE OF OTHER ROOMS. THERE WERE SECRET PASSAGEWAYS AND SLIDING PANELS AND TRAPDOORS.

The Enchanted Forest itself is particularly resonant. When King Mendanbar discovered that wizards were causing destruction in the forest, leaving sad dead patches, he worked on restoring some of them: CAREFULLY, HE REACHED OUT AND GATHERED A HANDFUL OF MAGIC. IT FELT LIKE TAKING HOLD OF A HANDFUL OF THIN CORDS, EXCEPT THAT THE CORDS WERE INVISIBLE, FLOATING IN THE AIR. PULLING GENTLY ON THE INVISIBLE THREADS, MENDANBAR STEPPED SLOWLY BACKWARD. WITH A SUDDEN WRENCH, EVERYTHING SNAPPED INTO PLACE.

Later, he felt the power of the forest washing over him, AND AS IT DID HE SAW PATTERNS IN IT. HE SAW HOW TO SHIFT THE PATTERN JUST A LITTLE, FILLING IT IN WITH THE POWER STOLEN FROM THE FOREST AND STORED IN THE SWORD, TO REPAIR THE DAMAGE THE WIZARDS HAD DONE. It's the physicality of the magic that brings this world to life; besides the threads of power in the forest (which sound like the rays activated when you turn on an alarm system), there are shield spells and fireproofing potions and talking mirrors and defective flying carpets that must go to the repair man. Cimorene and Mendanbar navigate all this with good sense and gumption, working to protect delicate alliances among the various communities—humans, dragons, good witches and sorcerers, and assorted bizarre creatures.

Marvelous Places

Roxaboxen, a 1991 picture book written by Alice McLerran and illustrated by Barbara Cooney, creates a wonderful play town created by children in an Arizona desert village. The author's mother and aunt and half a dozen friends did, in fact, create such a town when they were children. MARION CALLED IT ROXABOXEN. THERE ACROSS THE ROAD, IT LOOKED LIKE ANY ROCKY HILL—NOTHING BUT SAND AND ROCKS, SOME OLD WOODEN BOXES, CACTUS AND GREASEWOOD AND THORNY OCOTILLO—BUT IT WAS A SPECIAL PLACE. . . . A TOWN BEGAN TO GROW, TRACED IN LINES OF STONE: MAIN STREET FIRST,

EDGED WITH THE WHITEST ONES. AT FIRST THE HOUSES WERE VERY PLAIN, BUT SOON THEY ALL BEGAN TO ADD MORE ROOMS. THE WOODEN BOXES COULD BE SHELVES OR TABLES OR ANYTHING YOU WANTED. They added more streets, ice cream parlors and shops, a fort, jail, and cemetery. THE ONLY GRAVE IN IT WAS FOR A DEAD LIZARD. AND SPRING CAME, AND THE OCOTILLO BLOSSOMED, AND EVERYBODY SUCKED THE HONEY FROM ITS FLOWERS, AND EVERYBODY BUILT NEW ROOMS, AND EVERYBODY DECIDED TO HAVE JEWELED WINDOWS. Fifty years later, they all remembered Roxaboxen. Cooney's earthy pictures glow, showing how the children's imagination made something thrilling out of dry nothingness.

Deeply sedimented in the minds of fiction readers, there are special places like Roxaboxen, full of magic and meaning (though they may not know what the meaning is): the garden of tumbling peonies in *Tom Kitten*, the warm barn in *Charlotte's Web*, the Hundred Acre Wood in *Winnie-the-Pooh*. They may be indoors, personal places like Mole's home in *Wind in the Willows* or Peter Pan's cave. They may be outdoor settings—open, with wide vistas like Ibbotson's Island of the Aunts, or marvelous enclosed green spaces like *Tom's Midnight Garden*. Enchanted places appear in realistic stories, of course, like *The Secret Garden*, but they take on a particular shimmer when the whole work is fantasy.

These marvelous places are found most often in celebratory, light fantasies, those harmonious worlds where conflicts are resolvable. Often opposing characters or groups are reconciled during a visit to what Northrop Frye (in *Anatomy of Criticism: Four Essays*, 1957) called the Green World. Think of *As You Like It* scenes in the Forest of Arden, and picnics in Jane Austen's novels, where people find their true selves. It's a movement away from habit and system, outward to freedom and insight, and back again. The other kind of marvelous place goes not outward but inward, to some restorative womblike shelter: a cave, a cabin, a kitchen.

In the darker fantasies, either there exists no special harmonious place (that's partly why it *is* a darker world), or else such a place appears for a brief, fragile moment of brightness within a continuing danger or gloom. Tolkien's Rivendell and Lorien are such places, momentary sanctuaries; his hobbits' homes are cozy places from which they set out, which never are the same when they return. Even most of the lighter books suggest that these marvelous places are vulnerable. When Christopher Robin had to leave the Hundred Acre Wood for school, when Mole visited his underground home but didn't live there anymore, there is a sense of loss, muted, rueful, though not tragic. The special place is somehow out of the world it nestles in but ultimately subject to its laws; it is a moment both in and out of the natural cycle of time. Generations of children have read with delight in *The Secret Garden* where Mary finds and explores the abandoned walled garden. You might think this would be unexciting—a grumpy child rooting around among dry rose branches—but you would be wrong.

When I was six years old, I spent much of my free time (when I wasn't reading) blissfully sitting under our baby grand piano, having draped the outside with blankets and furnished the inside with various talismanic objects. My sons built a similar but more spacious cave out of dining room chairs, and I let it stay, remembering my piano house. A popular children's toy is the plastic cover that looks like a house, with a little peaked roof, a door, and painted windows. When you fit it over a card table, you can sit there for ages, celebrating and restoring your soul and eating potato chips. You can even read, by the dim light that comes through the plastic cover, and thus travel to new marvelous places, inside your own marvelous place.

❧ ❧

P. L. Travers's Mary Poppins (1934) spent her Day Out with Bert the Match-Man inside a chalk picture Bert had sketched on the pavement. Bert DREW HER RIGHT OUT OF THE STREET, INTO THE VERY MIDDLE OF THE PICTURE. HOW GREEN IT WAS THERE AND HOW QUIET, AND WHAT SOFT CRISP GRASS UNDER THEIR FEET! THEY MOVED ON TO-GETHER THROUGH THE LITTLE WOOD, TILL PRESENTLY THEY CAME UPON A LITTLE OPEN SPACE FILLED WITH SUNLIGHT. AND THERE ON A GREEN TABLE WAS AFTERNOON-TEA.

THEY DRANK IT AND HAD TWO CUPS MORE EACH, AND THEN, FOR LUCK, THEY FINISHED THE PILE OF RASPBERRY-JAM-CAKES. AFTER THAT THEY GOT UP AND BRUSHED THE CRUMBS OFF. "THERE IS NOTHING TO

PAY," SAID THE WAITER, BEFORE THEY HAD TIME TO ASK FOR THE BILL. "IT IS A PLEASURE. YOU WILL FIND THE MERRY-GO-ROUND OVER THERE!" This adventure inside Bert's picture, which occurs early in the book, sets up in pure form some basic delights—a "little open space filled with sunlight"; food with a friend; playful, whirling motion on the merry-go-round. On other occasions, Mary Poppins included Jane and Michael and the twins, showing them wonderful places within the mundane geography of London. Through Mary Poppins's magic, the children visited the land under the sea, the animals' dancing party at the zoo, the circus show of constellations in the sky. From their nursery window they saw in the park their nanny and some wooden figures from a Noah's Ark, creating the spring: FROM THE PILE OF PAINTED WOOD NELLIE-RUBINA AND MARY POPPINS EACH TOOK A LONG SPRAY OF LEAVES AND, LEAPING INTO THE AIR, ATTACHED THEM SWIFTLY TO THE NAKED FROSTY BRANCHES OF THE TREES. NELLIE-RUBINA AND MARY POPPINS SEIZED THE REMAINING WOODEN SHAPES AND RAN SWIFTLY ABOUT THE PARK TOSSING THE BUTTERFLIES INTO THE AIR. AND THE CURIOUS THING WAS THAT THEY STAYED THERE, POISED ABOVE THE EARTH, THEIR BRIGHT PATCHES OF PAINT SHOWING CLEARLY IN THE STARLIGHT. Despite the harrumphings of Mary Poppins in her role as nanny—"SPIT-SPOT INTO BED"; "DON'T BITE YOUR BUS TICKET!"—this is a world of celebration.

Mystery, magic, and celebration, in Mary Poppins's London, are hidden in special places: experiences tucked away inside normal, dull life, made especially powerful by their hiddenness. In J. M. Barrie's *Peter Pan* (1911), magic is not hidden within the everyday world but separate, in another realm called Neverland. Just as that playful place is isolated from real life, its mood is ambiguous, less celebratory: Peter Pan will never grow up; childhood and adulthood can never be integrated, nor can work and play, reason and imagination. Peter is pathetic as well as sprightly, and the world is imbued with a sense of loss. The children in *Mary Poppins* were safer, and they had more fun. They were always aware that loss would come eventually to the haven of their nursery—that Mary Poppins would leave them some day—but the threat seemed distant, and it seemed part of the natural order of things.

❧ ❧

Fantasy authors who write from a religious perspective (and they are many) see the sheltering place, and the moment out of time, as partaking of the sacred and attained by ritual. Those special states are equally important in thoroughly secular stories, where the complex muddle of ordinary life requires some extraordinary condition, safe and free, to clarify our view and provide perspective. The concept of "liminality"—thresholdness—is discussed by Victor Turner in *The Ritual Process* (1969) and Tom Driver in *Liberating Rites* (1998): participants in a ritual go from their everyday state through a threshold, or ritual pathway, to a new, renewed state. The liminal, transitional position involves simplicity, humility, and "communitas" (a sense of relatedness with humanity and the universe), while the everyday state involves complexity, status, and hierarchy.

Fictional characters who find marvelous places are like participants in religious rituals going through "threshold" activities. The most memorable scenes in fantasy stories are often the moments of transition: like C. S. Lewis's children crawling into the old wardrobe and coming out in Narnia, Alice falling down the rabbit hole, or Dorothy flying through the cyclone in her house.

Elizabeth Goudge is probably the Queen of the Liminal Fantasy Writers. In *The Little White Horse* (1946) and *Linnets and Valerians* (1964), there are dozens of splendid special places and thresholds leading into them—gates, hidden entrances, little doors. Her child characters climb winding staircases and come out in snug, peculiar, shining rooms; they push through tunnels of green bushes into entrancing little gardens. Goudge lets her children find perfection, and she lets them stay there. For those who don't mind a high sugar content in their reading, Goudge's books are superb. You can't take celebration much further. ROBIN ENVELOPED HER IN A GREAT BEAR HUG THAT NEARLY TOOK HER BREATH AWAY. AND ALL THE ANIMALS (WHO HAD COME RIGHT INTO THE HALL) GATHERED ROUND THEM IN A CIRCLE AND ROARED AND BARKED AND WHINNIED WITH JOY.

When orphaned Maria, in *The Little White Horse*, came to her distant cousin in Moonacre Hall, she found some ancient quarrels that were easily mended, along with joyful people and beasts and a plethora of marvelous places. MARIA STEPPED INSIDE AND FOUND THE KITCHEN TABLE SPREAD WITH A FAIR WHITE CLOTH, AND UPON IT WAS A PLATE OF PINK-ICED CAKES, A FOAMING MUG OF MILK, AND A SMALL SILVER DISH FULL OF CANDIED CHERRIES. . . . THE HILLS STOOD ALL ROUND THE VALLEY LIKE A GREAT WALL. THEY WERE BROKEN ONLY IN ONE PLACE, WHERE THEY FELL AWAY LIKE PARTING CURTAINS TO SHOW A SHINING SLAB OF MOTHER-OF-PEARL THAT LOOKED LIKE THE DOOR-STEP TO HEAVEN. IT WAS THE SEA.

The entrances to these places were at least as exciting as what was beyond them: MARIA WALKED ROUND THE ROCK, AND THERE BE-HIND IT, ALMOST HIDDEN BY A ROWAN-TREE THAT DROOPED OVER IT FROM THE HILLSIDE ABOVE, WAS A DOOR IN THE HILL. The narrow, low door to Maria's room in the old stone tower was LIKE THE DOOR OF HER VERY OWN HOUSE. IT WAS OF SILVERY GREY OAK STUDDED WITH SILVER NAILS, AND IT HAD A KNOCKER MADE OF THE SMALLEST HORSE-SHOE MARIA HAD EVER SEEN. The round room beyond this door pre-sented infinite delights, including a vaulted stone ceiling ribbed like tree branches, and a blue box filled with biscuits.

Goudge's later book, *Linnets and Valerians,* contains a darker note, as the lady of the village had lost her son and husband to pin-sticking spells of the local witch. But four innocent children drove up in a magic pony cart, to live with their uncle, the vicar, defeat the witch, and replace the adult melancholy with the joy of Eden. Marvelous places and thresholds range from the shadowy church—LIKE A CAVERN UNDER THE SEA LIT WITH DIM GREEN LIGHT, WITH SUNBEAMS THAT HAD PIERCED DOWN THROUGH MILES OF WATER FROM THE WORLD ABOVE—to the sexually explicit cave: THERE WAS THE WIDTH OF A DOORWAY BETWEEN THE ROCK AND THE NARROW EN-TRANCE TO THE CAVE, HARDLY MORE THAN A LONG CRACK THROUGH WHICH A BIG MAN COULD SQUEEZE WITH DIFFICULTY. It's a sheltering world, where Uncle Ambrose taught the children with an ideal mix of freedom and structure, where young Nan imagined good spirits holding over her an umbrella of safety. And there are the bees, who must be treated courteously. "MADAM QUEENS AN' NOBLE BEES," SAID EZRA, "THERE BE FOUR CHILDREN COME TO BIDE IN THIS 'OUSE. THEY BE GOOD CHILDREN. 'AVE A CARE OF 'EM AND LET NO 'ARM COME TO 'EM.

'AVE A CARE OF 'EM IN THE WOOD AND ON THE 'ILL. GOOD NIGHT FROM ALL THAT LIVES AN' BREATHES IN 'OUSE AN' GARDEN, THE MICE IN THE WAINSCOT AN' ALL THAT WEARS FUR OR FEATHER IN YOUR DOMINION."

This peaceful universe is a long distance from Alice's rabbit-hole leading to chaos, or Ged's grim wall by the desert land of death in Le Guin's *The Farthest Shore*. Celebratory fantasies like Goudge's are alien to the spirit of the twenty-first century, where we know that evil is not so easily destroyed. Maybe some people still want to read them, for just that reason. Maybe, if we are courteous, the bees will let no harm come to us.

3

꧁❧ ❦ ꧁❧

Shifting Worlds: Playing with Time and Space

Little Stephen, in Joyce's *A Portrait of the Artist as a Young Man*, wrote on the flyleaf of his geography book:

> *Stephen Dedalus*
> *Class of Elements*
> *Clongowes Wood College*
> *Sallins*
> *County Kildare*
> *Ireland*
> *Europe*
> *The World*
> *The Universe*

Real and fictional children often make this kind of list as they try to understand their unique positions in space and time. After you grasp, as a toddler, that your self is separate from everything outside the self, in the next years you need to figure out: What is this non-self like? What are its parts? and Where does your own self fit in? I have been discussing books in which a simple, happy, celebratory world surrounds the self. Such marvelous safe places are appealing, but they are not enough. Here I will consider books that break ordinary laws of time and place and proportion. Reading these books, we are freed from normal, confining rules and can gradually figure out new rules that apply in these fantasy circumstances—all of which hints that our firmly held assumptions about the world may be too rigid. We come to realize that there is a weird but revealing view to be seen only from the other side of Alice's looking-glass.

Of course, all fantasy stories break natural law. Sometimes two different worlds are both presented fully; other times, there is an excursion of characters from the primary world (like our own real one) into a more fully described secondary (fantasy) world, or else an incursion by characters, spirits, creatures, or objects, from the secondary into the more fully developed primary world. Dorothy goes to Oz; the Psammead comes to England. The present chapter will consider the type of book that emphasizes not the different universes themselves but the changes and contrasts, not the rules found in these worlds but the rules governing the shifts—the magic. Readers who enter the shifting worlds of this kind of book may become very big or very small, or both, like Alice; may zip back in time or forward; may destroy gravity and fly on wings or carpets. They look and listen and think from dazzling new perspectives.

One of my earliest memories is of an object displayed on my grandmother's desk, a set of Russian nesting dolls. The rounded, rudimentary shape of the wooden dolls seemed wonderful, and the bright patterned colors, and the startling way each one fit inside another. For some reason, I dipped the tiniest doll into my grandmother's ink bottle, thus introducing the stain of original sin to the smallest baby in its wooden womb. This made me feel nervous and guilty, but I still loved the nesting dolls. They told me there was more than the obvious world around me, that there were worlds inside and outside other worlds.

Even the everyday universe contains much that seems mysterious to children. Fantasy fiction lets them practice the skill of making sense of confusion, using logic and imagination together. A child's mind can enjoy and even invent for itself strange, creative perspectives and explanations. My niece's four-year-old son once asked his mother, "How do elevators change things?" Not everybody likes viewing the world from a weird new perspective, of course; not everybody is comfortable with the discomfort of the strange. It takes a hardy type of child to enjoy the moment when Alice tried the "DRINK ME" bottle: SHE WENT ON GROWING AND GROWING, AND SHE TRIED LYING DOWN WITH ONE ELBOW AGAINST THE DOOR, AND THE OTHER ARM CURLED AROUND HER HEAD. AS A LAST RESOURCE, SHE PUT ONE ARM OUT OF THE WINDOW, AND ONE FOOT UP THE CHIMNEY, AND SAID TO HERSELF, "NOW I CAN DO NO MORE. WHAT *WILL* BECOME OF ME?" Cautious children are disturbed by Alice's adventures, but others find them exciting and appealing.

Lewis Carroll's existential chaos ("WAS I THE SAME WHEN I GOT UP THIS MORNING? BUT IF I'M NOT THE SAME, WHO IN THE WORLD AM I?") is the opposite extreme from the more orderly magic encountered, for instance, by E. Nesbit's characters in *Five Children and It* (1902). Alice was truly alone, while Nesbit's four children took care of each other and the baby. They tried to follow the rules of their own pleasant "real" world (except for a few naughty outbreaks), and when they got involved with magic creatures and objects, they tried to understand and follow the appropriate magic rules. While the conflicting rules of society, nature, and magic created funny, impossible disasters in Nesbit's fantasy books, even the conflicts there were logical and made sense. Alice too wanted to be polite and obedient, but her universe was totally beyond control. The rules of Wonderland shifted and turned upside down; old gentlemen in trains turned into sheep. A kind of logic is present in Wonderland, but it floats teasingly beyond our reach, telling us the only certainty is uncertainty.

Think of all the new things a young person needs to figure out. To Piaget and his followers, children up to seven or eight years old have no sense of the perspectives of others—it takes years for them to outgrow their egocentric limitations. Other psychologists, including Maureen Cox (1991) in *The Child's Point of View* (p. 20), insist that young children can understand other viewpoints; Cox describes studies supporting this view. "From birth, the child enters a visual world in which objects in space are jointly available to all observers. The child is not imprisoned by her own point of view, although she may use it as a starting point from which to infer what another person can see." Games and puzzles and stories help growing children develop this skill, this sense of many social and physical realities. To discover what things and people mean, how things and people connect, children, and many adults too, make collections of odd objects; build elaborate structures like blocks and Legos and train sets; play board games and video games and card games. They like to tinker with miniature worlds like dollhouses. There is a strong satisfaction for some in the creation of a tiny bonsai that resembles a big tree. In each of these activities they are creating a story, an organizing, clarifying perspective—another kind of temporary world. So they don't feel like Alice.

The Big, the Little, and the Good

Alice's size changed with jarring frequency—huge and tiny and once again normal. When Robert in Nesbit's *Five Children and It* said of the baker's boy, who had kicked him into a heap of sand, "I WISH I WAS BIGGER THAN HIM," he activated a magic wish that turned himself into a ten-foot-high giant. Robert and the other children made some money exhibiting him at the local fair, which was gratifying. They had a problem, though, because they knew their magic wishes reversed themselves at sunset and Robert would be revealed to the fierce proprietor as merely a little kid. Using their ingenious problem-solving skills, the children managed to sneak Robert out of the tent, now normal size at sunset, and they all dashed home.

In stories of changing time, space, or proportion, the physical changing process—how it happens and what it feels like—is central and fascinating, described in detail. In addition, there is always some moral or social element that the storyteller and characters care about, some way of thinking and behaving. In *Five Children and It*, the children wanted to have fun in new and exciting ways, unsupervised, but they also cared greatly about being fair, honest, and polite. The challenge for them lay in coping with magical circumstances without compromising their basic values (or getting in trouble). Thus, when they found themselves ravenously hungry from flying around on magical wings, the wings prevented their buying food in the customary manner. So they took food from the larder window of a strange house and left money with an apologetic note. WE ARE VERY HUNGRY BECAUSE OF HAVING TO FLY ALL DAY, AND WE THINK IT IS NOT STEALING WHEN YOU ARE STARVING TO DEATH. WE WILL ONLY TAKE THE NESSESSITIES OF LIFE, AND NO PUDDING OR PIE, TO SHOW YOU IT IS NOT GREDINESS BUT TRUE STARVATION. OUR INTENTIONS ARE QUITE HONOURABLE IF ONLY YOU KNEW. Similarly, when Robert was a giant, he insisted on being paid only for one day, knowing he would not remain big after sundown. In good fantasy, the subjective, personal element is always interesting. Science fiction more than fantasy offers objective accounts of possible events, extrapolating from existing science, and often leaves out the subjective altogether. That's why many readers find the most extreme, pure science fiction boring.

In fantasy tales about different sizes—huge or tiny people—questions of power and responsibility arise naturally; the use and misuse of power is the most common theme. Dozens of books describe children of normal size who encounter groups of small magic people (fewer describe children whose size changes, like Alice). Looking at smallness is the novelty, since real children in their real lives are all too often used to looking at large, gross, powerful people. Thus, while normal-sized characters confronting little people are not themselves transformed in size, they seem so to a reader, who is not used to being the gigantic, powerful one. The Lilliputians in *Gulliver's Travels* have appealed to young readers since the eighteenth century; the voyage to Brobdingnag, where Gulliver became the tiny person among giants, is less popular.

Mistress Masham's Repose (1946), T. H. White's story about a colony of Swift's Lilliputians discovered by a child in twentieth-century England, raises questions of freedom and tyranny. White's answers are serious, but his style is playful—funny and charming, though overloaded with obscure jokes about eighteenth-century English culture, whose language and customs the Lilliputians still practiced. Nonetheless, the heroine, Maria, and her adventures are enthralling. Orphaned heir to a dilapidated estate—the house was ABOUT FOUR TIMES LONGER THAN BUCKINGHAM PALACE, BUT WAS FALLING DOWN—Maria was ONE OF THOSE TOUGH AND FRIENDLY PEOPLE WHO DO THINGS FIRST AND THINK ABOUT THEM AFTERWARD. Discovering the tiny Lilliputians established on a hidden, overgrown island, she scooped up a barely visible baby and its terrified mother and took them home. SHE WANTED TO PLAY WITH THEM, LIKE LEAD SOLDIERS, AND EVEN DREAMED OF BEING THEIR QUEEN. Her moral growth was uneven; only after a series of disasters caused by her attempts to bully them and run their lives did she truly come to respect them as independent beings.

In fact, the economic and social arrangements of these small people were wise and mature: no wars, few laws, no established religion, families run by the mothers. They were moral giants compared to Maria's guardians, the Governess and the Vicar, who robbed the ducal estate and, when Maria wouldn't turn over the crucial documents, threw her into the deepest dungeon. (THE FURNITURE CONSISTED OF INSTRUMENTS OF TORTURE. THE FLOOR WAS COVERED WITH RUSHES, EXCEPT WHERE SAND OR SAWDUST WERE NEEDED, TO SOAK UP BLOOD.) Fortunately, the Lilliputians were smarter than the guardians as well as more virtuous. Helped by the good Cook and the Professor, they rescued her. The fortune was restored; the mansion and grounds became a paradise retreat for people large and small.

❧❧ ❧❧

Perhaps the best children's books about tiny people are *Mistress Masham's Repose* and Pauline Clarke's *The Return of the Twelves* (1962). The best known, however, are Mary Norton's *The Borrowers* (1953) and Lynne Reid Banks's *The Indian in the Cupboard* (1980). The *Borrowers* series is unusual in being told from the viewpoint of the tiny people; the perspective of normal-sized children who discovered the borrowers appears only occasionally. So these books are concerned not with the proper exercise of power but with survival, ingenuity, and courage—with the dangerous choices that the weak have to make when surrounded by the strong.

The Clock family, Pod and Homily and young Arietty, had always lived in an apartment down a tunnel behind the hall clock in a big old house. Until recently, friends and relations lived in the walls and under the floors. Life was constricted because of danger from "human beans," but pleasant: they lived by "borrowing" bits of food and small objects left around the house, like safety pins and bottle tops. Furnishings included a matchbox chest, a bed in an ornate cigar box, and portraits of Queen Victoria that had been stamps. THEY BATHED IN A SMALL TUREEN, WHICH ONCE HELD *PÂTÉ DE FOIE GRAS.* The other families had emigrated, and now the Clocks were alone.

Arietty, the strong-minded girl borrower, yearned for freedom and fresh air. Even though borrowers dreaded being "seen," she struck up a friendship with a lonely human boy. Arietty's narrow horizon was broadened when she learned from the boy that borrowers were not the center of the world. This was hard to believe. She asked him, "SURELY YOU DON'T THINK THERE ARE MANY PEOPLE IN THE WORLD YOUR SIZE? THERE WOULDN'T BE ENOUGH STUFF IN THE WORLD TO GO ROUND AFTER A BIT! MY FATHER SAYS IT'S A GOOD THING THEY'RE DYING OUT. . . . JUST A FEW, THAT'S ALL WE NEED—TO KEEP US." "WHAT DO YOU MEAN," ASKED THE BOY, " 'TO KEEP US'?" "OH DEAR," SHE GASPED, "YOU ARE FUNNY! HUMAN BEANS ARE *FOR* BORROWERS—LIKE BREAD'S FOR BUTTER!" The boy, equally self-centered, insisted that billions of large people exist and that Arietty would probably be the last living borrower. These are not sentimentally drawn characters; when the two first met, the boy threatened to hit her with a stick: "IN CASE YOU CAME AND SCRABBLED AT ME WITH YOUR NASTY LITTLE HANDS." They became reconciled, but servants discovered the borrowers' home through a hole in the floor and called in the police and ratcatcher. Just as the human beans started to smoke them out with poison gas, the boy broke open a grating so the borrowers could escape into the fields and seek refuge with some cousins.

The second book, *The Borrowers Afield* (1955), tells how the borrowers struggled to reach that goal, defending themselves against weather, cats, and gypsies. In their tidy camp, they discovered that THE SHELF WAS FLOWING OVER WITH A HEAVING MASS OF SLUG. A SLUG THAT SIZE CANNOT EASILY BE TACKLED BY A BORROWER, BUT LUCKILY THIS ONE SHRUNK UP AND FEIGNED DEAD: ONCE THEY HAD PRIZED IT OUT OF ITS CLOSE-FITTING RETREAT, THEY COULD BOWL IT OVER THE SANDY FLOOR AND ROLL IT AWAY DOWN THE BANK. Though frightened, Arietty exulted in this new, open world; even her conventional mother became reconciled to leaving the Edwardian bric-a-brac behind, inside the dark walls. THERE WAS A SMELL OF WILDNESS, OF SPACE, OF LEAVES AND GRASSES, AND ANOTHER SMELL— FRAGRANT, SPICY. IT WAS THE SMELL OF WILD STRAWBERRIES. Arietty crawled inside a hedge, looked up at the twigs, then climbed up to see the view: UP AND UP AS FAR AS SHE COULD SEE—THERE WERE LAYERS AND STORIES OF GREEN CHAMBERS, CROSSED AND RECROSSED WITH SPRINGING BRANCHES. WHAT A WORLD—MILE UPON MILE, THING AFTER THING, LAYER UPON LAYER OF UNIMAGINED RICHNESS!

❧ ❧

The Indian in the Cupboard and its sequel tell a memorable story, despite Banks's pedestrian style (for instance, THE WHOLE BUSINESS NEARLY BLEW OMRI'S MIND EVERY TIME HE THOUGHT AT ALL DEEPLY ABOUT IT). When Omri got an old bathroom cupboard for his birthday, he casually placed a plastic Indian inside it. Then, after he locked and unlocked the cupboard with an old key, he discovered that the tiny Indian and his horse had become warm and real. More sensitive than Maria with her Lilliputians, Omri knew that he must act responsibly toward the three-inch-tall Indian. HE WOULD HAVE LIKED TO FEEL HIM ALL OVER, HIS TINY ARMS AND LEGS, HIS EARS—YET WHEN HE SAW HOW THE INDIAN, ALTOGETHER IN HIS POWER, FACED HIM BOLDLY AND HID HIS FEAR, HE LOST ALL DESIRE TO HANDLE HIM—HE FELT IT WAS CRUEL, AND INSULTING TO THE INDIAN, WHO WAS NO LONGER HIS PLAYTHING BUT A PERSON WHO HAD TO BE RESPECTED. He was delighted when the horse emitted a miniature pile of manure and when the cupboard made doll-sized plastic objects become real, like medical supplies and weapons. But he was horrified when his thoughtless friend Patrick put a plastic cowboy in the cupboard, thus bringing to life an enemy for Little Bear and causing trouble for the boys.

The scornful, stoic Indian is the most compelling character. When Omri gave him food and asked, "DO YOU FEEL BETTER NOW?"—"I BETTER. YOU NOT BETTER," SAID THE INDIAN. "YOU STILL BIG. YOU STOP EAT. GET RIGHT SIZE. TOMORROW TALK. YOU GIVE LITTLE BEAR MEAT—FIRE—MUCH THINGS." HE SCOWLED FIERCELY UP AT OMRI. "GOOD?" Little Bear built a fine longhouse to live in but could not be dissuaded from fighting with Boone, the surly cowboy. The Indian almost killed Boone with an arrow, then felt remorse and agreed to swear blood brotherhood with his enemy.

Omri, realizing it was wrong to own these miniature people, put them back in the cupboard and sent them to their own worlds. While they would live real and full-sized lives back there, their plastic forms would remain for the boys to keep. Looking at their last tiny campfire all together, Patrick said, "I FELT AS IF I WERE THE SAME AS THEM. I WISH WE *WERE* ALL THE SAME SIZE. IF WE COULD ENTER THEIR WORLD—SLEEP IN THE LONGHOUSE, RIDE THE HORSES—" Though the themes are somewhat muddled, it's clear that Omri and Patrick have been forced to acknowledge the reality of people who originally had seemed like objects; the boys have grown in responsibility, tolerance, and empathy.

❧ ❧

Since Max, in Pauline Clarke's *The Return of the Twelves*, is only eight, you might think the book is just for younger readers. In fact, it is more richly written and subtler than *The Borrowers*, *The Indian in the Cupboard*, and even *Mistress Masham*, which is clever but arch and heavy-handed. Recently moved to an old house in the village noted for the Brontë family homestead, Max discovered twelve wooden soldiers dumped in a dusty attic corner; he neatly lined them up. When he returned and found the soldiers alive, smartly marching around the attic, he gently won their trust and friendship. He kept secret that his toys were alive, especially because it became clear that these were the valuable wooden soldiers played with long ago by Charlotte, Emily, Anne, and Branwell Brontë, the same soldiers who starred in the elaborate stories composed by those four genius children but had slept, frozen, for more than a century.

Each soldier had his own personality and remembered his own history, battles, and journeys. As they explored the house and garden, Max helped inconspicuously, but HE REALIZED THAT PART OF THEIR LIFE DEPENDED ON THEIR BEING LEFT TO DO THINGS BY THEMSELVES. HE COULD OVERSEE AND SUGGEST, BUT NOT DICTATE. When the most adventurous soldier got lost outside, Max resisted the impulse to carry him off to safety, and watched Stumps bravely climb a vine to the bedroom window. HE WONDERED WHETHER IT FELT TERRIFYING TO BE SO LITTLE IN SUCH A HUGE WORLD, UNDER SUCH AN ENORMOUS MOON-WASHED SKY. MAX THOUGHT OF ALL THE OTHER SMALL CREATURES, MICE, TOADS, BEETLES, SOME MUCH TINIER THAN STUMPS. NO DOUBT TO GOD, HE, MAX, SEEMED QUITE AS SMALL AND NEEDING HELP. HE FELT HE WOULD LIKE TO PROTECT ALL THE CREATURES, AND WONDERED WHO DID. HIS JOB NOW WAS TO PROTECT STUMPS.

The real Brontë children did in fact call themselves the Genii and their toy soldiers the Young Men, named Stumps, Bravey, and so on. In Clarke's story, the soldiers addressed Max, and later his sister and the wise vicar, as the new Genii, which means Guardian Spirit as well as Person of Great Intellect. When Max put his imagination to work about the soldiers (as when he figured out where the missing Stumps would be), he was actually creating the event. Max figured this out: "I WONDER WHO MADE ALL THIS UP? BECAUSE THEY KNOW THEIR NAMES AND AGES AND ALL ABOUT GOING TO AFRICA. COULD THEY MAKE IT ALL UP THEMSELVES? I THINK IT'S THE GENII WHO HAVE TO MAKE THINGS UP. LIKE I DID ABOUT STUMPS WANDERING AROUND THE KITCHEN AND GETTING OUT THE DOOR. AND THEN IT WAS REALLY TRUE, HE REALLY HAD."

IT DID NOT SEEM ODD, BECAUSE THIS WAS EXACTLY HOW THE GAMES YOU MADE UP WORKED. OF COURSE THEY WERE TRUE. IN YOUR MIND. IT WAS ONLY THAT THIS HAD GONE ONE STEP MORE AND COME ALIVE. It happened because Max loved them. The Brontë children had loved them too.

There was much public interest in locating the Brontë toy soldiers and increasing suspicion that this beat-up collection found by a local boy was the real thing. Learning that a collector was coming to take them to America, the soldiers made a plan to escape the collector by marching cross-country to their original home in the Haworth parsonage, now a Brontë museum. Max supervised the dangerous march. The Young Men reached their destination and settled in as authenticated exhibits. WERE THEY DOOMED TO PERPETUAL FROZENDOM, NOW THAT THEY WERE ON SHOW IN THEIR ANCESTRAL MANSION? NO; THEY KEPT THEIR FACULTIES AS SHARP AS EVER, AND INDULGED IN NIGHT LIFE. Max could visit them, and the townspeople who had glimpsed them on their epic march thought it was only a dream; so the soldiers were happy at last. Two girls in a field remembered a lovely scene: THEY SAW A COLUMN OF LITTLE MEN THREADING THEIR WAY THROUGH THIS FOREST, HOLDING A TINY BLUE FLAG ALOFT. THEY HEARD THIN, CAUTIOUS SINGING. THE TROOP OF TINY MEN, DRESSED LIKE SOLDIERS, SOME WITH FEATHERS IN THEIR HATS, SEEMED SO AT HOME IN THE OATS, AND THE GREEN FIELD-PATH WAS SO SILENT AND MAGIC, THAT THE LITTLE GIRLS ONLY NUDGED EACH OTHER, AND EXCLAIMED, AND LAY WATCHING AS IF THIS WERE NOTHING MORE THAN YOU MIGHT EXPECT IN A FIELD OF OATS ON AN AUGUST DAY.

Max's bringing to life the sleeping toy soldiers is a metaphorical version of the artist's act of creation. Fantasy fiction offers not just escape but metaphor, the symbolic virtual worlds discussed by Susanne Langer that give delight and insight. A patronizing remark about metaphor appears in a book on spiritual matters by Thomas Moore, *The Re-Enchantment of Everyday Life* (1996): "I try to find a middle path between the psychological reduction of enchantment to projection or metaphor, and a literal, too simple belief in a spirit world" (p. xix). To me, metaphor is not a reduction but a triumph, an illuminating way of looking at life, including its enchantments—at a distance and at the same time up close. Metaphor is not a psychological gimmick like projection. It's not something to apologize for.

Masters of Magic

The three classic creators of children's magic fantasy are E. Nesbit and her disciples Mary Norton and Edward Eager. All three wrote about cheerful children in an ordinary, stable world who stumbled into adventures caused by magic, involving physical transformations or travels in time or space. *The Story of the Amulet* (1906), the third in Nesbit's *Five Children* series, was the first children's book to use time travel: the children visited ancient Britain, Egypt, and Babylon; they chatted with Julius Caesar. While all this is fun, her two earlier books are more inventive and energetic. Magic is a complicated thing, in both *Five Children and It* and *The Phoenix and the Carpet*: the children must not just decide how best to use it, they must negotiate with the grouchy Psammead—a furry, fat, brown Sand-fairy from prehistoric times—exactly how the magic worked. It was exhausting for the Psammead to hold its breath and swell up in granting wishes, so he promised them only one wish a day, which would last only until sunset. The children asked and the Psammead agreed that the servants should not notice any results from a granted wish. After some mistakes from hasty wishing, they decided to take turns. It's like children settling on the rules of a new game, which is itself a kind of practice for adult life, where they will discover confusing rules that others set for them and also useful rules that they themselves establish.

Then there is the eternal question of how to wish wisely, a question just as important in realistic fiction and real life as in fantasy. The children suffered through badly worded wishes (one resulting in heavy, unspendable gold guineas) and accidental wishes (one causing everybody else to want their annoying baby brother and try to kidnap him). No one enjoys lectures about actions leading to consequences, but such lectures become appealing when buried within the delightful episodes of *Five Children and It*: this is what will happen if you carelessly wish to be beautiful, rich, beloved, bewinged, bigger, or older. The children did not want to recognize the harm they could cause so casually, as when Cyril wished there were "Red Indians" in England. "NOW THERE ARE, AND THEY'RE GOING ABOUT SCALPING PEOPLE ALL OVER THE COUNTRY, LIKE AS NOT." "PERHAPS THEY'RE ONLY IN NORTHUMBERLAND AND DURHAM," SAID JANE SOOTHINGLY. IT WAS ALMOST IMPOSSIBLE TO BELIEVE THAT IT COULD REALLY HURT PEOPLE MUCH TO BE SCALPED SO FAR AWAY AS THAT. The children worried about the maid and cook, though:

"THEY WOULDN'T NOTICE ANYTHING, BUT YOU CAN'T BE REALLY
SCALPED OR BURNED TO DEATH WITHOUT NOTICING IT, AND YOU'D BE
SURE TO NOTICE IT NEXT DAY, EVEN IF IT ESCAPED YOUR ATTENTION AT
THE TIME," SAID CYRIL.
The logic of rules and events is followed inexorably. One bor-
ing, indoors day, they wished to be in a besieged castle. THE CHIL-
DREN FOUND THEMSELVES IN A BIG PAVED COURTYARD, WITH THE GREY
WALLS OF THE CASTLE RISING DARK AND HEAVY ON ALL FOUR SIDES.
NEAR THE MIDDLE OF THE COURTYARD STOOD MARTHA, MOVING HER
RIGHT HAND BACKWARDS AND FORWARDS IN THE AIR. THE COOK WAS
STOOPING DOWN AND MOVING HER HANDS ALSO IN A CURIOUS WAY.
Robert figured it out: "THE CASTLE IS ON THE SAME PLACE WHERE
OUR HOUSE IS, AND THE SERVANTS HAVE TO GO ON BEING IN THE HOUSE,
OR ELSE THEY WOULD NOTICE. SO WE CAN'T SEE THE HOUSE, BECAUSE WE
SEE THE CASTLE; AND THEY CAN'T SEE THE CASTLE, BECAUSE THEY GO ON
SEEING THE HOUSE." When Martha brought them invisible, unfeela-
ble dinner, they were stumped only for a while. Cyril LEANED OVER
THE TABLE WITH HIS FACE ABOUT AN INCH FROM IT, AND KEPT OPENING
AND SHUTTING HIS MOUTH AS IF HE WERE TAKING BITES OUT OF AIR. . . .
CYRIL STOOD UP WITH A GRIN OF TRIUMPH, HOLDING A SQUARE PIECE OF
BREAD IN HIS MOUTH. DIRECTLY HE BIT A PIECE OFF, THE REST VANISHED;
BUT IT WAS ALL RIGHT, BECAUSE HE KNEW HE HAD IT IN HIS HAND
THOUGH HE COULD NEITHER SEE NOR FEEL IT.
In *The Phoenix and the Carpet* (1904), the same children were
given a rolled-up secondhand Persian carpet for their nursery playroom. It contained an egg, from which sprang a gorgeous phoenix.
The vain and loquacious bird told them about his ancient lives and
advised them about the use of the carpet—a flying carpet, of
course. The subsequent journeys were full of wonders, but complicated: events were woven together in a dense texture, just as the
strands were woven in the hard-working carpet. The cook, joining
the children on a trip to a tropic isle, chose to remain and become
queen of the friendly savages. Later the children met a burglar
(breaking into their house), who helped dispose of the 198 cats the
carpet had kindly brought to the nursery. (When asked to provide
food for the cats, it brought 396 rats.) The police seized the burglar as a catnapper, but the children rescued him with a carpet

journey to the tropic isle, where he met and wed the queenly cook. A clergyman brought from London by carpet, to marry the couple, later turned up in another chapter. So the different episodes, while remaining discrete adventures, are interwoven and interdependent. In a Nesbit fantasy, things are not organized into a neatly structured world, but everything is connected.

Many readers love Nesbit's *The Enchanted Castle* (1907), a shimmering story of children with a wishing ring, stone dinosaurs, moonlit banquets with Olympic gods, and terrifying Ugly-Wugly people made of hockey sticks and umbrellas. Magic jewels, green labyrinths, mysterious tunnels—there are too many ingredients here, like a luscious pudding overstocked with spices, chocolate bits, fruits, and macaroons. *The Magic City* (1910) is a better-designed book and just as exciting. Ten-year-old Philip, lonely and sullen, created in the parlor an elaborate city made of blocks, books, candlesticks, chess pieces, and all manner of household objects. THERE WERE TOWERS AND TURRETS AND GRAND STAIRCASES, PAGODAS AND PAVILIONS, CANALS MADE BRIGHT AND WATERLIKE BY STRIPS OF SILVER PAPER, AND A LAKE WITH A BOAT ON IT. Despite the cruel governess, who broke down his beautiful toy city, Philip managed to shrink (or did the city grow?) and enter the passageways and buildings he had created. His old friend the carpenter, who had originally built some of the blocks, explained: "ALL THE CITIES AND THINGS YOU EVER BUILT—AS YOU MADE 'EM, YOU'VE THE RIGHT TO COME TO THEM. AND ALL THE PEOPLE WHO HELPED TO MAKE ALL THEM THINGS YOU USED TO BUILD WITH, THEY'RE ALL HERE. D'YOU SEE? MAKING'S THE THING. IF IT WAS NO MORE THAN THE LAD THAT TURNED THE HANDLE OF THE GRINDSTONE TO SHARP THE KNIFE THAT CARVED A BIT OF A CABINET. THEY'RE WHAT'S CALLED THE POPULATION OF YOUR CITIES." Weather and animals came to this world from the pages of books used in the city's construction; when an evil creature escaped from a book, it had to be forced inside and the book closed firmly.

Philip accomplished the seven noble tasks that proved him Deliverer of Polistopolis and was honored by the city. Back in his everyday world, he no longer felt isolated and gloomy. He had saved himself by acts of courage and kindness, and especially by his efforts to construct a world of his own that would be beautiful and well made. HE WAS ACCUSTOMED TO THE JOY THAT COMES OF MAKING THINGS. This is, in fact, the same joy gained by readers, young and old, who build their own worlds as they enter the fictional worlds constructed by fantasy writers.

ঔ⊛ ⊛ঔ

Mary Norton's book about nice children on magic journeys seems mechanical compared to Nesbit's—the *Borrowers* series was Norton's masterpiece. Even so, *Bed-Knob and Broomstick* (1957) has its own commonsense charm. As is usual in this type of story, the children were staying in the country for the summer. THEY PLAYED BY THE RIVER, AND THEY PLAYED IN THE LANES AND ON THE HILLS. THEY WERE PUNCTUAL FOR MEALS BECAUSE THEY WERE VISITORS AND GOOD CHILDREN AT HEART. Befriending a shy piano teacher next door, they discovered she was studying to be a witch and persuaded her to give them a magic device. She put a spell on the brass bed-knob that Paul carried in his pocket, and after they screwed the knob back onto its post, the three children started to learn the rules for using it. You had to screw the knob one direction to travel on the bed to a different place, the other direction for a different time. When they wished to see their house in London, the bed landed on the sidewalk outside, and the children landed in jail for bed stealing. They planned the next trip more carefully, to the obligatory desert isle, taking Miss Price, the would-be witch, along as chaperone; but they still ran into trouble with savages and barely escaped. Getting things right was important in all matters, magical or not. Doing right—playing fair—was important also: Is it taking unfair advantage to grow a rose by magic for the flower show? (But what about people who can afford special fertilizers? That's unfair too.) Such questions bothered Miss Price, so much that she vowed to give up magic.

Two years later, the children returned and persuaded her to let them use the bed again, to go very carefully into the past. THEY HAD SEEN HOW MANY TWISTS THE BED-KNOB ALLOWED, AND THEN MADE A ROUGH CALCULATION OF PERIOD. CHARLES CLEVERLY HAD MADE A SCRATCH WITH A PIN, DOWN THE BASE OF THE SCREW. AND PAUL WAS SUP-

POSED TO TWIST UNTIL THE TWO ENDS OF THE SCRATCH MET EVENLY. Their planning paid off; they arrived in 1666 London before the Great Fire, and eventually Miss Price stayed in the past to marry Emelius Jones, a genial magician's assistant she had rescued from being burned at the stake. In the book's last sentence, Miss Price's voice reached the children from the seventeenth century, reminding them to be good and follow the rules: "CAREY, COME AT ONCE OUT OF THOSE LETTUCES."

❧ ❧

Edward Eager moved the nice-children-with-magic story to the United States, in seven clever books published between 1954 and 1962. Each one postulates a type of magic that is unique but totally logical. In *Seven-Day Magic*, a library book recorded in its pages the children's own adventures as they happened: they visited Oz and advised the wizard; they helped their father become a singing star. Another tale, *Magic or Not?*, describes ambiguous events and happy endings that were probably caused by magic, but just might have happened by chance and luck; it's not clear which.

Eager's most ingenious books are the four that tell about two generations of a family. The best known is *Half Magic*, in which four children found an ancient coin that granted their wishes, but only half of each wish. This special clause they deduced only after they had wished their mother home and she was transported to a lonely spot halfway home; and after Martha had wished to be away from a boring movie and found herself half-away, transformed into a ghostly half-presence. (But, thought her sister, better that it was half of *all* of Martha rather than a pair of gruesome legs or a severed head and shoulders.)

The children learned to word their requests wisely and compensate exactly: one time in Camelot, Katharine rescued the imprisoned Sir Launcelot by WISHING THAT THEY WERE TWICE AS FAR AS THE DUNGEON DOOR AND THAT SHE HAD TWO KEYS TO THE DUNGEON IN HER HAND. For seven days the magic charm made the children happier and happier, culminating by arranging the wedding of their mother to a perfect stepfather, and then it stopped working. They realized it had given them all it could. Martha suggested they might still be able to use it to make other people happy. MARK SHOOK HIS HEAD. "THAT'S NO GOOD. WE'D GET SO WE WANTED TO TELL EVERYBODY WHAT TO WISH. I THINK THAT WOULD BE KIND OF AGAINST THE RULES. IT CAME TO US OUT OF THE UNKNOWN, AND I THINK THAT'S WHERE IT OUGHT TO GO AGAIN. I THINK WE OUGHT TO LET SOME UTTER STRANGER FIND IT." They dropped it on the sidewalk as a tired-looking little girl approached, then hid and watched as the girl picked it up: soon, her heavy baby brother magically floated up into the air and back to her arms.

The same children stayed in a rented cottage named (like the book) *Magic by the Lake*. When Martha said of the cottage's sign, "DON'T YOU WISH IT WERE TRUE?" THERE WAS A SILENCE. THE TURTLE STUCK ITS HEAD OUT OF ITS SHELL. "NOW YOU'VE DONE IT," IT SAID. "YOU HAD TO BE GREEDY AND ORDER MAGIC BY THE LAKE, AND OF COURSE NOW YOU'VE GOT A WHOLE LAKEFUL OF IT, AND AS FOR HOW YOU'RE GOING TO MANAGE IT, I FOR ONE WASH MY HANDS OF THE WHOLE QUESTION!" The rest of their vacation was spent taming the lake magic and, as they could get wishes every three days by touching the lake water, using their wishes. Their goal was laudable—to find buried treasure that would keep their stepfather's bookstore from going bankrupt—but they went too far and broke the wishing rules. The turtle complained: "HARDLY A MINUTE TO REST UP BETWEEN TIMES, WEARING A POOR LAKE OUT!" "WHAT DOES IT MATTER!" SAID JANE. "WHEN THE MAGIC GETS SHALLOW WE CAN JUST WISH ON YOU, AND FILL IT UP AGAIN." "NO," SAID THE TURTLE, "THAT'S JUST WHAT YOU CAN'T DO. IT'S OUT OF MY HANDS NOW. MAGIC HAS A BALANCE, AND WHEN YOU BREAK THE RULES, YOU UPSET IT. THERE'S NO TELLING WHAT IT MIGHT DO NEXT!"

The lake was placated and the bookstore saved. The book ends with Martha wondering whether they would ever again see the strange children, Ann, Roger, and Eliza, who rescued them when the magic adventures of the two groups overlapped on the desert island. The turtle answered, "TIME WILL TELL. BUT WHETHER YOU'LL KNOW THEM OR NOT, IS ANOTHER STORY." The joke is that those strange children were actually the heroes of two other Edward Eager books, in which Ann and Roger had a mother named Martha, and Eliza's mother was Katharine. Thus the two mothers and their children crossed paths in a magic adventure, without knowing it.

In *Knight's Castle* the younger set of Eager children went into Roger's toy castle and had an adventure with the cast of *Ivanhoe*. As Eliza, the arrogant one, said of the magic: "TRYING TO TEACH *ME* MORAL LESSONS! MAYBE THAT'S WHY IT CAME INTO OUR LIVES, TO MAKE NOBLE CHARACTERS OF US. I LEARNED NOT TO BE BOSSY, AND ANN LEARNED TO BE BRAVE AND THINK FOR HERSELF." "AND I LEARNED WISDOM," SAID ROGER, LOOKING SO SMUG AND HOLY THAT JACK AND ELIZA SAT ON HIM AND TICKLED HIS FEET. Then in *The Time Garden*, they nibbled leaves of thyme in a historic garden and traveled to past times to help people: slaves on the Underground Railroad, a poor family visited by Jo March and her sisters, Queens Elizabeth and Victoria in various predicaments, and—quite logically—four children about to be cooked in a pot on a desert island. These were (as readers realize, but not the characters) their own mothers, aunt, and uncle, who had the same adventure from the other perspective in *Magic by the Lake*. Eager is brilliant at examining odd shapes and viewpoints of human experience, deliciously stretching his readers' imagination.

The magic tales of Nesbit, Norton, and Eager—written in the 1950s or earlier—differ from later children's fantasies in some important ways. The adventures are safe; the risks are minor. Although the children face titillating dangers, they are under the protection of magical beings. In addition, the rules of the magic provide a safety net, such as the knowledge that the spell will end at sundown. If a real physical danger looms, you know it will be averted—the whole spirit of these books assures you that nothing bad will happen to the children, except maybe being scolded and sent off to bed. Style and tone tell you they will be safe, and so does context, because these pre-1960s fictional children lived in safe worlds. Children who lived in *unsafe* worlds, with problems more serious than a lost jacket or a quarrel with a friend, were not being written about then. But by the 1970s, fictional nice children would no longer be allowed to go off just anywhere on a magic carpet, any more than real ones would be allowed to take a subway alone at night.

Time Travel Is Good for You

Another kind of fantasy, not so lighthearted but not pessimistic, flourished just after the Edward Eager–Mary Norton period, from the late 1960s through the 1980s. In many such stories, an attractive but self-involved child travels to a past time, learns about a world different from his or her own, helps the people there in some way, and returns home wiser and more empathetic. It's the Junior-Year-Abroad type of fantasy. Most of these are good books, earnestly concerned about the personal growth of the characters. Some, like Penelope Lively's *The House in Norham Gardens*, are subtle and incisive, while others are thin or heavy-handed.

An early version is *Fog Magic* (1943) by Julia L. Sauer, a sweet, soft book set in Nova Scotia. Greta, wandering through the fog, discovered that an old ruined village occasionally came back to life; villagers welcomed her into their homes and holidays. After her twelfth birthday, she was no longer able to find them in the fog—only cellar holes where the houses had been. Still, she learned her sympathetic father had had the same experience as a child, and (to use Sauer's stilted language) she knew she would always hold the town of Blue Cove in her heart.

In *A String in the Harp* (1976), by Nancy Bond, a widowed American professor took his children to a coastal Welsh village for a year. Although teenaged Peter at first was depressed and sullen, the odd artifact he picked up on the beach and hid from archeologists—an old, carved harp key—opened his mind to the present and past power of this austere part of the world. The key would hum strangely in his hand, and he would suddenly be watching scenes and hearing conversations from the life of Taliesin, the great sixth-century Welsh bard. Villagers too, while Peter was nearby with the key, would witness unaccountable events, such as a ghostly funeral procession in the night. Peter's task, it turned out, was to return Taliesin's lost harp key to his wild gravesite and keep it from the chilly national museum. This story is unusual in that Peter and his friends found themselves inside the world of Taliesin but only as invisible observers. Reading *A String in the Harp* is a

thoughtful—though glacially slow—experience, a mournful rumi-
nation on how a present world can and cannot intertwine with
its past.

Penelope Farmer, in *Charlotte Sometimes* (1969), beautifully
creates the clammy atmosphere of a girls' boarding school, both in
mid-twentieth-century England and in 1918. The time travel device is intriguing: Charlotte woke up in the right boarding-school
bed but the wrong year; she had switched times with a girl named
Clare, who slept in the same bed. Although the two girls never
met, they managed to leave notes for each other giving hints about
how to behave in the unfamiliar world. Questions of identity
hover: the two looked somewhat alike, and the strange switch was
never noticed. Charlotte remembered LOOKING IN A MIRROR, HOW
AFTER SHE HAD BEEN STARING AT THEM FOR A WHILE HER FEATURES
SEEMED NO LONGER TO MAKE HER FACE OR ANY FACE. PERHAPS IF YOU
STARED AT ANYONE LIKE THAT, THEIR FACES WOULD DISINTEGRATE IN
THE SAME WAY. WOULD YOU KNOW WHO YOU WERE YOURSELF? It
turned out that Clare had died of flu shortly after she and Charlotte returned permanently to their own times. A friend who knew
the secret said of Clare, "SHE WAS A SORT OF GHOST, WASN'T SHE? A
PRETTY SOLID SORT OF GHOST, OF COURSE, IF BONY." "I SUPPOSE I MUST
HAVE BEEN A SORT OF GHOST, TOO, IN 1918—IF YOU CAN HAVE GHOSTS
FROM THE FUTURE." They decided that Clare had come into the future only because she died; if she had lived forty years longer, there
would have had to be two Clares alive at once. The questions here
are provocative, though the whole doesn't quite add up.

In Cynthia Voigt's *Building Blocks* (1984), twelve-year-old
Brann fell asleep in his New York basement, having crawled into
a giant fortress of old wooden blocks to avoid his parents' quarreling, and woke in the Pennsylvania bedroom of his father, Kevin,
age ten. The cause of the adult Kevin's timid, passive behavior,
which always infuriated his son, was explained: Kevin's own
father bullied and beat his children, and Kevin was frightened but
brave. Going back to the present through the building blocks,
Brann was able to drop his resentment and build a better relation-
ship with his parents.

❤ ❤

Some of these Junior-Year-Abroad fantasy heroes change the past time they visit, as well as learn to understand it. In Robert Westall's *The Wind Eye* (1977), three children on the British coast sailed in a small boat to a holy island where they helped and were helped by medieval St. Cuthbert. Perhaps the most evocative of these books is *Playing Beatie Bow* (1980), by Ruth Park. Here the angry modern teenager is Australian, journeying from her highrise apartment in Sydney back to the same district, crowded and rickety, in the late nineteenth century. One day at dusk Abigail watched children play in a city and saw a shabby little girl watching too, and smiling. In their game, the children danced in a ring chanting, "OH MUDDA, WHAT'S THAT, WHAT CAN IT BE? THE WIND IN THE CHIMNEY, THAT'S ALL, THAT'S ALL," until somebody crept toward them covered in a sheet, wailing. "IT'S BEATIE BOW," SHRIEKED MUDDA IN A VOICE OF HORROR, "RISEN FROM THE DEAD!" As night fell, Abigail followed the shabby little girl into the past, into a warren of seedy streets with broken-down shanties and goats on the roof. Her ankle was broken when a drunk lunged at her, and she was carried into the home of the poor family whose lives became entangled with hers—the family of the shabby little girl, who lived in the 1890s and whose name was Beatie Bow.

The story involves Abigail's attempts to get back to the present and to deal with the kind Bow family while in the past. Granny, the matriarch, explained that in each generation one member had the Gift of second sight and healing; every fifth generation, one member died young, one was barren, and the Gift would die out unless the appointed Stranger appeared and protected the Gift by some important action. This time, Abigail was the Stranger. Everyone assumed the person to die young would be Gibbie, the obnoxious little boy invalid: "I BEEN THINKING ON MY FUNERAL," GIBBIE SAID PLEASURABLY. "SIX BLACK HORSES I'LL HAVE, WITH PLUMES, AND A DEAD CART COVERED IN FLOWERS. BUT MY COFFIN WILL BE WHITE BECAUSE I'M JUST AN INNOCENT CHILD."

Even though Abigail detested Gibbie, when the house burned down she rescued him. Back in the present, she saw a genealogy showing that Gilbert Bow lived a long life and had children. Gibbie, then, was not the one who died, and Abigail had indeed saved the Gift and the Bow family. She also changed the past by persuading the cleverest child to go to school: Beatie Bow became a famous headmistress, striking fear into her pupils and inspiring the chasing game still played by children generations later. While the story's convolutions are intriguing, even more so is the thick atmosphere of lower-class Victorian Sydney: hardworking families, slum lowlifes, stinks and diseases and boats in the harbor. This is an unusual, haunting story.

❧ ❧

In some books, a time-traveling child changes not events in the past but the present interpretation of past events. *The Court of the Stone Children* (1973), by Eleanor Cameron, tells the romantic but appealing story of Nina, a San Francisco teenager (angry and depressed in the beginning, like all such protagonists) who was drawn to a small museum of French art and its furnished rooms brought there from a chateau. The ghost of young Dominique, who had lived in these rooms in France, appeared to Nina and begged her to discover the truth about her father, Comte de Lombre, accused of murder in 1804 by Napoleon's officials. Nina, working as an assistant in the museum, used a portrait and a diary to piece together evidence that exonerated de Lombre and revised the standard historical version of the incident.

Penelope Lively's *The House in Norham Gardens* (1974) is wittier and deeper than *The Stone Children*. Clare Mayfield had lived happily for years with her great-aunts, scholarly Oxford spinsters who were old but keen. At fourteen, she began to worry—about the aunts' health, the finances of their huge house, her own place in time and the universe. At the start of each chapter is a passage describing a remote tribe and what happened after the arrival of white anthropologists in 1900. It becomes clear this was the tribe discovered by Clare's great-grandfather, whose diary and treasures remained in their attic.

Finding a primitive painted, wooden shield in a trunk, she leaned it against a wall and left it there. IT SEEMED TO SAY SOME-

THING: IF THIS KIND OF THING, THIS PATTERN, WAS A LANGUAGE, THEN IT MUST HAVE BEEN A SHOUT, ONCE, TO SOMEONE. NOW, UP HERE IN THE ATTIC, IT WAS A WHISPER, A WHISPER YOU COULDN'T EVEN UNDERSTAND. Clare became obsessed by the shield; in dreams she began to visit the New Guinea island it came from. The villagers seemed to want something of her and became importunate, lurking around the house in Oxford now, in vivid hallucinations. Clare learned that the people of the tribe did not know time, only the cycles of life and death; they worshiped their ancestors' spirits, in the form of tamburans, or ceremonial shields; she herself saw time as rushing past and was desolate.

The shield in the attic, battered and faded when she found it, slowly became smoother and brighter, its colors and design more vivid. But the people slowly entered the modern world—she saw their village with Coca-Cola and radios—and they stopped wanting her to return the shield to them. Advised by an African anthropology student, she gave the shield to the Pitt Rivers Museum, where it would be appreciated and protected. Clare, reconciled to her own moment in time and its relation to past and future, planted a young tree for her old great-aunt's birthday. EVERYTHING HAD SEEMED UNREAL. THERE HAD BEEN PEOPLE WHERE NOW THERE WERE ONLY DARK STIFF BRANCHES IN MRS RIDER'S GARDEN. THE STORY SEEMED TO BE FINISHED. But the passage about the tribe starting the final chapter gives the reader a hopeful note to end on: the villagers LEARN TO DRIVE CARS, USE TELEPHONES AND SCREWDRIVERS. THE CHILDREN LEARN HOW TO READ AND WRITE. ONE DAY, THEY WILL DISCOVER AGAIN THE NEED FOR TAMBURANS, AND THEY WILL MAKE A NEW KIND OF TAMBURAN FOR THEMSELVES, AND FOR THEIR CHILDREN, AND THEIR CHILDREN'S CHILDREN.

Tangled Times

Three authors of time-shifting fantasy, all of them English, go far beyond the somewhat conventional patterns I have been discussing. William Mayne's *Earthfasts* (1966) is a sad, brooding but very satisfying book about the mysteries of time. L. M. Boston's *Green*

Knowe series (1954–1964) and Philippa Pearce's *Tom's Midnight Garden* (1958) are beautifully designed, joyful stories about a child's experiences of time, loss, love, and community.

In Mayne's *Earthfasts*, two smart, normal teenagers were startled at the sight of a uniformed drummer boy stepping out of a crack in a rural hillside. A legend said that King Arthur slept below the castle nearby, surrounded by his knights and his treasure, waiting for the right time to awaken. In the eighteenth century, some young soldiers had tried to locate the treasure: this boy had walked into an underground passage at the castle, drumming loudly so his friends could follow along the ground above. They never found him, and he reappeared more than two hundred years later, carrying a strange bright candle. "WHAT FOR DID YOU COME OUT OF THE GROUND LIKE THAT?" SAID KEITH. "I WERE IN IT," SAID THE DRUMMER BOY, "WHAT FOR ELSE?" "WHAT WERE YOU IN IT FOR?" SAID KEITH, "WERE YOU DEAD?" "WOULD I BE DEAD AND OUT HERE?" SAID THE DRUMMER BOY.

The boy was thankful that Keith and David fed him, but he refused to believe he was in the twentieth century. He marched stoically through the castle grounds, now ruined, where he had been based, to his home, where an old man told him a family tale: the old man's grandfather's uncle as a lad had walked into a hill and never came out. Convinced now, but unwilling to live out of his own time, the boy went to the place where he came out, insisting he would return home. A CRACK COULD BE SEEN, BLACK IN ITS DEPTH, AND NO MORE THAN EIGHT INCHES WIDE, AND CLOSING AS IT DEEPENED. "DARK," SAID NELLIE JACK JOHN. THEY LOOKED AT THE DARKNESS WITH HIM, AND IT SEEMED A WHOLE WORLD OF DARKNESS, STRONGER THAN THE SUNLIGHT. He had lost his ever-burning candle, taken from King Arthur's chamber, so the boys gave him a flashlight and he entered the earth again.

Then supernatural things started happening, such as the circle of standing stones turning into rampaging giants and a prehistoric wild boar attacking the town. Later, Keith realized that WHEN NELLIE JACK JOHN TOOK UP THIS CANDLE AND BROUGHT IT OUT FROM ITS PLACE HE DISTURBED THE TIME THAT SLEPT AND HE WOKE WHAT WAS ASLEEP BEFORE. THE KING'S TIME STOOD STILL WHEN THE CANDLE WAS

IN ITS PROPER PLACE UNDER THE GROUND, BECAUSE KING ARTHUR'S TIME WAS NOT YET COME. It was Keith's task to return the candle they had found again, because David was considered dead: he had disappeared on the hillside, drawn back into the dark ancient place. Keith walked into the hill, put back the candle, found David and Nellie Jack John, and brought them out again, alive. The drummer boy never got back to his own time, but found a home with a kind farmer. *Earthfasts* is wildly original, though it contains traditional elements; its style is rich but terse.

❧❧ ❧❧

Lucy Boston's books about an old house called Green Knowe embody a perspective that is wide, loving, and playful. *The Children of Green Knowe* (1954) brings little Tolly to stay with his great-grandmother. The mansion and garden were steeped in layers of the past; ITS THICK STONE WALLS WERE STRONG, WARM AND LIVELY. IT WAS FURNISHED WITH COMFORTABLE POLISHED OLD-FASHIONED THINGS AS THOUGH LIVING IN CASTLES WAS QUITE ORDINARY. Mrs. Oldknow, the center of this world, HAD SHORT SILVER CURLS AND HER FACE HAD SO MANY WRINKLES IT LOOKED AS IF SOMEONE HAD BEEN TRYING TO DRAW HER FOR A VERY LONG TIME AND EVERY LINE PUT IN HAD MADE THE FACE MORE LIKE HER. The place was full of mirrors, doubles, shadows, and lively ghosts.

Children depicted in a family portrait, who had lived at Green Knowe in the seventeenth century, played hide-and-seek with Tolly, remaining invisible until they trusted him. Mrs. Oldknow told him they had all died of the Great Plague, on the same day. Toby, Alexander, and Linnet became his friends. They sometimes distressed him by vanishing, but they rescued him when the one evil spirit in the garden, a hideous topiary bush called Green Noah, lumbered down the path to grab him. HE NO LONGER FEARED THAT THE CHILDREN WOULD NEVER COME BACK. HE FELT THAT THEY WERE LIKE BROTHERS AND SISTERS WHO COME AND GO, BUT THERE IS NO NEED FOR WORRY: THEY ARE SURE TO COME HOME AGAIN.

In the second book, *Treasure of Green Knowe* (1958), Mrs. Oldknow told Tolly more stories of the house's past, this time about blind Susan from around 1800 and the black boy Jacob, brought back from Barbados by Susan's sea-captain father to be her companion. Overprotected Susan learned from him how to climb trees and run; Jacob learned from her how to read; and modern Tolly joined them as they played. While this was a delicate, lyrical world, it was not soft. It contained brutal elements too: Susan's brother and mother tormented Jacob. The Chinese boy Ping, in *A Stranger at Green Knowe* (1961), was welcomed by Mrs. Oldknow but felt lonely and isolated, until he made friends with an escaped gorilla hiding in the woods and also with Tolly. In *An Enemy at Green Knowe* (1964), a witch of unspeakable evil and vulgarity tried—sending plagues of maggots, cats, and snakes—to force Mrs. Oldknow to sell the place and its treasures. But Green Knowe always won out, strengthened by its beauty and by its people, who came together from many different times and places.

❧ ❧

Philippa Pearce's *Tom's Midnight Garden* is thought by many to be the best children's fantasy book ever written. They may be right. Tom's summer promised to be claustrophobic: he was quarantined for his brother's measles inside the treeless apartment of an obtuse aunt and uncle, who made him sleep too much and stuffed him with food. IN AUNT GWEN'S LARDER THERE WERE TWO COLD PORK CHOPS, HALF A TRIFLE, SOME BANANAS AND SOME BUNS AND CAKES. AS A MATTER OF FORM, HE LAID HOLD OF A STALE BUN. THEN, A GREAT WEARINESS OF ALL FOOD OVERCAME HIM, AND HE PUT THE BUN DOWN. Restless in the night, he opened the building's back door to the paved courtyard for garbage cans, but instead found himself in a big moonlit garden of flowerbeds, paths, and trees.

Each summer night, when the grandfather clock struck thirteen, he stole down the stairs and out to play in this garden, which had once adjoined the house. Tom was invisible then; his body had no weight, but he could force it through a door. Hatty, the lonely little girl who played there, treated cruelly by her aunt, was the only one who could see Tom. They played wonderful games together, teasing the birds and building a treehouse. TOGETHER THEY HUNTED FOR FROGS UNDER THE LEAVES OF THE STRAWBERRY-BED AND SET THEM HOPPING. They quarreled about which one of them was a ghost, until

Tom figured out that DIFFERENT PEOPLE HAVE DIFFERENT TIMES, AL-
THOUGH OF COURSE, THEY'RE REALLY ALL BITS OF THE SAME BIG TIME.
SHE WOULD BE NO MORE A GHOST FROM THE PAST THAN I WOULD BE A
GHOST FROM THE FUTURE. WE'RE NEITHER OF US GHOSTS; AND THE GAR-
DEN ISN'T EITHER.

Tom's visits to the garden seemed to skip around in time: seasons shifted, Hatty appeared to be different ages; one night the big
fir tree was felled in a storm, but the next night it was whole again.
At the end of the book, old Mrs. Bartholomew, the landlady in the
top-floor apartment, revealed that she was Hatty herself, redream-
ing her childhood every night. NEVER BEFORE THIS SUMMER HAD SHE
BEEN ABLE TO REMEMBER SO VIVIDLY WHAT IT HAD FELT LIKE TO BE THE
LITTLE HATTY—TO BE LONGING FOR SOMEONE TO PLAY WITH AND FOR
SOMEWHERE TO PLAY. MRS BARTHOLOMEW HAD GONE BACK TO WHEN
SHE WAS A GIRL; AND TOM HAD BEEN ABLE TO GO BACK WITH HER, TO
THAT SAME GARDEN.

Tom recognized the old woman now as truly Hatty, the bright
black eyes and voice and laugh. They had shared all these adventures. Once he had asked Hatty to always keep her ice skates in a
hiding place under a floorboard; then Tom looked for the old
skates, which were still there, in his own time. The next night,
when he went into the magic garden, he brought them along, and
the two of them skated down the glittering river: TWO SKATERS ON
ONE PAIR OF SKATES, WHICH SEEMED TO TOM BOTH THE EERIEST AND
THE MOST NATURAL THING IN THE WORLD. *Tom's Midnight Garden*
is itself both eerie and natural, like all the best fantasy books.

Friends have told me of childhood imaginings: being Robin Hood
or Odysseus or Wendy learning to fly. Many people do identify
with characters, but I didn't. While I loved favorite characters de-
votedly, I simply wanted to admire them, puzzle out their lives,
understand their histories and their maps. Surely many readers are
like that, wanting to put things together as observers, rather than
putting themselves inside the story. When not reading (a very small
percent of the time), I was happy playing parcheesi or backgam-
mon with my mother, games in which you moved by skill and luck,

through a mysterious abstract universe. For at least a year, after dinner, my grandmother, mother, father, and I would sit at a card table and play canasta, a soothing, order-making activity my sister was baffled by—but then, she doesn't read fantasy books either. Playing clock solitaire, where you hope individual cards will fall into the right harmonious pattern, gave me the same kind of satisfaction as reading about Oz—the Emerald City nicely surrounded by the four kingdoms, blue, purple, yellow, and red—the comfort and excitement of a good design. When a book truly combines this strong sense of organizing pattern with a sense of wonder and of human significance, then that's a triumph—like *Tom's Midnight Garden*.

The Middle of the Journey: Looking Around

In discussing the different kinds of fantasy worlds in children's fiction, my chapters follow the chronology of children's growth outward, starting from their own small world of picture books and moving toward the vast universes of high heroic fantasy. At the same time, the chapters follow a path from light, happy stories to darkest sagas about evil powers. You cannot divide these types strictly into light books for children and dark books for adults, however. Although it's true that young children can't understand the most complex dark epics, it is also true that adults can enjoy reading small, light, happy fantasies as well as large, dark, solemn ones. In addition, some middle-level children reach for the more challenging books and are excited by what they find.

A fictional fantasy world can be viewed as a circle. In Chapter 1 (A Child Goes into the World), the circle is light, optimistic, with a tiny bit of darkness in the center, which is easily smothered in the course of the story. In Chapter 2 (Lighter Worlds: Living in Harmony and Balance), the light circle contains a more substantial circle of darkness, but the lightness still comfortably contains the darkness. In Chapter 3 (Shifting Worlds: Playing with Time and Space), the circle is variable: the ball of darkness is bigger and more ominous in some of these works and smaller in others, but all of them present the light as still surrounding, dominating, the dark.

In Chapter 4 (Bigger Worlds: Finding the Way), you see an intermediate sort of story, one that can be called the junior epic. Although the fantasy worlds of these intermediate books contain dark forces of evil (much more threatening than the bits of darkness discussed in earlier chapters), they are still kept inside a larger, light circle of reassuring goodness. To authors of the junior epic, good wins out over evil; their worlds contain only a quasi-darkness, not the real darkness of the true epic fantasy—not Tolkien's sad certainty that much of the good in Middle-earth will ultimately be overcome by darkness despite the best efforts of its heroes.

Both of the last two chapters examine worlds where now the dark circle surrounds the light, where indestructible evil squeezes the hopeful circle of good, which struggles within the dark, refuses to surrender, and wins some temporary victories. Chapter 5 (Worlds Stained by Humankind: Making Choices) deals with a narrower focus and smaller worlds than Chapter 6 (Battlefield Worlds: Fighting Tyranny and Chaos), which describes the large universes of high epic fantasy. But those narrower stories, smaller worlds, of Chapter 5 are just as dense and dark as the broader ones.

So these chapters follow a chronology of darkening, expanding fantasy types, which appeal to children as they change and grow. In general, the historical chronology follows an analogous pattern. Early children's fantasy books, from the late nineteenth and early twentieth centuries, tend to have a lighter, more cheerful perspective; late-twentieth-century fantasies are bleaker and more pessimistic. For most people, the world of 2000 seems darker than the sheltered, late Victorian and Edwardian world was around 1900; we have moved from Nesbit's buoyant *The Phoenix and the Carpet* to Pullman's somber *The Amber Spyglass*. But that is a general trend, and many individual works ignore the trend.

This sequence of different kinds of fantasy does not run from the least to the most successful books, or from trivial to great. All these types include both masterpieces and dull imitations, with all levels of quality in between. The only possible exception is the junior epic of Chapter 4: any other type of fantasy can reach perfection of its kind, as in *Where the Wild Things Are* or *The Wizard of Oz* or *Tom's Midnight Garden*. The junior epic, though much loved by many children, points toward a level of complexity that it seldom attains; often, it is a tentative version of serious high fantasy. This classification of types is suggestive rather than rigid— simply a way of looking at a large and varied field. What's important, and exciting, is the uniqueness of each book or series.

4

Bigger Worlds: Finding the Way

Publishers turn out an abundance of pleasant, conventional fantasy series for middle-level children. These series create a wider world than the single book, with more movable parts to fit together, but they do not stretch the reader's mind alarmingly. This is the one type of children's fantasy that adult readers may find exasperating, sometimes simple-minded or heavy-handed. The youngest fantasy books, like *Winnie-the-Pooh* and *Sylvester and the Magic Pebble*, are not simple-minded at all; they are accessible even to the very young but are evocative for all—like poetry, you might say. It's the middle level, those primitive versions of a more sophisticated genre (the epic or heroic fantasy series) that advertise their immaturity. Lloyd Alexander's Prydain books are fun and popular and harmless, and so are Anne McCaffery's Harper Hall stories, countless books by Tamora Pierce, and dozens of other series. They're just not as richly original or as brilliantly written as series by Le Guin, Hamilton, McKinley, Nicholson, or Pullman, to name a few; and some sink to the formulaic level.

After *Peter Rabbit* and *Where the Wild Things Are* (those picture books with very little text), and after the easy-reader stories like Elsie Minarik's *A Kiss for Little Bear* (where the proportion of text is greater), comes what young children proudly call "the chapter book." They want bigger worlds to explore and longer stories that can't be read all at one bedtime session. The ultimate challenge after the chapter-book phase is the series, which differs from the single book in its relation to reality. Even when a series is thin and childishly limited, readers must work to absorb its whole fictional world; they must move out from and back into their real lives and must follow the connections among the parts of the various books. If reading a fantasy story is like putting together a big jigsaw puzzle, reading a series is like working a puzzle that has an extra dimension. Even a shallow series is doing something important—though a profound series does it much better.

All people, always, put together their own stories, trying to make them make sense. A recent type of psychological counseling involves narrative therapy: a client examines the story of his or her life and self, to see destructive aspects and assumptions in that taken-for-granted narrative, then constructs a new story, leading to freer, healthier behavior and outlook. Traditional therapy also works to rewrite patients' personal narratives. Humankind being a narrative animal, we are drawn to continuing stories about a known cast of characters—everything from tales of the ancestors told every night around the fire, to long Victorian novels published in periodical installments, to television sitcoms that go on for years.

Sometimes, when television viewers get involved in a television drama series, they can't stand to watch a rerun even if they hated missing it the first time around, because it's out of sequence: it destroys the almost-real level of reality they normally find in the series and introduces a third, really-unreal level. So, if I catch a glimpse of an *NYPD Blue* episode featuring Detective Bobby Simone, I turn it off—he was a great character but hey, he's dead. Many viewers and readers have intense respect for the extended story, as long as it follows its own path vividly and logically. If all fiction combines the familiar with the strange, fantasy series fiction combines the most familiar (characters and places that keep reappearing) with the most strange (whole worlds that are weird and magical).

Junior Epics and Animal Magic

While books by Lloyd Alexander, Anne McCaffrey, and Tamora Pierce are less good than the finest fantasy series, they are still considerable accomplishments—much superior to the popular *Redwall* series, about bloody battles of heroic, medieval mice and squirrels, and the nasty new series about Artemis Fowl, a rich, Irish, twelve-year-old criminal mastermind who fights like James Bond against a race of horrible, violent fairies. And those three children's writers—Alexander, McCaffrey, Pierce—produce better books than supposedly adult works like Andre Norton's *Witch World* series, which some find tedious, and the hilariously awful Conan books. Here is a passage from Robert Jordan's *Conan the Invincible* (1982), written in the overwrought Tarzan tradition; if this is adult, I'd rather be childish. THE AX LEAPED TOWARD CONAN, WHO DANCED BACK, BROADSWORD FLICKERING IN SNAKELIKE THRUSTS. THE MIGHTY BARBARIAN SWUNG, FELT HIS BLADE BITE THROUGH BONE, AND AX AND SEVERED HAND FELL TOGETHER. BLOOD PUMPED FROM THE STUMP IN REGULAR SPURTS. THE MAN HURLED HIS ROUND SHIELD AT CONAN'S HEAD. "CONAN!" HE SCREAMED. "YOU WILL DIE!" CONAN'S BLADE LEAPED FORWARD ONCE MORE, AND THE HELMETED HEAD ROLLED IN THE DUST. "NOT YET," THE CIMMERIAN SAID GRIMLY.

In the five Prydain books by Lloyd Alexander, Taran's career follows a traditional path toward self-knowledge, maturity, and leadership. This is a great series for children who shy away from overly challenging books. The Prydain stories, published between 1964 and 1968, create a solid, funny, sometimes moving world. Young Taran, Assistant Pig-Keeper in Caer Dallben, loved his rustic home and his guardians, the old sorcerer Dallben and the bald farmer Coll, but yearned to explore the world, prove himself a hero, and learn the identity of his parents. Like any traditional hero, he set out to find his fortune, acquired a mentor and assorted companions, and ran into exciting but chastening adventures. Prydain is loaded with predictable, Tolkienian elements: crotchety dwarves, elusive Fair Folk, treacherous warriors, a sneaking king's steward. Arawn Death-Lord and his minions threatened to come out of the evil land Annuvin and overwhelm all good people and beasts. Taran joined the forces of Prince Gwydion, in a fellowship with Princess Eilonwy, a bubbly but smart teenager, a loyal caveman-like creature who talked a bit like Tolkien's Gollum, and others.

In Book 1, Taran's gang killed Arawn's dreadful warrior, the Horned King; in Book 2, they destroyed the Black Cauldron, which had turned countless good knights fallen in battle into zombie Cauldron-Born, now fighting for the Death Lord. In Book 3, they rescued Eilonwy, who had been kidnapped and brainwashed. In Book 4, Taran, longing to be worthy of Eilonwy's hand, went to seek his own origins, and learned strange things about himself and his abilities. In Book 5, Taran helped defeat Arawn's troops and destroy the enchantments of Annuvin. Afterward, as his companions sailed off to live forever in the Summer Country, Taran and Eilonwy gave up their chance to go with them, choosing to stay and work for the good people of Prydain. Taran never discovered his parentage, but became High King of the land.

The Prydain quintet is derivative enough to make one yawn (here come the giant black birds of prey spying for the Dark Lord). Some important characters are genial cartoons. Fflewddur Fflam, the warrior who was also a would-be bard, carried a magic harp that snapped a string whenever he told a lie. This lying/string-breaking sequence becomes an embarrassing tic in the narrative. So does the rhyming speech of the lumbering Gurgi: his constant whine (that he feared smackings and whackings, or wished for munchings and crunchings) makes you want to clobber him on his shaggy head. Although younger children may enjoy this sort of formula, it makes the story seem artificial and lessens its impact.

Early in the series, then, the author seems like a patronizing on-looker; he doesn't believe in his invented world as intensely as, say, Baum believes in Oz. Gradually, though, Prydain comes alive, and Alexander's style loses much of its grating archness. There is nothing wrong with using traditional fantasy elements, if they are transformed with energy and conviction and thus become archetypes rather than clichés. Books 1 and 3 (*The Book of Three* and *The Castle of Llyr*) are the most afflicted with a slow pace and a cute style. Books 2, 4, and 5 (*The Black Cauldron*, *Taran Wanderer*, *The High King*) are less stilted, more natural, and more exciting.

Arawn's horrible servants were convincingly scary—the huge Huntsmen-Warriors who absorbed extra strength whenever one of their band died; and the unkillable, already killed, Cauldron-Born: THEIR FACES WERE PALLID; THEIR EYES LIKE STONES. THEY DID NOT BEAR SHIELD OR HELMET. THEIR MOUTHS WERE FROZEN IN THE HIDEOUS GRIN OF DEATH. Prydain's heroes movingly displayed values that adolescent Taran would gradually come to respect: Old Coll the warrior preferred digging turnips to fighting, though he died in battle. Brave soldier Adaon told the boy about peaceable pursuits: "THERE IS MUCH TO BE KNOWN," SAID ADAON, "AND ABOVE ALL MUCH TO BE LOVED, BE IT THE TURN OF THE SEASONS OR THE SHAPE OF A RIVER PEBBLE." Some characters are neither all good nor all bad. Sly, selfish Prince Ellidyr sacrificed himself to destroy the evil Cauldron; while great King Morgant betrayed his friends to the enemy. Prince Gwydion told Taran, "IT IS EASY TO JUDGE EVIL UNMIXED. BUT ALAS, IN MOST OF US GOOD AND BAD ARE CLOSELY WOVEN AS THE THREADS ON A LOOM. KING MORGANT SERVED THE SONS OF DON LONG AND WELL. UNTIL THE THIRST FOR POWER PARCHED HIS THROAT, HE WAS A FEARLESS AND NOBLE LORD. AND SO I SHALL HONOR MORGANT, FOR WHAT HE USED TO BE, AND ELLIDYR PRINCE OF PEN-LLARCAU FOR WHAT HE BECAME."

The most successful and freshest of the five books is *Taran Wanderer*. Young Taran was gaining skill and respect as a soldier and leader, but he envied the "honor" possessed by those of noble rank. Eilonwy's scolding did no good: "IT SEEMS TO ME THAT IF AN ASSISTANT PIG-KEEPER DOES THE BEST HE CAN, AND A PRINCE DOES THE BEST HE CAN, THERE'S NO DIFFERENCE BETWEEN THEM." When Taran left his home and friends to seek the truth about himself, instead of his parentage he discovered the shape of his world. Traveling in the Free Commots, whose people obeyed no lord but only the High King, he worked with a farmer and a shepherd, and studied the crafts of a blacksmith, a weaver, and a potter. Taran came to admire these sturdy citizens and their talents; and when Prince Gwydion appointed him to raise troops for the final battle against the Dark Lord, the men of the Free Commots admired him enough to follow him.

Taran chose to stay and work for his people, instead of sailing to the Summer Country. Old Dallben cautioned him that his tasks would be difficult, perhaps impossible, and his life would end like other mortals'. TARAN NODDED. "SO BE IT," HE SAID. "LONG AGO I YEARNED TO BE A HERO WITHOUT KNOWING WHAT A HERO WAS. NOW I UNDERSTAND IT A LITTLE BETTER. A GROWER OF TURNIPS OR A SHAPER OF CLAY, A COMMOT FARMER OR A KING—EVERY MAN IS A HERO IF HE STRIVES MORE FOR OTHERS THAN FOR HIMSELF ALONE." A journey through the Prydain books is more substantial, less silly and less simple-minded than it seemed at first.

ℛ℞ ℬℛ

Anne McCaffrey's first book about the people and dragons of Pern appeared in 1968. There are now more than fifteen, including a trilogy aimed at children—stories of the young musicians who trained at Harper Hall in Pern. McCaffrey created a huge, detailed world with a map, a history, and a strange science. A Red Star orbited the planet of Pern, emitting dangerous spores that fell in the form of killer Thread. To defend against Threadfall, the people of Pern built stone forts to live in and bred telepathic dragons that bonded with their human riders and destroyed Thread with their flaming breath.

Life on Pern is well described, its government, geography, and customs. With this imaginative background, McCaffrey tells her somewhat disappointing stories, mostly swashbuckling adventures of noble dragonriders. The children's trilogy has a different weakness: though earnest, the stories do not feel particularly original. The girl hero, Menolly, was badly treated by her family and forbidden to develop her talent; she escaped, found mentors who appreciated her, and became a much admired musician. The second book of the children's trilogy, *Dragonsinger* (1977), in which Menolly was an apprentice at the official crafthall studying voice, harping, and composing, is readable, but it amounts to a conventional boarding-school story in an exotic setting. And McCaffrey's style lacks economy: trivial scenes are spun out in too much detail,

and many sentences are ponderous (for example, THIS MILD DEVIA-
TION FROM THE ABSOLUTE OBEDIENCE TO HER FATHER'S RESTRICTION
ABOUT TUNING DID MUCH TO EASE MENOLLY'S GROWING FRUSTRATION
AND LONELINESS). Nonetheless, the reader roots for Menolly, who
is a spunky sort of girl.

The first book, *Dragonsong* (1976), is more successful, because
Menolly's physical and emotional pain is rendered with more intensity. Her father, Yanus, the strict leader of a remote seaside set-
tlement, allowed his musical daughter to assist the local Harper,
whose important songs provided teaching for the children and historical lore for all, but forbade her to practice the male skills of
songwriting and instrument playing. The old Harper died, and
Menolly took over the song teaching until a new Harper should be
sent from Harper Hall, so the children would not lose their school-
ing. Yanus, however, felt it was disgraceful to have a girl play the
Harper role and insisted this be a secret when the new Harper arrived. Her parents were so scornful and fearful of her talent and
her yearning to write songs that they kept her hidden, a Cinderella
who wasn't allowed to sing with the whole town. WHEN THE
HARPER BECKONED FOR EVERYONE TO JOIN IN THE CHORUSES, MAVI
PINCHED MENOLLY SO HARD THAT SHE GASPED. "DON'T ROAR. YOU MAY
SING SOFTLY AS BEFITS A GIRL YOUR AGE," MAVI SAID. SO SHE DIDN'T SING
AT ALL BUT SAT THERE BY HER MOTHER'S SIDE, NUMB AND HURT. When
her hand was badly cut, they deliberately allowed it to heal wrong,
too twisted and scarred ever to play an instrument.

The irony was that before he died, the old Harper had sent some
of Menolly's "tunings"—original songs—to the Masterharper at
Harper Hall, commenting only that this was the work of an apprentice. When the new Harper arrived, he searched in vain for the
brilliant young composer, not knowing it was the awkward girl he
saw cowering in the pantry. In despair, Menolly ran away and
lived in a cave, barely escaping death by Threadfall. Then her luck
turned. There was a rare and desirable species called fire lizards—
beautiful, tiny cousins of dragons, just the right size to perch on a
person's shoulder. Like the mighty dragons, fire lizards would be
Impressed by the first person to feed and caress them after they
hatched; the creature and its human friend would bond forever

and speak to each other telepathically. Menolly saved a clutch of fire lizards from Threadfall and Impressed all of them as they hatched.

She was now the guardian of nine coveted fire lizards, and eventually she was located by the Harper Hall masters and flown on a great bronze dragon to the place where she clearly belonged, accompanied by her nine warbling friends. Menolly was welcomed; her injured hand was treated properly so it would heal. The Masterharper was overjoyed to find the author of "TWO OF THE LOVELIEST MELODIES I'VE HEARD IN ALL MY TURNS OF HARPERING." As the dour composer Domick told her, "THE WHOLE POINT OF THE HARPER HALL IS TO EXTEND KNOWLEDGE. THAT'S WHAT'S WRONG WITH PERN; EVERYTHING'S KEPT IN SHALLOW LITTLE MINDS THAT RESIST NEW KNOWLEDGE, AND EXPERIENCE. THAT IS WHY I KNOW YOUR SONGS ARE AS IMPORTANT TO THE CRAFT HALL, AND PERN, AS MY MUSIC. THEY ARE A FRESH VOICE, FRESH NEW WAYS OF LOOKING AT THINGS AND PEOPLE, WITH TUNES NO ONE CAN KEEP FROM HUMMING."

The scenes in which Menolly could not believe that people wanted her to sing and play her own songs are pathetic and joyous. All people imagine a place where they will be appreciated and can warm themselves in the innermost circle, while those who were cruel and obtuse will be shut out in the cold.

⇛✳ ✳⇝

Since *Alanna* appeared in 1983, Tamora Pierce has finished four series of four books each and is well into a fifth. Three series are set in Tortall, a classic sword-and-sorcery country, feminism-for-children division. Pierce's stories, like McCaffrey's trilogy, are totally focused on the central child character; the angle of vision is small even though the setting is broad. Readers hear about other characters the way they hear about friends of a friend, and are mildly interested; but really they are made to care only about the hero. It's the innocent solipsism of the young teenager.

The Alanna books tell the traditional story of a warrior's training, with the twist that the boy who would be a knight was actually a girl. Alanna's twin, Thom, wished he could become a sorcerer instead of a knight, and Alanna dreaded the convent school.

She persuaded him to switch places: boy sorcerers studied at the convent, so the two forged letters announcing that Thom was on his way there and his brother "Alan" was coming to court as a page. Alanna faced the same school-story jealousy that McCaffrey's Menolly met at Harper Hall, with the extra challenge that she must bind her growing breasts and avoid swimming with the boys. Of course, "Alan" had more talent than anyone else and worked harder; proving herself the outstanding page, she was picked by Prince Jonathan to be his squire. She came to terms with her magical Gifts, accepting her mentor's advice—"MAGIC ISN'T GOOD OR EVIL BY ITSELF. USE IT WHEN YOU ARE CERTAIN YOUR CAUSE IS JUST"—and revealed that she was really Alanna.

In later books, Alanna became a member and shaman of the Bazhirs, a desert tribe skeptical of women. She killed in a public duel Prince Jonathan's evil cousin, who plotted to seize the throne. She led a dangerous expedition to the land of the Roof of the World and brought back the magic Dominion Jewel, for the protection and glory of Tortall. She took three lovers (not simultaneously); turned down the chance to be queen; and married the reformed, ennobled King of Thieves. Jonathan, now king, appointed her his personal knight, the King's Champion. Not bad. Little girls deserve their own heroes—though Pierce might have described a girl hero without copying the violence of boys' adventures: IN THE SPLIT-SECOND OPENING IN THE PATH OF HIS SWORD SHE RAMMED FORWARD, CRUSHING HIS WINDPIPE WITH ONE FIST AS SHE STRUCK HIS NOSE WITH THE OTHER, THRUSTING BONE SPLINTERS DEEP INTO HIS BRAIN.

In Pierce's second series, *The Immortals*, young Daine from a backwoods village learned to control her empathy with animals— her *Wild Magic* (1992). She worked on thought-talk—SOUNDS CRASHED INTO HER SKULL: BATS SEEKING INSECTS, CATS ON THE HUNT, HAWKS IN THE PALACE MEWS. IT WAS TOO MUCH TO HEAR ALL AT ONCE. Soon she could enter into the animals. JUMPING INTO A NOTCH IN THE STONE WALL, SHE LEAPED OUT, CHANGING AS SHE DID, TRADING HAIR FOR FEATHERS, ARMS FOR WINGS, AND LEGS FOR TALONS. AS A SPARROW HAWK, SHE STREAKED AFTER OZORNE. Tortall needed Daine's magic because they were threatened by human and inhuman enemies. Emperor Ozorne of Carthak, seeking ultimate power, had broken the barrier that kept Immortals out of the natural world—creatures that would never die unless defeated in battle. Some of the Immortals were friends to humankind, like dragons, but Ozorne hoped for support from Stormwings and Coldfangs, not to mention giant spidrens with FURRY SPIDER BODIES, THEY LEAPED AMAZING DISTANCES AND PREFERRED HUMAN BLOOD TO ANY OTHER FOOD. Daine led the victory over Ozorne. She penetrated the fortress as a squirrel and destroyed the magic device that protected it; she told her animal friends to damage enemy equipment; she summoned the emperor's museum of dinosaur bones back to vengeful life—the dinosaurs ripped apart Ozorne's palace.

In the fourth book, Daine found the father she never knew, the hunter god Weiryn; fought in a final battle to send Immortals back to their own realm; and ended up in the arms of the handsome sorcerer Numair. Once a timid, surly child, she now could say, when cautioned that "THERE MAY BE ENEMY SOLDIERS OUT THAT WAY. WAIT FOR A CLEANUP SQUAD," "IT ISN'T ME WHO HAS TO BE WARY OF THEM, THEY'D BEST BE AFRAID OF ME."

In Pierce's *Circle of Magic* series, starting with *Sandry's Book* (1997), four troubled orphans were selected to live in a cottage at Winding Circle Temple community and develop their magical gifts. Sandry, an aristocratic girl, yearned to weave fiber and light. Bitter Daja, from the scorned Trader tribe, had a genius for metalcraft. Angry Tris affected the weather: her moods created thunderstorms. The slum brat Briar had a mystical connection with growing plants. Each of the four became an apprentice and then an expert magician, using magic talent to solve community problems and repel enemies. These stories of crafts and useful skills are a welcome change from Pierce's other three series, with their warrior mystique. The four children at Winding Circle developed teamwork and loyalty like Alanna and Daine in Tortall, but in the service of curing plagues and controlling earthquakes.

Pierce seems to possess magic skills of productivity that delight her fans; bookstores offer shelves and shelves of her books. Readers respond to her earnestness and her endings in which the underdog triumphs. Although her style leans toward heaviness and cliché (DAINE THOUGHT HER EYES WOULD FALL FROM HER HEAD. . . .

PEOPLE ARE PEOPLE, AFTER ALL, SHE THOUGHT—BUT THAT WAS HOW THINGS WERE), there are touching scenes and fresh images, like the darkings in *The Realms of the Gods*. Evil Ozorne created these tiny beings, who looked like inkblot amoebas, out of his own blood so they could serve as spies in his war against Tortall. But three darkings were discovered by Daine and her friends, who named and befriended them. They turned against their creator and persuaded the other darkings to do so. Daine's guardian explained: "HERE, LIFE IS FORBIDDEN TO REMAIN A SLAVE OF ITS CREATOR. THE DARKINGS ARE FORMING THEIR OWN IDEAS AND WAYS TO COMMUNICATE." The one Daine called Gold-streak announced, "I GO. TALK TO DARKINGS. TEACH THEM—" IT RETURNED TO ITS HUDDLE WITH LEAF AND JELLY. THEY VIBRATED TOGETHER UNTIL GOLD-STREAK'S HEAD ROSE OUT OF THE MASS. "FREEDOM," IT SAID CLEARLY. "CHOOSING."

Reading these adventure stories is like going on a treasure hunt. Children find it exciting to gather with a few teammates and read the slip of paper that tells in cryptic terms how to take the next step in the journey. There is competition with the enemy team, and enough uncertainty to make the children shiver, along with certainty that the conclusion will be satisfactory and followed by ice cream.

In the Dragon's Belly, in the Skunk's DNA

If Alexander, McCaffrey, and Pierce give children appealing versions of traditional stories, Jane Yolen in the *Pit Dragon* series and K. A. Applegate in the *Animorphs* books tell their youth-against-bad-guys tales in remarkably fresh, vigorous ways. Yolen, who has written more than 300 books for all ages from toddlers to adults, imagines all her stories so precisely that familiar themes become alive and intense. Talking to dragons is a universally popular activity, described in Gannett's *My Father's Dragon* for the youngest children, in Le Guin's profound *Earthsea* series, and in books at all levels in between. Yolen ignores the chivalric tradition of dragons and knights, choosing instead to create the grimy, arid, twenty-fifth-century planet Austar IV, a land so inhospitable that every night the frigid temperature kills anyone left outside. Austar IV had been settled from Earth as a penal colony. Descendants of the guards and convicts bred elephant-sized native dragons to fight each other in stadium pits, developing an economy based on gambler-tourists from other planets. As a leftover from convict days, most people were bonders controlled by masters, but those who worked hard and filled their bond bags with coins could buy freedom. These are stories primarily for children, but unsentimental, tough, and complicated.

In *Dragon's Blood* (1982) and two sequels, Jakkin, a bondboy who cleaned stalls and scrubbed fighting dragons, stole a dragon hatchling and brought her up secretly (stealing one later was shameful but stealing one at birth was considered enterprising). SOON, HE KNEW ITS MIND BETTER THAN HIS OWN: A DEEP, GLOWING CAVERN OF COLORS AND SIGHTS AND SOUNDS. THERE HAD BEEN A RESONANT THRUMMING, A HUMMING THAT FILLED THE AIR AND THEN FILLED HIM. Constantly muttering the motto, "I will fill my bag myself," Jakkin was eager to become a brave, true man and buy his way out of bondage.

His world proved to be complex, however. On his first adult hunt for the giant predatory drakk birds, his behavior was timorous, but he boasted of his boldness while feeling ashamed of the lie: WAS THE PASSAGE FROM BOY TO MAN REALLY THAT EASY? AND WAS IT ALWAYS BUILT UPON LIES? Soon his dragon, Heart's Blood, began to fight in the pits and earned enough money for Jakkin to buy freedom from bondage. But people turned out to be not what they seemed. His world, instead of getting simpler with freedom, turned murky and dangerous from political turmoil. Jakkin and his girlfriend, Akki, ambivalent spies in in a rebel cell, unwittingly caused a bomb to explode in the dragon stadium, killing people and beasts. They escaped to the mountains with the dragon, but Heart's Blood was shot and killed.

Jakkin and Akki, with no shelter from the murderous cold at night, realized their only hope was the body of the gallant dragon. In a remarkable scene, Akki said, "WE CAN SHELTER INSIDE HER. HER BODY WILL HOLD ITS WARMTH FOR AT LEAST THE FOUR HOURS WE NEED." "INSIDE HER?"—THERE WERE NO WORDS FOR HIS DISGUST, HIS

TERROR. "LIKE A HATCHLING, JAKKIN. SHE PROTECTED US WITH HER BODY DURING THE FIGHT. SHE WOULD WANT TO DO IT NOW AS WELL." They sliced into her belly; HE COULD SEE INTO THE DARK, STEAMING CAVERN OF MUSCLE AND BEYOND IT THE GREAT ARCHES OF BONE. Warm, they slept until morning. They emerged like true hatchlings, covered with dragon blood and now blessed with dragon senses: the magical ability to see deeply and talk silently. The Pit Dragon books are resonant with archetypes at the same time that the people and events seem real and immediate.

≈≈ ≈≈

In her books about Animorphs, K. A. Applegate has created a series that is much better than might be expected, given the biggish print, simple sentences and vocabulary, and jokey teen dialogue. At first this looks like just another formula series for children— maybe like R. L. Stine's *Goosebumps* horror-book phenomenon. There is certainly a lot of "action," as the teenage characters turn into wild animals and battle evil aliens. The characters, however, are quite complex, the moral issues are provocative, and the detailed understanding of animals is impressive. The style is satisfyingly plain.

In Animorphs #1, *The Invasion* (1996), five ordinary kids crossing a construction site found a spaceship containing a dying Andalite prince. Andalites (good aliens who resembled small centaurs) were fighting with the Yeerks (horrible sluglike, parasitic aliens, who would coil inside the brain of any creature and take over the host's behavior). In his final moments the Andalite told the teenagers that Yeerks had already invaded hundreds of humans, wanting to control all of planet Earth. Andalites had a special power—they could temporarily morph into the bodies of other species—and he offered this power to the young humans so they could join the war against the Yeerks.

Jake, Marco, Tobias, Cassie, and Rachel (who called themselves the Animorphs) were now able to absorb the DNA of any animal, by touching it and concentrating. Then they could at any time morph into that animal, a process that took several minutes and looked most peculiar. Their city had a zoo, so they collected the

DNA of elephants, tigers, and crocodiles, as well as that of other beasts like skunks, birds, wolves, and insects. The Yeerks in human form, called Human-Controllers, soon realized that they were being subverted by a guerilla (sometimes gorilla) band of creatures who had morphed into animals, but they assumed these were Andalites, the only race known to have morphing abilities.

In each book, one of the Animorphs describes meetings and dangerous missions, using a first-person narrative. Episodes are well worked out and suspenseful, such as the time they infiltrated a picnic of The Sharing, a wholesome young people's organization run by smiling adults. The Sharing was actually a group designed to recruit voluntary Human-Controllers (who hoped for some benefit from allowing Yeerk-slugs to enter their brains) or involuntary victims (who were taken to the vile chemical pool full of Yeerks in their natural state and forced to become hosts). The Animorphs rescued innocent victims by morphing into an elephant, a tiger, a hawk; Tobias was forced to stay a hawk for more than the maximum two-hour period and could not morph back into human form. He remained in the group, joining their missions and flying in their windows to watch TV.

The most gripping aspect of these stories is not the foul or the kindly aliens but the animals. Applegate, who has researched and worked with animals, does a good job of conveying what it feels like to be a wolf or a dolphin or even a termite—what kind of smell, hearing, sight it has; what instincts direct its behavior; how it moves and eats and fights. I FELT MY JAW STRETCHING AND STRETCHING OUTWARD. THE BONES MADE A SLIGHT GRINDING SOUND AS MY SMALL, WEAK HUMAN MOUTH BECAME THE POWERFUL, CRUSHING JAW OF THE WOLF. MY KNEES REVERSED DIRECTION. ROUGH PADS REPLACED MY FEET. THE WOLF SMELLED EVERY FLOWER, EVERY LEAF, EVERY MUSHROOM. IT SMELLED WATER IN THREE LOCATIONS AND KNEW WHICH STREAM WAS SWEETEST. THE WOLF SMELLED A DOZEN SQUIRRELS, VOLES, DEER, A DEAD SPARROW, A RACCOON, NO, TWO RACCOONS.

That was one of Cassie's animal forms, and this is another: Pushing out of a chrysalis, I COULD SEE AGAIN! LIKE SOME LUNATIC ARTIST, SPRAYING EVERYING IN BRILLIANT, IRIDESCENT, GLOWING, IN-

SANE COLORS. COMPOUND EYES, I TOLD MYSELF. AND NOW, ANTENNAE THAT UNFOLDED FROM THE STICKINESS OF THE CHRYSALIS.

Beyond the typical war-of-good-and-evil and the empathy with animals, there are moral questions here that can challenge young readers and even their elders. Sometimes members of the group felt overwhelmed: Must they risk their own safety and that of their families in a futile fight against stronger forces? Animals kill by instinct and need, but should the Animorphs, as humans, choose to enter the tiger and the crocodile and savagely rip apart other beings? When these young people turned into predatory animals they mostly did so with horror, but some of them found they enjoyed it too much.

There is a subtle moment when Cassie, an ecologist who loved animals, was caught in a stalemate with a Human-Controller. In book #19, *The Departure*, she decided to give up being an Animorph—disgusted by her bloody activities and by waking up next morning after running as a wolf with bits of flesh stuck in her teeth. When she found herself alone in the forest with Karen, a pretty human girl parasitically controlled by a hideous Yeerk-slug, Cassie could not bring herself to kill the Karen/Yeerk. She listened to what the Yeerk-mind had to say: "IN OUR NATURAL STATE, WE CAN HEAR BUT WE CANNOT SEE. WE ARE BLIND, UNTIL WE ENTER A HOST. YOU CAN'T IMAGINE THE FIRST TIME YOU ENTER A BRAIN AND SEIZE CONTROL AND SUDDENLY, YOU ARE SEEING! IT'S A MIRACLE. DO YOU SEE THE SUNLIGHT? DO YOU SEE THE BIRDS FLYING? YOU HATE ME FOR WANTING THAT. YOU HATE ME BECAUSE I WON'T SPEND MY LIFE SWIMMING ENDLESSLY IN A SEA OF SLUDGE, WHILE HUMANS LIKE YOU LIVE IN A WORLD OF INDESCRIBABLE BEAUTY."

The style is aimed at children, but it's not stupid and it's not condescending. I have read five of the first nineteen Animorph books, and I enjoyed them. Applegate has finished the series at sixty books, fifty-six of which are already published. She said in an interview on the Scholastic Animorphs Web site that one of the five Animorphs dies in the final battles. "I couldn't leave the series with the conclusion that this war came out all right, no harm done. In wars people die, even good guys, even heroes." In the final book she leaves some ambiguity about whether the remaining Animorphs have permanently won the war. It's not far from the final mood of the Prydain series or *The Lord of the Rings*: you can't win it all and you can't win it forever; you only try your best, as long as you can.

The Comic Epics

Most of the junior fantasy epics are meant to be exciting and inspiring, with moments of humor. Some authors turn that proportion the other way around—a background of humor plus moments of excitement. These books are refreshing: they do not aspire fruitlessly to being "grown-up" the way the serious-minded junior epics do. Among the best funny epics are genial stories by John Bellairs and Bill Brittain, and clever, cool stories by Dav Pilkey, Louis Sachar, and Daniel Pinkwater.

Bellairs's stories are set in the friendly town of New Zebedee in the 1940s. Lewis Barnavelt, in *The House with a Clock in Its Walls* (1973) and *The Figure in the Shadows* (1975), was unhappy being fat and unpopular but happy living with his uncle Jonathan, a jovial, bearded, not-too-competent wizard. Their Victorian house was full of wonderful things: LOTS OF ROOMS TO EXPLORE: THIRD-BEST UPSTAIRS FRONT PARLORS AND SECOND-BEST BACK BEDROOMS; LINEN CLOSETS AND PLAYROOMS AND JUST PLAIN ROOMS. EACH ROOM HAD ITS OWN FIREPLACE MADE OF MARBLE THAT LOOKED LIKE BLUE CHEESE OR FUDGE-RIPPLE ICE CREAM OR GREEN HAND SOAP OR MILK CHOCOLATE. Some of the things were magical: THE MIRROR ON THE COAT RACK SHOWED YOU YOUR FACE—SOMETIMES. BUT MORE OFTEN THAN NOT, IT WOULD SHOW YOU ROMAN RUINS OR MAYAN PYRAMIDS. THERE WAS AN ORGAN IN THE FRONT PARLOR THAT SANG RADIO COMMERCIALS.

These magic delights were combined with ordinary comforts, like homemade cookies before bed and poker games with Uncle Jonathan and Mrs. Zimmerman, the kindly witch next door. But the household was troubled by an incessant ticking in the walls— the sinister sound of a clock hidden somewhere by the house's late owner, the evil Isaac Izard. Outside the house, Lewis was beaten up by bullies until, wanting a friend, he showed off his uncle's magic to one of the popular boys and boasted that he himself could raise someone from the dead. The spell Lewis had found in Mrs. Zimmerman's magic book proved successful; the corpse he revived was Mrs. Izard, who was just as bad as her husband. IN HER RIGHT HAND WAS A PLAIN BLACK ROD, AND IN HER LEFT SHE CARRIED WHAT LOOKED LIKE A SEVERED HAND WITH A LIGHTED CANDLE GROWING OUT OF ITS BACK. Lewis discovered that Isaac Izard had created the Doomsday clock, to bring about the end of the world. Tired of always being afraid, Lewis helped Uncle Jonathan and Mrs. Zimmerman find the secret room where the clock was hidden. He broke the clock and prevented the end of the world.

In *The Figure in the Shadows*, Lewis dreamed of a shadowy figure approaching him down the middle of a country road, getting closer in each dream. He heard the front-door mail slot opening at midnight and found a postcard bearing just one word, *Venio*, I come. Deep, universal fears like these run through the Bellairs books, along with fears about one's own share of the guilt: Lewis had taken the ghost's magic amulet; he had almost caused the end of the world by summoning Mrs. Izard from the dead. Lewis's fear and guilt were cushioned by his guardians' love and wisdom and by the ordinariness of their lives. Jonathan and Mrs. Zimmerman could drop a kidnapping murderer down a bottomless well and settle down again to poker, a picnic, or a movie.

Bellairs's grown-ups were perfect: they took children seriously, and also magic; got scared but did brave things; did not scold, and did not lie. Bellairs's universe contains both virtuous stability and hideous danger. But this is the land of the junior epics, where the great lump of evil is contained by the larger circle of good. Evil wizards are outwitted and outfought by the good guardians and the child. One thing that reduces the frightening effect of Bellairs's plots is the narrating voice—a confident, comical narrator who resembles the Uncle Jonathan character. It's like the Lemony Snicket books, where readers are cradled so safely by the storyteller that the unfortunate events seem bearable.

While Bill Brittain writes the same kind of folksy, humorous story as Bellairs, Brittain's are less scary and more truly mysterious. Bellairs's magic is fun but creaky, his Gothic effects too theatrical to be really terrifying—witches swooping out of the tomb, an old attic chest opening into a misty universe. Brittain's magic in the *Tales of Coven Tree* is closer to home, and it concerns the whole community rather than a single hero. Sensible old Stew Meat (nickname for Stewart Meade), owner of the general store, was the voice of the village, telling their stories in the first person. In *The Wish Giver* (1983), smiling, plump Thaddeus Blinn appeared in town and set up a tent at the June church social, with a small sign announcing, "I CAN GIVE YOU WHATEVER YOU ASK FOR ONLY 50 CENTS." To each of the four curious people who entered, he gave a card bearing a red dot. "EACH CARD CAN GRANT ONLY A SINGLE WISH, SO THINK CAREFULLY BEFORE MAKING IT. WHEN YOU'RE READY, PRESS YOUR THUMB AGAINST THE RED SPOT AND UTTER YOUR WISH ALOUD." The villagers dispersed, chuckling at the old humbug; each tucked away the card and forgot it. Until a great need arose.

Awkward Polly was bad tempered and made enemies. She wished that people would pay attention to her and smile at her; then she began croaking like a bullfrog any time she said something mean. Lovely Rowena wanted the handsome traveling salesman to settle down and marry her, so she pressed the red spot and said, "I WISH HENRY PIPER WOULD PUT DOWN ROOTS HERE IN COVEN TREE AND NEVER LEAVE AGAIN!" That night, when Henry walked down the forest path, his feet stuck to the ground. He turned into a handsome tree. Adam hated hauling water from the Crick for his Pa's dry farm, so he pressed the red spot and said, "I WISH WE HAD WATER ALL OVER THIS FARM," and it flooded.

Fortunately, the fourth villager with a wishing card, Stew Meat himself, had not used up his wish. Polly, Rowena, and Adam rushed to him, desperate. "THAT THADDEUS BLINN," I GROWLED. "I SHOULD HAVE KNOWN RIGHT OFF THE KIND OF A CREATURE HE WAS. I WISH THAT ALL THREE OF THESE YOUNG'UNS WILL HAVE THEIR WISHES CANCELED OUT THIS VERY MINUTE. AND MR. BLINN, I DON'T WANT ANY OF THE MISERY THAT USUALLY COMES WITH SUCH WISHING, EITHER." It's a familiar theme—the damage done by a careless wish—but Brittain fleshes it out nicely, giving a strong sense of the sturdy village of Coven Tree. The community was peaceful and harmonious but once in a while something strange happened, bringing a whiff from the darker, less civilized past. WITCHES HAVE ABOUNDED IN THIS PART OF NEW ENGLAND SINCE COLONIAL DAYS. THE VERY NAME OF OUR VILLAGE COMES FROM THE HUGE, TWISTED TREE DOWN AT THE CROSS-ROADS WHERE GROUPS OF WITCHES USED TO MEET. IMPS AND FIENDS HAVE APPEARED HERE FROM TIME TO TIME, TAKING THEIR PLEASURE FROM PLAGUING AND FRIGHTENING US POOR MORTALS. *The Wish Giver* and *Dr. Dredd's Wagon of Wonders* (1987) are satisfying stories.

❧ ❧

The apotheosis of silly is Dav Pilkey's *The Adventures of Captain Underpants* (1997). It tells of Ohio fourth-graders George and Harold, who created an original superhero, wrote and illustrated comic books about him, made copies when the school secretary wasn't looking, and sold them to kids for fifty cents each. An issue of the boys' comic book is included in the real book: "NIGHT AND DAY, CAPTAIN UNDERPANTS WATCHED OVER THE CITY, FIGHTING FOR TRUTH, JUSTISE, AND ALL THAT IS PRE-SHRUNK AND COTTONY." He destroyed the Inedible Hunk, a monster formed from school-cafeteria garbage ("HELP! THE INEDIBLE HUNK JUST ATE UP 15 FOLDING CHAIRS AND THE GYM TEACHER!").

We learn that GEORGE AND HAROLD WERE USUALLY RESPONSIBLE KIDS. WHENEVER ANYTHING BAD HAPPENED, GEORGE AND HAROLD WERE RESPONSIBLE. Mr. Krupp, the principal, caught them on videotape sabotaging the football team by sprinkling itching powder on their uniforms and other things. By threatening to give the video to the large, mean football players, Mr. Krupp blackmailed George and Harold into waiting on him—washing his car, mowing his lawn, clipping his toenails. They broke out of the principal's control by sending in a coupon for a 3-D Hypno-Ring and using it to hypnotize him. First they retrieved the blackmail video; then as a joke they told Mr. Krupp to turn into Captain Underpants. Tearing off his toupee and most of his clothes, the hypnotized principal raced out of the school, captured bank robbers, destroyed alien robots, and stopped a villain from blowing up the world. After all this, George and Harold got Captain Underpants/Krupp back in his principal's office and poured water over his head to break the

spell. They had thrown away the instruction sheet for the 3-D
Hypno-Ring without reading its warning: "DON'T POUR WATER ON
ANYBODY'S HEAD WHEN THEY ARE IN A TRANCE! THIS WILL CAUSE THE
HYPNOTIZED PERSON TO SLIP BACK AND FORTH FROM TRANCE TO REAL-
ITY WHENEVER THEY HEAR THE SOUND OF FINGERS SNAPPING." Now,
the principal went into his Captain Underpants mode whenever he
heard snapped fingers.

In Book 3, about the Cafeteria Ladies from Outer Space, the
real cafeteria ladies were so offended by George and Harold's
comic book about them ("NIGHT OF THE LIVING LUNCH LADIES"), that
they quit, thus allowing three hideous aliens named Zorx, Klax,
and Jennifer to become the new lunch ladies, who fed Evil Milk-
shakes to all the children so they would become Zombie Nerds
and take over the world. George and Harold and Captain Under-
pants/Krupp demolished the Alien Lunch Ladies.

So each real book contains a Captain Underpants comic book
drawn and written by the boys, along with an adventure in which
the boys and Krupp/Underpants take part. It's not exactly Jorge
Luis Borges, but it does involve sophisticated levels of reality.
Scholastic Inc. (the clever publisher that came out with Harry Potter) is making a lot of money and also providing a public service by
issuing these tales that appeal to those children called "reluctant
readers," as well as more literary kids. Even grown-ups can enjoy
Captain Underpants, if they don't mind compromising their dignity with silliness.

&& &&ampig

There are many funny fantasies in print that are set in some version of our contemporary world. Long before Pilkey introduced
Captain Underpants, Louis Sachar and Daniel Pinkwater were
making the children's book world giggle and sizzle. In the tradition
of Carl Sandburg's *Rootabaga Stories* (1922), Sachar's tall tales—
Sideways Stories from Wayside School (1978)—shock the reader's
perspective: WAYSIDE SCHOOL WAS ACCIDENTALLY BUILT SIDEWAYS. IT
WAS SUPPOSED TO BE ONLY ONE STORY HIGH, WITH THIRTY CLASSROOMS
ALL IN A ROW. INSTEAD IT IS THIRTY STORIES HIGH WITH ONE CLASS-
ROOM ON EACH STORY. The book consists of thirty very short, very

odd chapters, one for each child in the class on the top floor. The first teacher was a mean witch who turned the children into apples but turned herself into an apple too by mistake, and was eaten by Louis, the yard teacher. (Louis was the one telling these stories.) The new teacher was nicer; she cured Dana's itching mosquito bites by counting them and turning them into arithmetic problems. Everyone got along pretty well—they didn't mind when D.J. infected the class with wild laughter for no reason—THE DESKS WERE JUMPING UP AND DOWN, AND THE CHAIRS WERE SLAPPING ONE ANOTHER ON THE BACK. They weren't fazed by Kathy, who hated everybody, or Leslie, who tried to sell her toes because they served no useful purpose.

At the end, Louis, the yard teacher with a mustache of many colors, told a story about another school: "IN THIS SCHOOL EVERY CLASSROOM IS ON THE SAME STORY." "WHICH ONE, THE EIGHTEENTH?" ASKED JENNY. "NO," SAID LOUIS. "THEY ARE ALL ON THE GROUND. YOU MIGHT THINK THE CHILDREN THERE ARE STRANGE AND SILLY. HOWEVER, WHEN I TOLD THEM STORIES ABOUT YOU, THEY THOUGHT THAT YOU WERE STRANGE AND SILLY." "US? HOW ARE WE STRANGE?" "FOR ONE THING," LOUIS SAID, "NONE OF THESE CHILDREN HAS EVER BEEN TURNED INTO AN APPLE." "THAT'S SILLY," SAID DEEDEE, "EVERYBODY'S BEEN TURNED INTO AN APPLE. IT'S PART OF GROWING UP."

❧ ❧

Whatever the author's age, all the books discussed in this chapter are young in spirit: the serious adventure epics are earnest and full of feeling; the comic epics are playful and full of fun, delighting in the weirdness of human (also nonhuman) life and language. All of them remind us that, as Johan Huizinga pointed out in *Homo Ludens* (1949, p. 46), play is one of our most important, basic categories.

> The view we take is that culture arises in the form of play, that it is played from the very beginning. Even those activities which aim at the satisfaction of vital needs—hunting, for instance—tend, in archaic society, to take on the play-form. It is through this playing that society expresses its interpretation of life and the world.

In the best children's fantasy books, the authors do not focus on making money or winking at the audience; they are totally caught up in the playing of their newly created world. Some witty fantasy epics supposedly written for adults, like Douglas Adams's *Hitch-hiker's Guide to the Galaxy* books and Terry Pratchett's *Disc-world* series, seem to me too self-conscious and arch, less appealing than Sachar and Pinkwater.

Daniel Pinkwater enormously enjoys his own fictional worlds. *The Magic Moscow* (1980) introduces a kid narrator, Norman Bleistift, and his bearded boss, Steve Nickelson, owner of the Magic Moscow ice cream and health food stand in New Jersey. (One of their specialties was the Nuclear Meltdown. IT HAS NINE FLAVORS OF ICE CREAM, A SLICED RADISH, A PEACH, FOUR KINDS OF SYRUP, SUN-FLOWER SEEDS, BRAN FLAKES, A SLICE OF BAKED HAM, AND A PICKLED TO-MATO.) Steve, who spent his spare time watching reruns of the old TV show *Sergeant Schwartz of the Yukon and His Great Dog Her-cules,* was overjoyed when the actor who played Sergeant Schwartz appeared in the Magic Moscow and took part in a loud, messy ad-venture involving Steve's own slavering malamute and the streets of Hoboken. In the second book, Norman and Steve helped a bald fortune-teller friend cope with the fifth-century ghost he conjured up—Attila the Pun, the embarrassing brother of Attila the Hun. The masterpiece of this small trilogy is *Slaves of Spiegel* (1982), in which Sargon the Gross, leader of the junk-food planet Spiegel, kid-napped Norman and Steve so they could take part in the great In-terplanetary Cooking Contest. Back on Earth, a newscaster re-ported strange signals from space: "THEY CONSIST OF A SERIES OF GURGLING, CRUNCHING, AND SLOBBERING SOUNDS. ONE OF MY COL-LEAGUES SUGGESTS THAT THE SIGNALS RESEMBLE THE SOUND ONE WOULD HEAR IF ONE LISTENED TO A VERY LARGE GROUP OF SLOPPY EAT-ERS—SAY A THOUSAND PEOPLE EATING SPARERIBS AND CORN ON THE COB INTO A MICROPHONE. WE HOPE TO SOMEDAY DECODE AND ANALYZE THESE STRANGE NOISES."

Pinkwater's *Lizard Music* (1976) tells about other peculiar mes-sages coming over the airwaves: the lizard band that Victor no-ticed playing beautiful music on late-night television, though no such thing appeared in the TV guide. Victor's efforts to track down the elusive lizard folk are logical, ridiculous, and quite wonderful. *Alan Mendelsohn, the Boy from Mars* (1979), an even more wonderful book, has a plot I couldn't begin to describe. Here's a glimpse of the world of fat junior high student Leonard Neeble and his nerdy friend Alan Mendelsohn: AFTER LUNCH WE SAT AROUND AND GRANDFATHER TALKED ABOUT THE ITURI RAIN FOREST PYGMIES. HE SAID THEY RUN EVERYPLACE, AND CLAP THEIR HANDS WHILE THEY'RE RUNNING SO THEY WON'T SURPRISE A LEOPARD. They liked watching UNCLE BORIS'S MOVIE OF THE FEET OF EVERYBODY IN THE FAMILY, UNTO FOURTH AND FIFTH COUSINS. (If you don't find that sort of thing hilarious, you don't want to read Pinkwater.) After mastering Klugarsh's Mind Control Omega Meter and studying the Klugarsh course in Hyperstellar Archaeology, the boys could control the minds of people at school and could enter parallel planes of existence, which were overlapping in the same place and complicating people's lives.

A customer review posted on the Amazon.com Web site July 2, 1999, illustrates the kind of giddy response Pinkwater can arouse—and many other fantasy authors, for that matter. The Amazon review declares that *Alan Mendelsohn, the Boy from Mars* is "the most important novel in the history of mankind. I checked this book out of my public library at age 10, and renewed it every week thereafter for another reading. I probably read it over 200 times; it has had more influence on my life than my parents, television, Bill Gates, and God combined."

5

⤬⤬

Worlds Stained by Humankind: Making Choices

S ome amazingly dense, dark fantasy tales lead readers into depressing and terrifying levels of human experience. The rich complexity in these books draws some readers and distresses others, who prefer a less tangled universe—what Annie Dillard calls purity. In *Living by Fiction* (1982, p. 172), Dillard observed that "complexity is the truth of the world, and must be the truth of the art object which would imitate, order, and penetrate that world: complexity, and contradiction, and repetition, diversity, energy, and largesse. I am as attracted to purity as the next guy. But it must not happen here."

The dark texture of this kind of children's fantasy can be greatly satisfying, because the darkness still contains some hopefulness; things turn out all right in some of the books—or at least there is insight and reconciliation in spite of bad things happening. Adults can enjoy reading books that end hopefully and also books that end in total defeat and despair, because they have had years of experience to frame such stories, to set them in perspective among other narratives. But children, who have hardly any context, can find reading a hopeless story overwhelming. For them, a compelling book constitutes a much greater piece of their total emotional experience than it does for an adult. Young people need to deal with harsh truths, but they shouldn't be made to despair before giving life a chance. Works like *A Game of Dark* and *Behind the Attic Wall* take children very far toward the darkness but save them from hurtling into the abyss.

From *A Game of Dark*, by William Mayne: THEY WERE TRYING TO BRING IN SOME GREYISH BUNDLES THE SHAPE OF A BALL. "WHAT IS IT?" SAID JACKSON. "THEY ARE WHAT IT LEAVES," SAID CARRICA. "IT IS THEIR CLOTHES AND THEIR HAIR. THAT IS ALL WE HAVE TO BURY." THE BUNDLES WERE RAGS NOT LONG TORN, MINGLED WITH LONG HAIR. THE SMELL WAS STRONG ON THEM. "IT IS A HUGE WORM, THAT CAME FROM THE SEA AND LIVES UP THE VALLEY, AND LIVES ON PEOPLE FROM THE TOWN."

From *The Green Book*, by Jill Paton Walsh: AND SO FEAR GREW WITH THE WHEAT, A TERRIBLE FEAR THAT THERE WOULD BE NO WAY TO GROW FOOD ON THE NEW PLANET. AND WE COULD NEVER GO ANY-WHERE ELSE; THERE WAS ONLY A BURNT-OUT SPACECRAFT TO REMIND US OF FAR JOURNEYS, AND OF COURSE, THOUGH NOBODY EVER MENTIONED IT, EARTH WASN'T THERE ANY MORE.

Reading a good story, like these, you can feel the bones of its structure, savor its content, and learn to trust its narrating voice. Even when the story presents an unpleasant world and an unlikable narrator, if it all fits together right, you feel a brilliant explosion of meaning. Such explosions can be found in excellent fantasy books written in the last half century by William Mayne, Penelope Farmer, and Sylvia Cassedy, Virginia Hamilton, Alan Garner, Jill Paton Walsh, and Jane Yolen, Robert O'Brien, Louis Sachar, Peter Dickinson, Lois Lowry, Franny Billingsley, and Natalie Babbitt. These consider, in dramatic, fantasy form, probing questions about individual psychology and identity; about relationships in a family or community; about grim aspects of our world's past and grimmer prospects for our future; about death and love and choosing.

Mind Has Mountains, Cliffs of Fall

One type of dark fantasy is built around the progagonist's psychological state. In William Mayne's *A Game of Dark* (1971), fourteen-year-old Don Jackson shifted strangely between his depressing home world and a stark land where poor villagers were besieged by a monster. In Don's silent Methodist home, his schoolteacher mother grew more remote as his paralyzed father grew sicker. The boy felt only revulsion toward his austere father and shame at that revulsion; he wished the local Church of England priest were his father instead. The chill of his home grew stronger, and the whispers, and the suffering. With increasing frequency, then, Don would find himself slipping into his other world—no magic amulet, just a sudden awakening in another cold, awful land where he didn't know what to do.

His time in that land was hideously real. A POWERFUL AND TERRIBLE SMELL FILLED HIS THROAT AND MADE HIM VOMIT. THE STENCH ROSE FROM THE GROUND ROUND HIM, WHERE IT WAS TORN AND CRUSHED IN A BROAD BAND LIKE A TRACK, MARKED ACROSS THE HILLSIDE THROUGH THE BROKEN TREES AND TRAMPED BRACKEN. OVER THE GOUGED MARKS IN THE EARTH LAY THE FROZEN SLIME FROM WHICH THE STENCH CAME. HE STOOD IN IT WITH BARE FEET. It was the trail of the sickly white worm, ninety feet long, who slid down the hill each night for its dinner of townspeople.

Soon a pattern of father figures becomes visible to the reader. The boy became squire to the local lord, who was in charge of destroying the worm. A hired knight fled when he saw the monster: neither he nor the lord could protect the villagers. Despite their official status, the priest in one world and the feeble knight in the other both failed to offer true help. The lord, in turn, resembles Don's stoic father; each faced death with no hesitation because of his belief, and in each case the traditional code was futile, bringing only pain. Believing in order and duty, the lord must fight the worm; of course, he was devoured. But first he told Jackson, "YOU WILL HAVE TO RULE. YOU ARE THE ONLY PERSON, DEAR BOY, WHO KNOWS HOW TO. YOU'RE THE ONLY PERSON WITH ENOUGH WIT AND WILL."

Knowing he could not survive under the old rules, the boy broke the worm-fighting code: he killed it by stabbing its belly from a pit underneath. The town condemned his "dishonorable" behavior, but he had saved them, and the code was meaningless anyway. He left their land forever, able to reconcile with his real world. The phallic worm had been a version of Don's cold, pale, destructive father, sliding around ominously in his wheelchair. The worm's cry was a BUBBLING, GULPING, HOWLING—the dying father made horrid noises breathing. The Oedipal meaning is there, but by the end it's apparent that the disgusting worm Don fought was not primarily the bad father, but death, sickness, passivity, and his own childish despair.

❧ ❧

Penelope Farmer's *A Castle of Bone* (1972) presents two girls and two boys who go into a magic world through an old cupboard. Hugh, the protagonist, was an aloof, artistic boy. After he and his father bought a cupboard from a junky antiques shop for his bedroom, strange things happened. Hugh dreamed repeatedly of approaching a beautiful, distant castle and each time woke with some evidence—like wet slippers and forest leaves—that the dream had been real. One time HE WENT ON TOWARDS THE CASTLE. IT LOOKED ALMOST TRANSPARENT TONIGHT, IT MIGHT HAVE BEEN MADE OF GLASS OR ICE. IN PLACES THE WALLS WERE SO WHITE, SO STARING, THEY WERE LIKE MIRRORS REFLECTING MOONLIGHT, WHILE ELSEWHERE THEY WERE SO BLACK IT WAS AS IF HUGH LOOKED THROUGH THEM TO THE NIGHT SKY ITSELF. Another night it looked opaque, as if made of bone.

While the castle dreams are a bit tedious, the cupboard transformations are startling and great fun: Hugh, his sister, and two neighbor children were looking at the cupboard, and someone set a leather wallet inside it. A moment later, a squealing sound erupted. A LARGE WHITE SOW FELL OUT AND BLUNDERED, TERRIFIED, ACROSS THE ROOM—UNMISTAKABLY A REAL PIG, WITH HANGING DUGS AND CRUDE, PREHISTORIC-LOOKING SKIN. After chasing the pig into the woods, the children figured out that the cupboard transformed any contents back to an earlier state: an old toothpaste tube became full; matches became a fir tree.

There was one problem: YOU COULD NOT DETERMINE THE STAGE OF ITS PAST TO WHICH YOU WANTED SOME OBJECT TO REVERT, BY THE LENGTH OF TIME YOU LEFT IT IN THE CUPBOARD. THE CUPBOARD

WORKED TO ITS OWN TIMINGS. The children fell to squabbling and pushing; Penn, the more assertive boy, landed in the cupboard and emerged as a toddler. Efforts to reverse the change made it worse: putting him back in the cupboard only turned him into a newborn. The three remaining children were advised by the old man in the antiques shop, "GO INTO THE CUPBOARD. DON'T WAIT FOR IT TO PULL YOU, ENTER OF YOUR OWN WILL. AND GO ON INTO YOUR CASTLE." They went into this mysterious world, got Penn restored to his normal state, and made it back to the cupboard and the bedroom.

WALLS HAD CLOSED ROUND HUGH, IMPRISONING HIM IN THE NARROWEST OF CASTLES; THE CASTLE OF BONE, HE THOUGHT. THIS CASTLE OF BONE WAS HIMSELF. But he had been able to move out of his isolated self and make the necessary choices. This makes sense, but still *A Castle of Bone* has a problem with coherence. There is an elaborate but unclear pattern of tree magic; a murky connection between the cupboard transformations and the castle dreams; clogged scenes where too much is happening. The style, too, gets clotted: THE CASTLE WAS WHOLE, SLUMBERING, PEACEFUL. YET IT WAS ALSO THE CENTRE OF A VORTEX, DRAWING EVERYTHING IN TOWARDS IT ON INVISIBLE THREADS. IT WAS LIKE THE TWIST OF A KALEIDOSCOPE. Still, it's fascinating to read about the cupboard, when they put in Jean's plastic purse: THEY FOUND ONLY AN OILY AND MALODOROUS LIQUID, SLIGHTLY WARM AND DEFINITELY UNPLEASANT. And about the old cat, who wandered into the cupboard. Hugh's mother couldn't imagine where he went, but she was comforted by a nice newborn kitten that appeared in the house that night.

೧ⴾ ⴾ೧

One of the most astonishing tales is Sylvia Cassedy's *Behind the Attic Wall* (1983), a fierce, unsentimental variant on the familiar dolls-come-to-life theme. You are confused as you read this story, but from ignorance, not incoherence; the elusive truth is there to discover, though mystery remains. Twelve-year-old Maggie, a surly orphan, had been thrown out of nine homes. While her outside was dreadful—bony, scowling, with greasy, chewed-on hair—

her inner life teemed with games, patterns, and imaginary friends that helped her survive horridness and feel a slight sense of control. Now she approached her newest home, where two great-aunts had agreed to take her in.

Maggie's imagination conjured up TWO GREAT WOMEN WITH GREAT WHITE APRONS AND SMILING GREAT WHITE SMILES. WHEN SHE STOOD BEFORE THEM ON THE WOODEN PORCH THEY WOULD KISS HER AND SAY, "WHAT A LOVELY FACE." Instead, they were mean, shriveled crones. Upon meeting Maggie, THE AUNT IN GREEN SPOKE: "THERE'S NO COLOR TO HER FACE." THE AUNT IN BROWN: "LOOK HOW SHE STANDS. HER SPINE MUST BE CROOKED." "HER HAIR IS IN STRINGS." "IT HASN'T BEEN WASHED IN MONTHS." She settled into the gloomy stone mansion, went to the local school, and bore up under instructions such as "DON'T DRAW PHLEGM INTO YOUR THROAT LIKE THAT. YOU WILL BLOCK YOUR EAR PASSAGES PERMANENTLY."

Maggie thoroughly earned the aunts' verdict—"SHE'S A DISGUST-ING CHILD"—by taking a necklace, ruining some satin shoes, over-flowing the bathtub, and throwing the new clothes bought for her into the charity bin. The one person to show humanity was Uncle Morris, who carried a bowler hat and silver-knobbed walking stick. He teased Maggie in a kind and antic manner. "I'M TWELVE," SHE SAID. "TWELVE!" HE EXCLAIMED. "HOW VERY NICE. WOULD THAT BE INCHES OR DOLLARS?" Uncle Morris was seldom around, however, and Maggie turned to imaginary friends. She invented the five ad-miring Backwoods Girls, to whom she explained things in a supe-rior voice: this is what a dresser is, and a stocking, and so on. They invariably answered "OOH! HOW WONDERFUL."

Then other voices began to speak in the walls, not created from inside Maggie. Tracking them down, she was disappointed to find, in a hidden garret, only two friendly old dolls and a china dog. The magic did not bother her—they did indeed speak and move about, though creakily—but the fact that the magic was patheti-cally incomplete: Timothy John and Miss Christabel were alive, and the dog did bark, but their activities, like pouring tea and visit-ing the garden, were only pretend. Enraged, she shouted and threw them across the room. "IT'S STUPID TO WATER WALLPAPER ROSES, AND ANYWAY THERE'S NO WATER IN THIS KETTLE, AND NO MILK IN THE

PITCHER, AND THAT'S NOT REAL BREAD—IT'S JUST PIECES OF WOOD. AND YOU'RE JUST A COUPLE OF OLD DOLLS." But she fixed their injuries and, in some touching scenes, was won over by the dolls' calm affection and good cheer. Her party for them, with cake and presents, was a success until the great aunts broke in and discovered the silk scarf Maggie had cut up for ribbons and their valuable figurine she had purloined as a gift for Miss Christabel, smashed in a game of blindman's buff.

Maggie didn't mind being sent away for her wickedness, but she was desolate that the dolls now were lifeless, having been "seen." In her last days she conducted heartbreaking conversations with them in the attic, speaking back and forth as a child would with normal dolls. (MAGGIE NODDED TIMOTHY JOHN'S HEAD FOR HIM. SHE MADE HIM SAY, "YOU ARE OUR SPECIAL FRIEND. WE LOVE YOU, MAGGIE.") She was even more desolate when Uncle Morris suddenly died of a heart attack. But on the last day, just before leaving for the train, she heard "MAGGIE! WHATEVER IS KEEPING YOU? THE TEA IS GETTING COLD!" Visiting once more to say goodbye, she was told, "WE ARE THREE UP HERE NOW. HE'S COME, YOU KNOW. IN THE GARDEN. OUR NEWCOMER." In the corner she saw a small doll's bowler hat and a little walking stick with a silver knob, just like Uncle Morris's. Passages at the beginning and end of the book tell us that Maggie moved on to a happy family, where she had new sisters and didn't need imaginary Backwoods Girls anymore. She never told anyone about the quasi-human dolls who made her wholly human.

Unraveling the Past

A good book needs to be read several times. It doesn't matter whether the book is considered juvenile or young adult or adult, whether the reader is young or old. A second-time reader discovers much that is wonderful—details and patterns created by the author consciously or sometimes unconsciously. While lesser fantasy stories sustain you through a few hours in an airport, comforting you with familiar language and themes (after which you gladly leave the books behind), the ones discussed in this chapter get better as you read them again. They are fascinating and beautiful, but they are not comfortable and, mostly, they are not what would be called fun. Many readers, whatever their age, don't like them, but those who do get into them find them dazzling.

Besides those psychological books that focus on the individual child, there are fine books that describe the intricate relations between people, the frightening lovely dance of love and hate, past and present. If it takes magic and ghosts to convey this properly, then so be it, according to Virginia Hamilton and Alan Garner.

Hamilton's *Sweet Whispers, Brother Rush* (1982) tells the history of a family through the ambivalent mind of fourteen-year-old Teresa, called Tree. While M'Vy (mother Viola) worked hard as a practical nurse to support Tree and her brother, she would leave them alone for a week or more while on a job. Tree became a responsible child, cooking and cleaning and caring for her retarded older brother Dabney. Both loving and resenting her mother, she couldn't understand M'Vy's frequent absence. Although Brother Rush, a handsome, pale-brown ghost in a pin-striped suit, frightened Tree by appearing suddenly in her little playroom and beckoning her into another place and time, she was grateful too: he guided her toward a complicated understanding of her family and herself. Each time she entered the oval mirror-space held in the ghost's hand, Tree found she was herself a ghost, living through events from a dozen years back, events she had never known about. Visiting this nice house in the country, she entered the mind of the young Viola, her mother, on the porch swing; then she saw the same events through her own eyes as a baby-girl on her mother's lap; then she became an unseen presence in the car accident in which her uncle—Brother Rush—had been killed.

Thus the horrors of the family past started to swirl around her. Her young mother had turned against retarded Dabney, beat him for clumsiness, kept him tied to a bedpost. Her mother's brother, Brother Rush, was ravaged by a genetic disease, porphyria, under his handsome suit and his gloves. TREE STARED AT RUSH'S BARE HANDS. THE SKIN WAS THICK WITH SORES AND WHITE-LOOKING SCARS. PAINFUL HANDS, FULL OF SICKNESS. She saw that Viola's hatred of

Dabney grew partly out of her fear and helplessness in the face of the disease that killed the men in her family.

The reader puzzles all this out slowly, along with Tree. Between visits to the past, she lived her young life mostly alone with her beloved Dabney, who needed to be told how to take a bath and when to sit down. The child's matter-of-fact competence is sad and beautiful: SHE GRATED CHEESE AND PUT A CUP OF IT WITH CHOPPED ONION IN THE SAUCE. LATER, TREE WENT INTO THE KITCHEN TO SEE ABOUT THE MACARONI. IT WAS BUBBLING. SHE MADE SALAD OF CABBAGE AND CARROTS, WITH MAYONNAISE TO HOLD IT TOGETHER. "YEAH," SHE SAID, SMELLING THE GOOD SMELL OF MACARONI.

In his better moments, Dabney would do a little happy dance for her, in his running shoes with the electric lights in the toes. Tree couldn't control the world, though. Dab fell horribly ill and died. After much grief and rage, Tree reconciled with M'Vy and her new boyfriend, a big man who brought hope and lunch in the hospital coffee shop. "THIS PLACE GOT A LOT TO OFFER," SHE SAID. "MORE THAN MY SCHOOL CAFETERIA." SHE'D NEVER SEEN SUCH GOOD-LOOKING JELL-O, GREEN AND YELLOW AND RED AND ORANGE. Life had possibilities, after all, but its terrible contradictions could never be dispelled. Tree would always long for Dabney and would always be haunted by the whispered truths she learned from Brother Rush.

&� �&

Alan Garner's *The Owl Service* (1967) deals with ghostly centuries rather than decades. Three teenagers who met in a Welsh valley—Gwyn, the housekeeper's son; English Allison, who inherited the old vacation house there; and Roger, whose father married Allison's mother—became the new embodiments of an ancient, tragic feud. Scratching sounds from the attic led them to discover a dust-covered dinner service, a pile of dishes painted with a design that looked like flowers from one angle, owls from another. Once friendly, the three became strange and estranged—Allison obsessively tracing drawings of the owl pattern; working-class Gwyn and posh Roger developing a jealous distrust of each other.

Weird, muttering Huw, who did odd jobs, told the legend of the local curse when the children asked about the Stone of Gronw, a slab of rock with a hole through it. Centuries ago, Lleu wanted a wife, and Gwydion made him a lovely woman out of flowers, Blodeuwedd; but she fell in love with Gronw, who killed her husband. "THERE IS A MAN BEING KILLED AT THAT PLACE," SAID HUW: "OLD TIME. HE IS STANDING ON THE BANK OF THE RIVER, SEE, AND THE HUSBAND IS UP THERE ON THE BRYN WITH A SPEAR: AND HE IS PUTTING THE STONE BETWEEN HIMSELF AND THE SPEAR, AND THE SPEAR IS GOING RIGHT THROUGH THE STONE AND HIM." "WHY DID HE STAND THERE AND LET IT HAPPEN?" SAID ROGER. "BECAUSE HE KILLED THE HUSBAND THE SAME WAY EARLIER TO TAKE THE WIFE."

After the violence, Blodeuwedd, no longer a thing of sweet flowers, had turned into a cruel, hunting owl, and ever since the story had been repeated with new trios of angry lovers.

Gwyn discovered the more recent triangle. His mother, Nancy, had been involved with the landowner Bertram, Allison's uncle, from whom she inherited the house. Nancy's other suitor, Huw, had caused Bertram's death on a motorcycle, perhaps accidentally, perhaps not. Huw was in fact Gwyn's father. The tension and belligerence in the air became overpowering. Allison's owl drawings kept disappearing; a portrait of the beautiful Blodeuwedd was revealed under plaster in a stable; the young people quarreled.

When Nancy tried to leave the valley, knowing murderous powers were being unleashed again, she was turned back by flooded roads and menacing townspeople. ALL ALONG THE ROAD PEOPLE WERE STANDING AT THEIR GATES, AND NANCY HAD TO PASS THEM. "FORGOTTEN SOMETHING, HAVE YOU?" "CHANGED YOUR MIND?" "YOU GO HOME, NANCY. YOU GO HOME, PET." Gwyn too tried to escape but was treed by dogs. The eternal story had to play itself out. Old Huw told Gwyn: "WE OF THE BLOOD MUST MEET IT IN OUR TIME. IN THIS VALLEY: NOW. THAT IS HOW THE POWER IS SPENT. THROUGH US, THE THREE WHO SUFFER EVERY TIME. BECAUSE WE GAVE THIS POWER A THINKING MIND. WE MUST BEAR THAT MIND, LEASH IT, YET SET IT FREE, THROUGH US, IN US, SO THAT NO ONE ELSE MAY SUFFER. SHE IS HERE, THE LADY, AND YOU HAVE MADE HER OWLS: SHE WILL GO HUNTING. BUT DON'T LET HER DESTROY."

At the house, a stuffed owl attacked and clawed Allison, until Roger placated the spirit of Blodeuwedd, and the torrent of feathers smothering the girl turned to flower petals. The story (a version of a Mabinogion tale) would seem ridiculous in less skillful hands. As Garner tells it—in a voice combining agility and intensity—we are convinced and enthralled.

The Child in Worlds Where Evil Rules

The Owl Service created a narrow world of past and present inter-tangled. Another of Alan Garner's tales, *Elidor* (1965), widens the worlds where characters struggle. Not far from the Watson home in Manchester was a bombed, rubbled wasteland. Exploring the debris, one of the four children threw a football through the window of a ruined church, and they found themselves in a ruined castle, looking out on the equally dead landscape of another world. THE VIEW SHOWED ONLY DESOLATION. PLAIN, RIDGE, FOREST, SEA, ALL WERE SPENT. EVEN COLOR HAD BEEN DRAINED FROM THE LIGHT, AND ROLAND SAW EVERYTHING, HIS OWN FLESH AND CLOTHES, IN SHADES OF GRAY, AS IF IN A PHOTOGRAPH. THREE CASTLES. THEN—IT CAME, AND WENT, AND CAME AGAIN. IT'S A LIGHT. ON A HILL. VERY FAINT—LIKE A CANDLE—GOLDEN TOWERS!

The hero Malebron appeared and told Roland about Elidor and its four castles at the land's corners. Three were destroyed by the enemy; Gorias retained its light, but that too was menaced. Male-bron gave the children the four Treasures of Elidor to take back to their own land and protect, thus fulfilling the prophecy and help-ing to disperse the darkness: "IT IS NOT EASY TO CROSS FROM YOUR WORLD INTO THIS, BUT THERE ARE PLACES WHERE THEY TOUCH. THE CHURCH, AND THE CASTLE. THEY WERE BATTERED BY WAR, AND NOW THE LAND QUAKES WITH DESTRUCTION. WASTELAND AND BOUNDARIES—PLACES THAT ARE NEITHER THE ONE THING NOR THE OTHER—THESE ARE THE GATES OF ELIDOR."

Holding the shining, jeweled spear, stone, sword, and cauldron, the children escaped their pursuers and fell back into the dust of the slum church in their own world. ROLAND HELD A LENGTH OF IRON RAILING; NICHOLAS, A KEYSTONE FROM THE CHURCH. DAVID HAD TWO SPLINTERED LATHS NAILED TOGETHER FOR A SWORD; AND HELEN,

AN OLD CRACKED CUP. The Treasures, although disguised in these forms, emitted energy that alerted their enemies (and caused televisions to fail and electric mixers to buzz madly in neighborhood kitchens). One of the children, Nicholas, wanted to stop protecting the Treasures, let the enemy trace them, and give up on Elidor. "WHAT IS IT ONCE YOU'VE GOT USED TO THE IDEA? IS IT ANY BETTER THAN OUR WORLD? IT'S ALL MUD AND DUST AND ROCK. IT'S DEAD, FINISHED."

But they persisted and won, dissolving the attacking warriors. And they flung their battered Treasures back into Elidor, through the windows of the wasteland. FOR AN INSTANT THE GLORIES OF STONE, SWORD, SPEAR, AND CAULDRON HUNG IN THEIR TRUE SHAPES, ALMOST A TRICK OF THE SPLINTERING GLASS, THE GOLDEN LIGHT. THE CHILDREN WERE ALONE WITH THE BROKEN WINDOWS OF A SLUM. Usually, in fantasies, a secondary world contrasts forcefully with the characters' normal world. What's most gripping about Elidor is the sad way the two worlds echo each other. The four children defeated, for a time, the evil forces that were destroying Elidor; in their own war-scarred world of Manchester, it seems, it would not be so easy to bring back the light and the hope and the greenness that should flourish there.

      ❦ ❧

Jill Paton Walsh's *A Chance Child* (1978) follows the astonishing journey of a sickly little boy called only Creep, whose mother had pretended he didn't exist, locking him in a closet and starving him. His half brother fed him enough to stay alive, until he escaped and wandered through the dump to an oily canal next to a corroded, stinking factory. Stumbling upon an abandoned flatboat, he crawled in and slept; then he set off up the canal just to get away, hauling the boat's chain. But the boat started moving along by itself, as if purposefully. Christopher, his half-brother, came looking for him and tracked him partway along the canal before being brought back home.

This sounds pitiful but not mysterious, until you realize that the boat carried the boy into another century. As in Elidor, the two worlds Creep experienced were similar, both being cruel and exploitative. In a coal-mining tunnel he heard a girl sobbing and fol-lowed the sound through the darkness. HIS HAND MET SOMETHING SOFT, DAMP, AND THE VOICE SHRIEKED IN HIS EAR, " 'ELP ME OUT!" "S'ALL RIGHT," HE SAID. "AVEN'T YER GOT A CANDLE?" "I'VE ETTEN IT," THE VOICE REPLIED. When Creep returned the tiny lost girl to a man with a lantern, the man could not see him: he was invisible to adults. As the boat floated him out of the tunnel along with Tom, an abused apprentice running away, it becomes apparent that Creep did not need food. The two wandered through grisly scenes, meeting seven-year-old Lucy, called Blackie, as she worked in a foundry: HANGING ON A LOOP OF SOOTY ROPE FROM THE ROOFTREE, A LITTLE GIRL DANGLED, ONE FOOT ON A CROSSBEAM, AND THE OTHER TREADING UP AND DOWN ON A BELLOWS HANDLE, TO BLOW THE FIRE TO FURNACE HEAT. Blackie joined them. The children did all right in their rusty boat until Tom fled, terrified by Blackie's innocent dreams for their future. He shouted, "DOUBT IF ANYONE'LL MARRY THEE; BUT I KNOW I WON'T!" because of her face: A HUGE CRINKLED PINK AND BLACK SCAR LAY ACROSS HER VISAGE; HER MOUTH WAS PULLED CROOKED AT THE CORNER, HER EYE WAS DRAWN TIGHT AND HALF SHUT, AND HER EYE-LASHES WERE GONE. When they first met, she explained why the scar was black. "THE SKIN'S GROWED OVER THE COAL DIRT FROM THE FIRE. IT HURT TOO MUCH TO WASH IT OFF."

This is not light reading for a child relaxing on the beach. Un-speakable details pile up about life in the dark, satanic mills of the early nineteenth century. Yet Paton Walsh writes with such in-tense, loving conviction that the effect is exhilarating. Alternating chapters, back in the present 150 years later, tell of Christopher's efforts to learn what happened. After seeing "Creep" carved into an old stone bridge, the letters worn, grooved, and overgrown with lichen, he understood that his brother had left a sign for him to follow but had slipped off to an earlier century. So he sought out a teacher from a fancy school and asked how to look up an ordinary person in the past, from when there were canals. As Creep and Blackie were working and traveling then, Christopher was, now, in a library stubbornly reading old parliamentary pa-pers that interviewed working people about factory conditions.

One day at a cotton mill, as an enraged mother started to beat the supervisor who had beaten her son, Creep let out a great laugh—and immediately became visible to all; also hungry. Like Pinocchio, he became a real boy. Perhaps it was the sight of a real mother taking care of her child that caused his transformation. In the parliamentary papers, Christopher found an 1833 interview with one Nathaniel Creep: HAS WORKED AT SUNDRY OCCUPATIONS. MARRIED. FOUR CHILDREN. The entry mentioned notes that Mr. Creep had given the interviewer about his life; Christopher found them in the local archive. The notes told how Creep's mother locked him in a cupboard, how he escaped, worked in the factories, became a printer's assistant, and married his friend Lucy (Blackie). Christopher rejoiced that Creep had made it after all. He was better off in that earlier brutal world than he would have been in his own home. Both then and now a child could be lost, could fail to exist. Once while working in the factory, Blackie had watched as a boy was beaten: THE MACHINES STARTED UP AGAIN, AND WIPED OUT HIS SCREAMS, SO THAT BLACKIE, WITH TEARS IN HER EYES, COULD SEE HIS STRETCHED MOUTH, AND HIS SCREWED-UP EYES, BUT COULD NOT HEAR HIM. Paton Walsh has succeeded in making us hear the screams of these children.

❧ ❧

Jane Yolen, in *The Devil's Arithmetic* (1988), managed to tell an even more difficult story. By sending an American girl from the 1980s back in time to a concentration camp, Yolen gets enough distance that a reader can grasp the truth and the horror without being destroyed by despair; she can provide a partially good ending where there can be no happy endings. A twelve-year-old girl in a New York suburb, Hannah Stern resented her family Seders in the gloomy apartment in the Bronx, where her grandfather shouted and brooded about his time in the camps. "PASSOVER ISN'T ABOUT EATING," HER MOTHER BEGAN, "IT'S ABOUT REMEMBERING." "I'M TIRED OF REMEMBERING," HANNAH SAID.

Bored with the child's ceremonial task of opening the door to welcome Elijah to the Seder—SHE DIDN'T BELIEVE THAT THE PROPHET ELIJAH WOULD COME THROUGH THE DOOR ANY MORE THAN SHE BE-

LIEVED DARTH VADER WOULD—she walked through, into a old-fashioned farmyard in Poland. The happy peasant family were about to celebrate the wedding of Shmuel, Aunt Gitl's brother. To them, Hannah was Chaya, the adopted niece whose parents had died in an epidemic. Chaya had also had the fever, which explained her confusion about obvious facets of Polish life.

Hannah thought this must be a dream, about life in 1942; then as the wagon of the singing wedding party approached the bride's town, it became nightmare: IN THE MIDDLE OF THE BROWN LANDSCAPE, LIKE A DARK STAIN, WERE THREE BLACK OLD-FASHIONED CARS AND TWELVE ARMY TRUCKS. Yolen's telling of the tale so familiar—but not familiar to most child readers—is immediate, full of details, but economical. Hannah and her relatives traveled days in a suffocating boxcar, lost jewels and clothes and hair, saw friends beaten and shot, and learned to survive in the barracks. They learned that when the commandant came around, children too young to work had to burrow into the garbage mound to hide. An experienced girl prisoner, Rivka, gave Hannah hints on how to act. For one thing, you must memorize your own number and those of people close to you; it could be important. Many were "processed" for death: EVERYONE KNEW THAT AS LONG AS OTHERS WERE PROCESSED, THEY WOULD NOT BE. A SIMPLE BIT OF MATHEMATICS, LIKE SUBTRACTION, WHERE ONE TAKEN AWAY FROM THE TOP LINE BECOMES ONE ADDED ON TO THE BOTTOM. THE DEVIL'S ARITHMETIC.

But Rivka insisted, "AS LONG AS WE BREATHE, WE CAN SEE AND HEAR. AS LONG AS WE CAN REMEMBER, ALL THOSE GONE BEFORE ARE ALIVE INSIDE US. MY MOTHER SAID, BEFORE SHE DIED, THAT IT IS HARDER TO LIVE THIS WAY AND TO DIE THIS WAY THAN TO GO OUT SHOOTING. CHAYA, YOU ARE A HERO. I AM A HERO." RIVKA STARED AT THE SKY AND THE CURLING SMOKE. "WE ARE ALL HEROES HERE." When a guard chose girls for "processing," including her friend Rivka, who was wearing a head scarf, Hannah thought fast: herself, SHE HAD LIVED, WOULD LIVE IN THE FUTURE—SHE, OR SOMEONE WITH WHOM SHE SHARED MEMORIES. BUT RIVKA HAD ONLY NOW. When the guard turned away, Hannah snatched the scarf, sent Rivka off to hide, and put the scarf on her own head to deceive the guard. She walked into the building with the smokestack, from which no one returned. But she was in her grandfather's apartment at the Seder table.

Hannah had always stared at the long number on her Aunt Eva's arm. Now she recognized the memorized number, and Aunt Eva explained her name had been Rivka until she came to the New World; she was grateful to Chaya, the friend who saved her and died. Chaya's Aunt Gitl had survived, too, and worked in Israel with survivors. Probably this book could not have been written as a straight narrative, without Hannah's shift in time. The fantasy element makes it possible for reader and writer to stand back and still to witness the story of love and evil, as it happened to those who were there, the real witnesses.

❧ ❧

Elidor, A Chance Child, and *The Devil's Arithmetic* all move into a past world to reveal something about the present. Louis Sachar's *Holes* (1998) brings some of the past—a hundred-year-old curse and a hundred-year-old murder—into the present in a beautifully shaped revelation. Of course, none of these simplified, linear summaries of plots can hope to convey the confusing, nonchronological paths that these novels actually take. You plunge into a book like *A Chance Child* or *Holes* holding your breath, peering all around to get your bearings. For a long time you don't know where you are, what has happened, where you're heading, but you try to absorb each passing sight and sound; gradually patterns become clear. By the end, puzzle pieces fall into place, and you can see the whole picture. Some parts are still fuzzy and mysterious, but the whole is a fine thing. A tolerance for uncertainty is a useful quality, in fantasy and also in real worlds. You have to be patient, as you figure out these stories. It's like untangling small knots in a necklace.

In his theory of child development, L. S. Vygotsky described a "zone of proximal development." (*The Vygotsky Reader,* 1994) He disagreed with Piaget's claim that children move automatically through fixed stages, from egocentric to rational, saying instead that a child at each moment has an area of potential growth and needs help from an older, more experienced person to move into that area. Vygotsky stressed that the child matures by interacting with social forces, not just by undergoing biologically determined processes. Within children's zones of proximal development, then, good teachers and parents encourage them to climb to higher levels of understanding. So do good books. When children and adults as well read complex kinds of fantasy fiction, their capacity for insight expands, and their ability to create order.

Holes is one of those works, challenging but deliciously readable, with three intertwined, fateful stories. Stanley Yelnats was a nerdy kid from a bad-luck family. Though innocent, he was arrested for stealing sneakers and sentenced to Camp Green Lake in the stifling desert, where there was no lake. The warden, a sadistic Amazon, decreed that each boy at Camp Green Lake had to dig a hole in the sand each day, five feet deep and five feet across. Breakfast was at 4:30; the heat was boiling; deadly poisonous yellow-spotted lizards hid in the sands. Stanley made friends with a silent boy named Zero and taught him to read. But when the smarmy counselor ("YOU'RE ALL SPECIAL IN YOUR OWN WAY. YOU'RE NOT COMPLETELY WORTHLESS") announced, "ZERO'S TOO STUPID TO LEARN TO READ. THAT'S WHAT MAKES HIS BLOOD BOIL. NOT THE HOT SUN," Zero bonked him with a shovel and took off into the immense desert, with Stanley following.

By this time, the reader has also heard about Stanley's great-great-grandfather Elya, who was cursed back in Latvia by a one-legged Gypsy woman for stealing her pig. That curse was the source of the Yelnats bad luck: for instance, Elya's son made a fortune in America but lost it to a famous desert bandit, Kissin' Kate Barlow. The true story was that the Gypsy, Madame Zeroni, gave Elya the pig to help him woo a Latvian maiden, after he promised to pay by carrying the Gypsy up a mountain to drink from a healing spring at the top. Betrayed by the maiden, Elya jumped on a ship to the New World without fulfilling his promise to Madame Zeroni, so she cursed him and his descendants.

By now the reader has also heard about the history of Green Lake, once a lush lakeside village where winsome Katherine Barlow taught school and made delectable preserved peaches. An arrogant, rich youth, horrified that she would kiss gentle Sam, the black onion peddler, but not him, shot and killed Onion Sam. No rain fell on Green Lake after that, 110 years ago. MISS KATHERINE SHOT THE SHERIFF WHILE HE WAS DRINKING A CUP OF COFFEE. THEN SHE APPLIED A FRESH COAT OF RED LIPSTICK AND GAVE HIM THE KISS HE HAD ASKED FOR. Kissin' Kate Barlow became a notorious outlaw and died of a yellow-spotted lizard bite without telling where she buried twenty years' worth of loot.

Stanley and Zero, whose real name was Hector Zeroni, were lost in the desert but survived by eating century-old jars of Kate's preserved peaches they found buried. Although Zero got very sick, Stanley dragged him up a mountain, where onion fields and water restored their health (Sam had long ago made excellent onion medicines there), and they cooked up a plan to sneak back to Camp Green Lake and dig in a certain hole where Stanley suspected Kissin' Kate's treasure was buried. The warden caught them with the suitcase full of jewels, but authorities showed up in time to see that the suitcase was labeled "Stanley Yelnats"—so he got to keep his great-grandfather's fortune. The boys had dug in a hole suddenly teeming with yellow-spotted lizards, but they were protected because the lizards never bit anyone with onion-flavored blood. And for the first time, Stanley's father had a stroke of good luck: one of his inventions succeeded brilliantly. STANLEY'S MOTHER INSISTS THAT THERE NEVER WAS A CURSE. THE READER MIGHT FIND IT INTERESTING, HOWEVER, THAT STANLEY'S FATHER INVENTED HIS CURE FOR FOOT ODOR THE DAY AFTER THE GREAT-GREAT-GRANDSON OF ELYA YELNATS CARRIED THE GREAT-GREAT-GREAT-GRANDSON OF MADAME ZERONI UP THE MOUNTAIN. The swirling pattern of cause and effect, coincidence and fate and free choice, was complete.

Where the Future Takes Us

Dismal place, the future: the countryside after a nuclear war; a new planet where the grass is glass; an overpopulated Earth where animals are dead and people dying; a loving society where everything is decided for you. Those are only four of the distinguished dystopia stories that should be considered fantasy rather than pure sci fi, because they emphasize people rather than scientific ideas. *Z for Zachariah* (1974), by Robert C. O'Brien starts a year after Ann Burden became the only survivor in her valley or anywhere else, as far as she knew. After the war, as radio stations went off the air, Ann's parents drove from their farm to town and never came back. Fifteen-year-old Ann kept a journal: I HAVE CLIMBED THE HILLS ON ALL SIDES OF THIS VALLEY, AND AT THE TOP I HAVE CLIMBED A TREE. WHEN I LOOK BEYOND, I SEE THAT ALL THE TREES ARE DEAD, AND THERE IS NEVER ANYTHING MOVING. I DON'T GO OUT THERE.

By some fluke, her valley was not contaminated; cows and chickens remained healthy and Ann kept some crops going. Of the two streams, one was clean. In the other, which came from outside the valley, dead fishes floated. She had a few books, a rifle, a well-stocked general store. Ann wished a living person would appear but feared it too. THE MAN ON THE RADIO, TOWARD THE END, SOUNDED CRAZY. HE SAID THAT MEN SHOULD ACT WITH DIGNITY IN THE FACE OF DEATH. HE PLEADED ON THE RADIO, AND I KNEW SOMETHING TERRIBLE WAS HAPPENING THERE. She decided, if people came, to hide until she felt safe. Seeing a campfire in the distance, she moved from the house to a cave.

Emerging from the dead land, the man wore a plastic suit and mask and pulled a wagon. Ann watched a few days, wanting to see what sort of person he was, this man bigger and stronger than she. When she decided to reveal herself, she didn't get there in time to keep him from bathing in the radioactive stream. A chemist who invented the protective suit before the war, John Loomis became ill from the water but survived; Ann tended him until he recovered. She allowed hope to lighten her stoic mood. THERE WAS NO REASON WE COULD NOT BE MARRIED IN A YEAR. IT SHOULD BE IN THE CHURCH, WITH FLOWERS. I MIGHT EVEN WEAR MY MOTHER'S WEDDING DRESS. WHAT WOULD IT BE LIKE, TEN YEARS FROM NOW, GATHERING GREENS SOME MORNING WITH CHILDREN OF MY OWN? But Mr. Loomis's manner, always abrupt, became tyrannical. He scolded her for spending time in the church and for not planting crops exactly as he would have.

Two things made Ann leave the farmhouse. In his delirium, he revealed that he had killed a colleague in the lab who asked to borrow the safe-suit, and one night he tried to rape Ann. When she fled, he went berserk, hunting her in the woods with a rifle and trying to shoot her in the foot so he could bring her back and control her. Realizing she could not live as his slave, Ann stole the safe-suit with its wagon of air- and water-purifying devices, and headed into the dead land. She shouted a goodbye. "DON'T GO," HE SAID, "DON'T LEAVE ME HERE ALONE." I SPOKE CAREFULLY. "IF I SHOULD FIND PEOPLE, I WILL TELL THEM ABOUT YOU. IN THE MEANTIME YOU HAVE FOOD. YOU HAVE THE VALLEY." Before she walked away, he softened enough to tell her he had seen birds to the west, a sign of life. AS I WALK, I SEARCH THE HORIZON FOR A TRACE OF GREEN. I AM HOPEFUL. The reader is not so sure.

❧ ❧

Although Jill Paton Walsh's *The Green Book* (1982) is barely a novella in length, its plight and its planet are thickly, movingly detailed. When Earth destroyed itself, there was time for space ships to gather supplies and set forth to colonize other planets. Each family received instructions. FATHER SAID, "WE CAN TAKE VERY LITTLE WITH US. SPADE, SAW, AX . . . ONE BOOK PER VOYAGER." Some chose the *Iliad*, or Grimm. Father, knowing he would need a technical reference book, wistfully put back a Collected Shakespeare. Little Pattie hid her choice until it was too late to change it: the silky green book was just an empty notebook, a sad waste. After a four-year journey, the new planet proved to have breathable air; the settlers stepped onto their new ground, filled with wonder. The youngest got to choose the name: "WE ARE AT SHINE, ON THE FIRST DAY," SAID PATTIE, SOLEMNLY.

The red trees were made into huts; jellyfish in the lake gave oil for lamps. Boulders in a valley hatched into beautiful giant moths, intelligent enough to play ring-around-a-rosy with the children. The Earth people watched the moth people in their stately ceremonial dance that turned into a mating flight, after which the moths laid eggs and died. Their wings provided fiber for thread. Life was good—except that the people feared they would starve. The rabbits they had brought died from eating gray, glassy grass, and there was only enough seed from Earth to sow one crop of wheat. If that was edible, they could manage; if not, they had painless, fatal pills to take. The wheat came up looking strange, its grains shiny hexagons. While the grown-ups debated its danger, Sarah snitched some grains, ground them, and made a pancake. After she and Pattie and Joe ate some, they told Father. Everyone waited, despairing, but the children didn't get sick: Shine would thrive.

Needing paper to write down harvest shares, Father insisted Pattie give up her empty notebook. PATTIE HID HER FACE. IT WAS FULL. IT WAS FULL OF WRITING, VERY LARGE AND ROUND AND SHAKY. "HEAVENS!" SAID FATHER. "WHAT'S THIS?" FATHER TURNED BACK AND BACK IN THE GREEN BOOK TO THE VERY FIRST PAGE, AND BEGAN TO READ: *"FATHER SAID, 'WE CAN TAKE VERY LITTLE WITH US'* . . ." You might call this mournful, hopeful story a postdystopia utopia.

&? &?

Peter Dickinson is a remarkable author whose *Eva* (1988) brilliantly imagines the unimaginable. Humankind was on the verge of giving up. Eva's city had half a billion inhabitants; pregnancies had to be licensed. MOST PEOPLE STAYED IN THEIR ROOMS ALL DAY. THEIR WORLD WAS FOUR WALLS AND THEIR SHAPER ZONE. (A shaper was a television and communication device.) Animals were dead, jungles and savannahs gone. Some chimps had been kept alive for research, and now that people regretted the loss of animals, the chimps were beloved by the public. Other animals they knew only by going into a shaper park to experience virtual flora and fauna.

When thirteen-year-old Eva awoke after an accident, strapped down with tubes, her thumb felt wrong, and if she squinted, she could tell her nose was different. Her own body was destroyed, so doctors had tried transferring the neural contents, the memories and thoughts, of her brain into another body: Eva was now a chimp. Her father was a leader in chimp research, so she had grown up loving the animals and understanding their ways. She could talk by using a keyboard and recorded discs of her old human voice. The procedure was tried with other chimps and dying humans, but all died of the shock; only Eva had an unconscious that could cross the shadowy edge between human and animal.

Then the personal story turned political. Like Eva's mother, I was upset to find she really *was* a chimp: she would move by "knuckling" and relax by rooting in her mother's hair for bugs to eat. But Eva was quite reconciled to that; what did sicken her was learning that researchers did not care about the lives of the real chimps, and that a huge corporation had financed her treatment and could force her to make commercials. Eva complied, but she won the public's adulation by her cheerful and intelligent interviews on the air and became a superstar (a company made a fortune by producing overalls like hers, with a stitched butterfly, and selling them as Evaralls). An eccentric young man connected to the corporation—Giorgio, called Grog—became her ally and turned the public fad into a mass movement protesting the treatment of the chimps. Grog wangled a trip for several dozen chimps to an undevelopable island with some remaining clumps of jungle trees, on the pretext of helping the now-vilified corporation by making lovely chimp commercials there and wildlife films showing how happy the animals were. But his real goal, and Eva's, was for her to escape with some of them out of the electrified enclosure and live forever in the jungle.

When this did happen, publicity forced the corporation to let them stay; the institute checked in occasionally. Twenty years later, Eva was dying content, though sad at the news from a visiting scientist: humans were committing suicide, starving themselves. No products were being made, no roads or bridges repaired. People had lost their will; the end was approaching. This was his final trip—equipment was breaking down. But the chimp community, who clustered around to comfort Eva, were thriving. She had taught them to make knots and baskets and fires and bone needles. Eva had always refused to mate with the stupider males and discouraged other females from doing so, but now she would be gone. Her human contribution came from her mind only: if later generations developed skills, NOT ONE HUMAN GENE WOULD BE THERE. ONLY, FAINTLY, CHANGED BY THEM AND CHANGING THEM, THE THREADS OF HUMAN KNOWLEDGE. Before the scientist left, Eva gave him her voice box machine to keep, with a final tape for the human world: I WANT TO SAY THANK YOU TO THE HUMANS FOR GIVING US

BACK THE LIFE THAT IS RIGHT FOR US. IF THE CHIMPS SURVIVE IT WILL BE
BECAUSE OF WHAT YOU HAVE DONE FOR US. *Eva* is read in many
schools, but it is hardly a children's book.

⁓

That is also true of Lois Lowry's *The Giver* (1993), an eloquent
dystopia story. Life was painless and choiceless, since the land
went to the Sameness. Jonas's school visited other communities,
but no one traveled to Elsewhere, far off. At each December Ceremony, that year's fifty children advanced a step: Baby Ones were
removed from the Nurturing Center and given names and families.
Eights started their volunteer hours and had their comfort object
taken away. Nines got a bicycle. The main event was the Twelves,
who were given job Assignments. Kind Elders chose Assignments
to fit each one's interests and abilities.

Jonas, an obedient Eleven who took part in his family unit's
compulsory sharing of feelings at dinner and telling of dreams at
breakfast, wondered what Assignment he was suited for. Jonas
was a typical child—for instance, his mother explained that a sen-
sual dream indicated his first Stirrings, at just the normal age, and
she started him on the daily pills to repress Stirrings for his lifetime. During the Ceremony, he was dumbfounded when the Chief
Elder skipped over his number, then called him to the stage at the
end: "JONAS HAS BEEN SELECTED TO BE OUR NEXT RECEIVER OF MEM-
ORY. HE IS TO BE ALONE, APART, WHILE HE IS PREPARED BY THE CURRENT
RECEIVER FOR THE JOB WHICH IS THE MOST HONORED IN OUR COMMU-
NITY." She cited his intelligence and integrity, potential courage and
wisdom. The current Receiver had found him most likely to have
the Capacity to See Beyond.

The position of Receiver, Jonas learned, brought honor but no
power, joy but also horrible pain. His teacher, the former Receiver
who now became the Giver, started gently by transferring into
Jonas's brain pleasant memories from the world's past: experienc-
ing a sled ride down a snowy hill taught Jonas what snow was (before Climate Control) and what a hill was (before all was leveled).
The Giver encouraged Jonas's primitive glimpses of color in objects, the ability to see color having been removed from all citizens

for centuries, after they went to the Sameness. Only the Receiver could have books, other than a dictionary and a directory. Ancient wisdom and ancient memories were kept alive in one Receiver each generation, because occasionally—rarely—the Committee faced a situation that could not be solved by familiar means, and memories sometimes helped.

While these new senses and experiences broadened and excited Jonas, they also made him suffer. He had to take part in war, discover lying, feel pain without asking for instant Relief-of-Pain. He learned that real anger and sadness went deeper than the petty frustrations discussed in the family unit's sharing of feelings. He experienced an old Christmas with a family where—astonishing!—old people sat right there with the children and parents instead of being sequestered in a House of the Old. The Giver told him the feeling in the air there was Love, a forbidden word in the community now. Worst of all, he learned what being "released" really meant. When an old person or sickly baby or repeat offender was released to "Elsewhere," that person wasn't sent to another land (as everyone was told) but was given a lethal injection.

The Giver shared Jonas's horror about the true nature of their society but thought nothing could be changed. Jonas asked: "WHY CAN'T *EVERYONE* HAVE THE MEMORIES? I THINK IT WOULD SEEM EASIER IF THE MEMORIES WERE SHARED." THE GIVER SIGHED. "THEN EVERYONE WOULD BE BURDENED AND PAINED. THEY DON'T WANT THAT." Together they figured how: if a Receiver disappeared, the memories he had absorbed would not go with him but would disperse among all citizens; they would have to come to terms with the memories. When Jonas's baby brother was scheduled for release, because he wouldn't sleep through the night properly, Jonas knew he had to go. It would change the community, and the former Receiver would still be there to help them bear it. He took the baby with him and set forth to find a real Elsewhere.

Weaving Wild Stories

Some of the finest fantasies do not seem to inhabit a world from our past, present, or conceivable future, yet illuminate our lives today, each from its unique angle. Russell Hoban's *The Mouse and Its Child* (1967), a sophisticated animal tale and outside my subject, is a fierce satire, in which two battered, wandering windup toys escaped from greedy or callous captors and created a happy ending for themselves and their friends. (Hoban's greatest fantasy masterpiece, *Riddley Walker*, 1980, is too complex to touch on here—a post–nuclear disaster story written in a splendid, barely comprehensible language.)

At another level, Nancy Farmer tried something original in *The Ear, the Eye and the Arm* (1994) but did not entirely succeed. Farmer, an American who has lived in Africa, created a sharply divided Zimbabwe of 2194: High officials lived luxuriously, served by robots. Poor workers lived in foul conditions, some kept in a toxic mountain of plastic garbage to scavenge, for the cruel boss called She-Elephant. Gangs terrorized people, and neighboring countries plotted to invade. Only the village compound called Resthaven preserved old African values, respect for ancestors, and traditional customs—keeping evil customs, including infanticide, as well as good ones. While the book has energy and interesting ideas, the style is perhaps too jokey and self-conscious, the characters too broad, and the startling details (such as mutant detectives with supernatural powers) unconvincing. The author seems to be thinking too much about her child readers, nudging and chuckling, rather than plunging herself and her readers into the intriguing story.

&⅗ ⅗&

Another recent writer, Franny Billingsley, has a surer touch and a stunning ability to evoke menace and mystery. *The Folk Keeper* (1999) is the journal of fifteen-year-old Corinna, who called herself Corin because only boys could hold the important, dangerous post of Folk Keeper for a village or castle. At the foundling home, willful Corinna had bullied the apprentice Folk Keeper into letting her take over. Now an expert, she sat silent in a damp stone cellar waiting to feed and control the vicious, lurking Folk creatures.

THEY'VE WORKED NO MISCHIEF FOR MONTHS. THE HENS GO ON LAYING, THE TOMATOES HAPPILY GROWING. I'M THE ONLY FOLK KEEPER IN RHYS-

BRIDGE WHO SITS WITH THE FOLK FOR HOUR UPON HOUR IN THE DARK, DRAWING OFF THEIR ANGER AS A LIGHTNING ROD DRAWS OFF LIGHT- NING. They consumed prodigious amounts of food (at one sitting: ONE BARREL OF HERRING, ONE DOZEN LOBSTERS, WITH MOST OF THE SHELL). On feast days they attacked. I NEVER SCREAMED. I HAVE THE BRUISES STILL. THEY SANK BENEATH MY SKIN, RIPPING THROUGH TISSUE AND FIBER INTO THE HEART OF MY BONES.

When Corinna was summoned to be Folk Keeper for Lord Mer- ton's household, she found an enemy in Sir Edward, a potential heir to the property. He flung her into the caverns where the Folk dwelt, sure that would be the end of her. But she had not known what her true identity could do—the heritage of her human half and the gifts of her supernatural half, which saved her in the cav- erns. AND WHEN I LOOSENED MY BRAID AND RAKED MY FINGERS THROUGH THE WEAVE OF HAIR: THE WORLD SHIFTED ABOUT ME, AND DID NOT COME AGAIN TO REST. I'D THOUGHT THE WORLD WAS FULL OF BOUNDED SPACE, DESCRIBED BY WALLS AND FOOTMEN AND CLIFFS AND COAL SCUTTLES. THAT'S ONLY THE SMALLEST PART OF IT. THE AIR IS AL- WAYS SHIFTING, BOILING AROUND YOU. I CAN SEE WITH MY HAIR.

Billingsley handles eeriness deftly, anchoring it with concrete- ness and wit. (When Matron insisted to Lady Merton that "OUR FOUNDLINGS TAKE THREE GOOD MEALS," Corinna noted, MATRON NE- GLECTED TO MENTION THAT NOT ALL THE MEALS ARE TAKEN ON THE SAME DAY.) It's hard to decide which is more admirable, *The Folk Keeper* or *Well Wished* (1997), another book full of dangerous beauty. THE TREES STOOD BLACK AND SLEEK AS SKELETONS, THEIR CRISP EDGES BLURRED TO VELVET BY THE FAILING LIGHT. BUT THERE WAS NOTHING BLURRED ABOUT THE WISHING WELL, WHICH ROSE FROM THE PALE WINTER GRASS IN A MASSIVE SWEEP OF GRANITE. AGNES, THE WELL'S GUARDIAN, WAS A MERE SHADOW BESIDE IT, KNITTING AS SHE ROCKED IN THE GREAT STONE CHAIR, ROCKING AND KNITTING JUST AS EACH GUARD- IAN HAD DONE FOR AS LONG AS ANYONE COULD REMEMBER.

The villagers kept from outsiders the Well's secret: any person could have one wish granted in a lifetime. For a month afterward you could ask to reverse the wish, but in that time you must not speak to anyone about your wish. Inside the Well was eternal spring—flowers and hummingbirds. But the Well was not benign; it would trick people into making bad wishes. Anyone who wished for an extra wish would become the new Guardian, sitting enchanted in the stone rocking chair for decades, until released by someone else wishing for more wishes.

Nuria, an impetuous ten-year-old, was lonely because someone had wished all the children away from the village. Her wise grandfather warned her not to risk a wish but promised to use his own, to get her what she wanted: a good friend. Catty, the resulting friend, was delightful; she was also in a wheelchair. Catty, watching Nuria run and skate, begged her to use her wish so that Catty could be cured (she had already used her own). But Nuria refused the risk, especially worried because ghostly images, knit by the Guardian out of smoke, were haunting her every night. When the smoke-things followed you, tradition said, you were next in line for a bad wish.

The two girls played happily until Nuria's jealous nature overcame her; she could not stand to share her grandfather's private songs and games with Catty, even though he pointed out that "SINGING ISN'T SOMETHING YOU USE UP, LIKE A PIECE OF CAKE. THERE'S PLENTY TO GO AROUND." Furious, she told Catty she would make a wish for her after all. The Guardian reminded her: when you wish something for another person, if you want to take the wish back, the other must agree. When Nuria proclaimed, "I WISH CATTY HAD A BODY JUST LIKE MINE!" the two girls were switched: Nuria was locked in Catty's body, and in her wheelchair. Catty wouldn't let the wish be revoked. *Well Wished* follows the logic of the situation cleverly and ends happily, each girl in her own body and Catty's body healthy again. It's a small book, but it contains, and understands, huge emotions.

❧ ❧

The dark deeds and emotions in these fantasy books, written since the 1960s, are not what you find in horror fiction, which is shock, suspense, and visceral fear of those various things that are out to get you. The stuff of fantasy also differs from traditional adventure stories, which celebrate conventional virtues and invite you to share a hero's career, and it differs from realistic problem fiction, which earnestly describes a possible outcome of a bad situation. Every work of fiction represents a worldview, of course, but usually it is implicit, not consciously presented by the author or ingested by the reader. Fantasy, though, knows what it's doing and doesn't hide it. By shifting you out of your world of normal limits and assumptions, a fantasy story inspires you to think, with all your mind and all your senses, about many questions, social, political, philosophical, and psychological. You see a pattern, hear a voice, and grasp a viewpoint perhaps more than when you read other kinds of fiction. You know you are mulling over a hypothesis, rather than just passing the time with a slice of life or a projection of your psyche. Suppose the contents of your brain were transferred into a chimpanzee. . . . Suppose you could save a parallel world from destruction. . . .

When I was a child, myopic mid-century readers didn't think they needed to consider many worldviews; they just *were* the world, a comfortable, fixed, middle-class American-centered place. For those of us lucky enough to be complacent, values meant uncomplicated choices between mean and nice, bad and good. Today, most choices are not simple, for young people and old. Many schools, realizing this, encourage lateral thinking and creative solutions. In *Wisdom* (1990), Robert J. Sternberg distinguishes wisdom, creativity, and intelligence. While these three qualities often overlap, an *intelligent* person solves specific, known problems and dissolves ambiguity. A *creative* person formulates new tasks and definitions. A *wise* person tolerates ambiguity, and looks for the meaning and structure of events (pp. 154–57). According to Deirdre A. Kramer, another contributor to *Wisdom*, wise people can tolerate uncertainty and paradox in the world: "Relativistic and dialectical thinking lead one to question the view that knowledge is absolute and unchanging, and thus both are suited to problem solving of an ill-structured nature" (p. 290). This may seem like a lot to lay on an innocent ten-year-old in a baseball cap, reading Harry Potter, but apparently fantasy reading fosters wisdom.

One of the wisest books is Natalie Babbitt's graceful, subtle *Tuck Everlasting* (1975). Winnie Foster, looking out from the fenced yard of her cottage to the green patch of woods nearby, decided to escape her confining world and look around. Discovering a handsome lad drinking from a stream in the center of the woods, she started to drink too but was grabbed by the boy, thrown onto a horse, and rushed frantically up the road away from the village. The four gentle members of the Tuck family took her to their disheveled home on a hidden pond and explained the odd kidnapping. Eighty years earlier, they had stopped to drink from that same stream. Since then, none of them had grown or changed; when Pa had a bad accident, he was unharmed. They realized that they could not die, and that this secret river of immortality could destroy the world.

In a boat on the pond, Pa Tuck told Winnie, "EVERYTHING'S A WHEEL, NEVER STOPPING. THE FROGS IS PART OF IT, AND THE BUGS, AND THE WOOD THRUSH, TOO. AND PEOPLE. BUT NEVER THE SAME ONES. ALWAYS GROWING AND CHANGING, AND ALWAYS MOVING ON. DYING'S PART OF THE WHEEL, RIGHT THERE NEXT TO BEING BORN." Winnie promised not to reveal the secret once she was back home. She understood the danger: IF ALL THE MOSQUITOES LIVED FOREVER—AND IF THEY KEPT ON HAVING BABIES—IT WOULD BE TERRIBLE—and people too. When a sinister stranger tracked them down and explained he had bought the woods and would sell the water, would force Winnie to drink some, and would use her for demonstrations, Ma Tuck knocked him out. He died, and Ma would be hanged; but her family knew she could not die and the secret would be exposed. Willingly getting herself in trouble, Winnie helped them rescue Ma from the jail. THE TUCKS—HER DARLING TUCKS—WERE GONE. Jesse, the younger son, had suggested that Winnie might join the family: wait seven years until she was seventeen and then drink from the stream; they would get married and have a grand old time, forever. But she had learned about the wheel of life. THERE WAS A FEELING THAT THE YEAR HAD BEGUN ITS DOWNWARD ARC, THAT THE WHEEL WAS TURNING AGAIN, SLOWLY NOW, BUT SOON TO GO FASTER, TURNING ONCE MORE IN ITS CHANGELESS SWEEP OF CHANGE. When the Tucks rode through the village again unchanged, seventy years later, the stream in the woods had been bulldozed and built over. They found Winnie's tombstone: "IN LOVING MEMORY, DEAR WIFE, DEAR MOTHER, 1870–1948." She had not jumped off the natural, cycling wheel. When you read the story, you're glad it worked out all right; you're a bit wiser.

6

*Battlefield Worlds: Fighting
Tyranny and Chaos*

My favorite childhood puzzle taught me the location and
shape of every state (I still think Montana is pink and
Texas purple). The view of my country was exciting—a vast perspective. Later, I noticed the same delight in my small son. He
crouched over a piece of driftwood on the beach, a flat rectangle
with a square piece missing from its upper right corner. "Utah,"
he explained, when asked what he was looking at. Shapes are important to us, and interconnections among places and peoples—or
at least they are important to the kind of person whose heart leaps
up at the sight of a map of Tolkien's Middle-earth or Le Guin's
Earthsea.

With our own universe so crammed with confusion, possibility,
and danger, readers in great numbers have embraced (and bought)
the biggest, most complex sort of fantasy fiction, what is called
epic or high heroic fantasy. These books satisfy the puzzle instinct,
the yearning for maps—the need to find meaning in large patterns
containing many interlocking shapes. In the spirit of great ancestors such as *Beowulf* and the tales of King Arthur, today's heroic
fantasies describe bands of fallible humans battling against evil in
a time of chaos. Readers care deeply about the fate of individual

characters and the fate of the cosmic battle. Darkness closes in on today's fantasy heroes and their worlds, as it does in the older epics; these wars can never be won conclusively. Nonetheless, heroes do win crucial battles, enabling the reader to experience what Tolkien called "eucatastrophe": "a catch of the breath, a beat and lifting of the heart, near to (or indeed accompanied by) tears" (quoted in R. J. Reilly, 1968, p. 148). These epic fantasy books acknowledge inevitable darkness while joyfully affirming the value of the struggle.

I am discussing here fantasy works of scope and even grandeur: C. S. Lewis, J. R. R. Tolkien, Susan Cooper, and J. K. Rowling, Madeleine L'Engle, John Christopher, Virginia Hamilton, and Ursula K. Le Guin, Robin McKinley, Patricia Wrightson, and William Nicholson, Diane Duane, Diana Wynne Jones, and Philip Pullman. These writers have created many worlds that are totally imaginary; many worlds that resemble some part of Britain; worlds that resemble Europe, Australia, and an Arab desert land; worlds that resemble Ohio, Long Island, and New England.

They use familiar, archetypal plot motifs and transform them utterly: The hero as a child, often growing up in ignorance of his or her real power and identity. The hero being trained and tested, often, as a youth, making some bad choice out of impatience or pride. The hero on a quest, one of great importance to the community, often a war against evil; helpers appearing, to share the task—animals, wise mentors, comrades, magic objects. And the hero returning home, usually successful, but at a cost—a sacrifice, a loss of normal life, a loss of special powers. These patterns are old, but each story is stunningly new. The few household names, the best-selling fantasy writers, fall into this high heroic category: Tolkien, Lewis, Rowling, Le Guin. They deserve their success, but they are not a pantheon far above all others. The other works discussed here also deserve close attention, much praise, and long life.

The Great Tradition

In some heroic fantasy series, the overall thrust of the story is a constant presence, while others wander through scenes without giving any sense of where they are heading. The most clearly purposeful is Tolkien's *Lord of the Rings*, where you know early on what the heroic task will be. While Susan Cooper's *The Dark Is Rising* series is less explicit about how the Dark powers are to be destroyed, her books also follow a clear path: an ancient prophecy lists nine tasks that must be accomplished before the final confrontation. Although J. K. Rowling's Harry Potter is still up in the air (literally, on his broomstick), with only four published of the proposed seven books, the shape of Rowling's series seems less linear than Cooper's or Tolkien's: probably events will continue to follow a winding rather than a straight path. No one fictional shape is intrinsically best.

❧ ❧

C. S. Lewis's seven Narnia books have an odd structure. They tell the whole life story of the land of Narnia—creation to destruction—from Lewis's Christian perspective. Instead of presenting a consecutive narrative from start to finish, though, with perhaps a few flashbacks, Lewis distances his beloved land from its readers: his stories are out of order, jumping around in time, and his cast of main characters changes often. The first two books (*The Lion, the Witch and the Wardrobe*, 1950, and *Prince Caspian*, 1951) follow a chronological sequence, with Lucy, Edmund, Peter, and Susan traveling from present-day England to magical Narnia and back in each book. The third (*The Voyage of the Dawn Treader*, 1952) follows chronologically, but Peter and Susan have disappeared, and a new child, nasty Eustace, has popped up from the "real world" to join Lucy and Edmund.

Book 4 (*The Silver Chair*, 1953) brings back a reformed Eustace and introduces Jill; Lucy and Edmund have vanished. Book 5 (*The Horse and His Boy*, 1954) suddenly tells a story that took place between Books 1 and 2, starring two children never met before, with bit parts played by the original four. Book 6 (*The Magician's Nephew*, 1955) moves backward to explain the origins of Narnia, involving two new children, Digory (who became the Professor who owned the Wardrobe, also great-uncle of Lucy-Edmund-Peter-and-Susan) and Polly. Book 7 (*The Last Battle*, 1956)—the only one in its proper chronological place—describes the sad but uplifting last days of Narnia; all the children appear in this one except Susan, who has ceased believing in Narnia. The writing of the Narnia books was fast and casual. Their chronological back-and-forthing was not part of a deliberate design. It looks as if Lewis turned out the first two, then wrote others to answer puzzling questions. He was a shy man, seemingly unemotional, who didn't know children. I suspect (though this is irrelevant to judging or reading the stories) that he shifted cast members and time sequences because it made him uncomfortable to get too close to his child characters. There were other people, too, that he didn't want to get close to: the narrator not only condescends to child readers (SHE WAS GIVEN DINNER WITH ALL THE NICE PARTS LEFT OUT AND SENT TO BED FOR TWO SOLID HOURS. IT WAS A THING THAT HAPPENED TO ONE QUITE OFTEN IN THOSE DAYS), but also displays painfully snobbish views of anyone who is not attractive, middle-class, and Anglo-Saxon. It is a troubling viewpoint, showing contempt for outsiders: fat, awkward children; sinister, swarthy citizens of a southern desert land; working-class cockneys; and any human female who is not totally docile.

Why bother with the Narnia tales, then, if they are wobbly in structure and obtuse in tone? Because when Lewis writes about things he cares about, it's vivid and moving: the land and denizens of Narnia; its loving creator, the great lion Aslan; the children moving poignantly between double lives as English schoolchildren and heroic rulers of Narnia. Adults I talk to sigh, "Oh *Narnia!*" and remember the thrill of finding a whole world through the back of a wardrobe: ALL FOUR CHILDREN STOOD BLINKING IN THE DAYLIGHT OF A WINTER DAY. BEHIND THEM WERE COATS HANGING ON PEGS, IN FRONT OF THEM WERE SNOW-COVERED TREES. A single, mysterious lamp-post stood shining in the snowy wood.

In Narnia, the children fought dreadful battles, and they journeyed to strange parts of the country, such as the island of Dufflepuds, who moved by jumping. EACH BODY HAD A SINGLE THICK LEG RIGHT UNDER IT, AND AT THE END, A SINGLE ENORMOUS FOOT WITH THE TOES CURLING UP A LITTLE SO THAT IT LOOKED RATHER LIKE A SMALL CANOE. They were harmless but chattery and stupid, full of remarks like "AH, YOU'VE COME OVER THE WATER. POWERFUL WET STUFF, AIN'T IT?" Dufflepuds washed dishes before dinner to save time. Narnia included both the silly and the sublime, which was Aslan. All good people and animals loved and feared the great, shaggy lion, who watched from the shadows and occasionally came forward to set things straight. HE WAS SOLID AND REAL AND WARM AND HE LET HER KISS AND BURY HERSELF IN HIS SHINING MANE.

Aslan created Narnia with his roar and chose some to be Talking Animals, wiser and nobler than ordinary beasts. He punished the cruel and wicked, but he allowed himself to be killed by the White Witch to save the life of sniveling Edmund, who had turned traitor to his friends. (Fortunately, Aslan came back to life through a loophole in the law.) At the end, when Narnia was overrun with evil, Aslan uncreated the land: WITH A THRILL OF WONDER (AND THERE WAS TERROR IN IT TOO) THEY ALL REALIZED WHAT WAS HAPPENING. THE SPREADING BLACKNESS WAS SIMPLY EMPTINESS. ALL THE STARS WERE FALLING: ASLAN HAD CALLED THEM HOME. The good characters retreated through the magical stable door to the "real" Narnia, a purer, immortal replica of the lost Narnia. You can love these books, if you revel in the wonderful details and the glorious history of Narnia and forget about the nasty bits where the author judges inferior people from on high.

❧❧ ❧❧

The best-loved and best-known (at least until Harry Potter) fantasy series is of course J. R. R. Tolkien's *The Lord of the Rings* trilogy and the earlier volume *The Hobbit*. Responses have been intense: in 1956, Edmund Wilson proclaimed *The Lord of the Rings* "juvenile trash." Some critics despise the books for being long, sentimental, and stuffed with familiar motifs from epic and romance—many critics and readers *love* the books for being long, emotional, and stuffed with familiar motifs from epic and romance. I think the greatest of Tolkien's strengths is his sense of design and rhythm, which orchestrates the whole enormous work, from the moment Bilbo smoked a morning pipe in his doorway in *The Hobbit*, to the end when Sam returned home after seeing Frodo off on the ship to the Undying Western Lands.

This does not mean Tolkien had from the start a complete plan: *The Hobbit* is a prologue, an adventure tale about chubby critters who eat lots of meals, told to children by a playful, avuncular storytelling voice that smacks of *Winnie-the-Pooh*. The trilogy's narrator is quite different—a serious moralist and scholar, who includes six long appendices about the history, prehistory, and languages of Middle-earth, with a chronology of events and family trees. Each of the three volumes contains two books, and Tolkien didn't even figure out where Frodo and the fellowship were going until the start of Book 2, when the council met at Rivendell. But the pattern and the purpose gradually take shape, and readers find themselves journeying through a great land with a precise geography (peaceful fields, tangled forests, mountain caves, wastelands, rivers), a land that encompasses various races with their own histories and their own relations to each other (small, earthy hobbits with hairy feet; heroic warrior men; tall, graceful woodland elves; tough, skillful, underground dwarves; ancient tree people; wizards).

Tolkien's fiction does not announce his religious convictions the way his friend and Oxford colleague C. S. Lewis's does, but his work is suffused with the knowledge that evil fell away from the good, burrowing into all Middle-earth, corrupting some members of each race. The most brilliant wizard, Saruman, turned his allegiance to the Dark Lord, Sauron; the terrifying Nazgul were perversions of hero warriors; vile orcs and trolls were fallen elves and dwarves. And ugly, whining Gollum was only a hobbit-like creature gone bad. But a mere diagram of different groups would not make for good reading—what draws us to Tolkien is the unity and intensity of the quest, the well-paced variety of the adventures (horror, hardship, battle, idyllic rest, suffering; despair followed by triumph followed by disillusion), and the stirring personal stories of individual characters buried inside the large history.

The questers were a fellowship of nine, journeying to blighted Mordor so that the hobbit Frodo could destroy the great Ring of Power in the fires of Mount Doom where it was forged, and thus defeat the king of all evil, Sauron. *The Fellowship of the Ring* (1954) tells how the good wizard Gandalf discovered that the gold ring of invisibility given to Frodo by his uncle Bilbo (who brought it home in *The Hobbit*) was Sauron's "ONE RING THAT HE LOST MANY AGES AGO, TO THE GREAT WEAKENING OF HIS POWER. HE GREATLY DESIRES IT—BUT HE MUST *NOT* GET IT." His strength was growing again; all Middle-earth was endangered. Frodo's response was a great understatement: "I WISH IT NEED NOT HAVE HAPPENED IN MY TIME." "SO DO I," SAID GANDALF, "AND SO DO ALL WHO LIVE TO SEE SUCH TIMES. BUT THAT IS NOT FOR THEM TO DECIDE. ALL WE HAVE TO DECIDE IS WHAT TO DO WITH THE TIME THAT IS GIVEN US." Tolkien, who fought and saw friends die in World War I, wrote just as World War II was starting; but Sauron is any murdering, corrupting tyrant, not an allegorical Hitler.

Knowing Sauron had sent his Nazgul to the hobbits' peaceful Shire, Frodo with the ring and three friends fled to the elf haven of Rivendell, barely escaping Nazgul attacks on the way. Great hero knights and elves met in council there with Gandalf and the hobbits, to decide how to meet the threat of the Dark Lord. The ring could not be used for good; it would corrupt anyone who owned it—the more powerful the wearer, the stronger the corruption; if hidden, it would still seek its master. The only way to keep it from strengthening Sauron would be to destroy it in his backyard, the pit of Mount Doom. A Ring-bearer must be chosen, and eight companions—Gandalf, men, hobbits, elf, dwarf—to help him on his way. Frodo yearned to stay peacefully at Rivendell. Nonetheless, "I WILL TAKE THE RING," HE SAID, "THOUGH I DO NOT KNOW THE WAY."

In the next book, *The Two Towers* (1954), the fellowship was separated, the others testing their courage and loyalty in battles against orcs and with warrior troops, while Frodo and his servant Sam went alone toward Mordor with the ring, finally entering Sauron's realm when his Eye was on the battles afar. In *The Return of the King* (1955), Frodo, exhausted, tortured by the increasing magic weight of the ring on a chain around his neck, nearly despaired but struggled on, supported by Sam. The disgusting creature Gollum, who had possessed the ring many years and was drawn to it obsessively, had followed the two on their journey and added to their dangers. Sam could not share the burden of carrying the ring, but on the last stretch, when Frodo was reduced to crawling, Sam carried his master on his back, stumbling up Mount Doom. As they reached the pit, where Frodo was finally overwhelmed by the ring's power and refused to throw it in, the crazed, bitter Gollum saved all Middle-earth by leaping at him, biting his finger off to get the ring for himself, and lurching with it into the fires of the pit.

It was not knightly prowess that defeated Sauron, but the courage and loyalty of small people—and their mercy too, because Bilbo and then Frodo had a chance to kill Gollum but took pity on him instead, thus saving him for the final meeting. The destruction of the ring marked the end of the Third Age of Middle-earth. High, noble beings would now have to leave the land: the elves with Gandalf would depart into the immortal West, taking poetry and beauty from the world, and leaving the future to men and hobbits. After a few years of rest back in the beloved Shire, Frodo the Ringbearer joined them to sail away. He told the desolate Sam that he was too deeply hurt to stay. "I TRIED TO SAVE THE SHIRE, AND IT HAS BEEN SAVED, BUT NOT FOR ME. IT MUST OFTEN BE SO, SAM, WHEN THINGS ARE IN DANGER: SOME ONE HAS TO GIVE THEM UP, SO THAT OTHERS MAY KEEP THEM."

Tolkien, a professor of Old English, revered both Christian and Anglo-Saxon virtues. As in *Beowulf*, the peoples of Middle-earth knew their world would not last: good and beautiful things were passing and would pass. Some day, Sauron would rise again. Even, *especially*, in such a world, the individual could only try his best (most were indeed *he*), and do his duty, as everything changed around him. The many songs underline the importance of the whole story: individuals must not only make brave and good choices themselves, they must also celebrate the courage and nobility of others, like Frodo and Sam (as Tolkien's books do). When the two small figures walked onto the triumphant field where armies waited, A MINSTREL KNELT AND SAID: "LO! LORDS AND KNIGHTS AND ALL FREE FOLK OF THE WEST, NOW LISTEN TO MY LAY. FOR I WILL SING TO YOU OF FRODO OF THE NINE FINGERS AND THE RING OF DOOM." Sam, the hero as commoner, was overcome, and wept; he had always loved songs about noble deeds. Those who dislike Tolkien probably resent his godlike presumption in painting such a huge canvas, in inventing mythologies and languages, and, most of all, in breathing new life into traditional themes and forms.

&? &?

While Susan Cooper's *The Dark Is Rising* series does not have the breadth and control of *The Lord of the Rings*, it is still a fine creation. The first book of the five, though, *Over Sea, Under Stone* (1965), can be dispensed with: a nice story but childish. The Drew children found a parchment map in their house in Cornwall; Great-Uncle Merriman read the inscription on it by one of King Arthur's knights and knew that this was important to the ancient, continuing, battle of the Light against the Dark. These ordinary children followed clues, found the grail cup bearing further instructions, and nipped it away from the villains just in time. In the fight, a crucial manuscript fell in the sea; the Dark didn't get it, and it was preserved in a metal case.

The Dark Is Rising (1973) is more gripping and energetic. Will Stanton, seemingly an ordinary boy, didn't know he was born to be the last of the Old Ones, a circle of people from different centuries bent on defending the world from the evil Dark Powers. On his eleventh birthday, he slipped into a past age of his Thames Valley countryside and was introduced by the oldest of the Old Ones, Merriman Lyon (who we come to realize is Merlin), to his new identity and his fearsome new duties. "IF YOU WERE BORN WITH THE GIFT, THEN YOU MUST SERVE IT. IT IS YOUR QUEST TO FIND AND TO GUARD THE SIX GREAT SIGNS OF THE LIGHT. YOU ARE THE SIGN-SEEKER, WILL STANTON." THE RHYTHMS OF HIS VOICE CHANGED SUBTLY INTO A KIND OF CHANTED BATTLE CRY. "FOR THE DARK, THE DARK IS RISING. THE WALKER IS ABROAD, THE RIDER IS RIDING."

From the start, the book has a mysterious, building tension. When Will woke and saw a sudden deep snow, and couldn't rouse his brother, he WENT OUT ONTO THE LANDING AND SHOUTED WITH ALL HIS MIGHT: "WAKE UP! WAKE UP, EVERYONE!" THERE WAS A TOTAL SILENCE, AS DEEP AND TIMELESS AS THE BLANKETING SNOW. Will walked slowly downstairs and out of the house. HE FELT VERY MUCH ALONE, AND HE MADE HIMSELF GO ON WITHOUT LOOKING BACK,

BECAUSE HE KNEW THAT WHEN HE LOOKED, HE WOULD FIND THAT THE HOUSE WAS GONE.

After a period of magic initiation and learning, Will passed through great dangers, weaving between present and past, to collect the six great Signs, which were disks marked by a cross: iron, bronze, wood, fire, water, and stone. Merriman told him, "WE OF THE CIRCLE ARE PLANTED ONLY LOOSELY WITHIN TIME." Will himself talked of "THE PART OF US THAT HAS NOTHING TO DO WITH YESTERDAY OR TODAY OR TOMORROW BECAUSE IT BELONGS AT A DIFFERENT KIND OF LEVEL. YESTERDAY IS STILL THERE. TOMORROW IS THERE TOO. AND ALL GODS ARE THERE, AND ALL THE THINGS THEY HAVE EVER STOOD FOR. AND," HE ADDED SADLY, "THE OPPOSITE, TOO."

In *Greenwitch* (1974), Merriman and Will joined the Drew children in the Cornish village where the lost manuscript was sought by both the Light and the Dark. The Greenwitch was a sea spirit made each spring by the village women out of branches and stones in an all-night ceremony, then flung over the cliff into the sea by the fishermen at dawn. Jane Drew was invited to watch the making. She thought the squat, mysterious shape of twigs looked lonely. Invited to touch the Greenwitch and make a wish, "OH DEAR," SHE SAID IMPULSIVELY, "I WISH YOU COULD BE HAPPY." The Greenwitch, who was subject to neither Dark nor Light, remembered this gesture of sympathy. When she found the metal manuscript case under the sea, she gave it to Jane, thus allowing Merriman to decipher the next clue in this cosmic treasure hunt. (Jane's only action is her instinctive kind wish for the Greenwitch. Women are bit players in Cooper, mostly passive.)

In *The Grey King* (1975), Will Stanton, visiting relatives in a Welsh village, found the hidden gold harp that could wake the six sleeping warriors, to fight against the Dark. His companion Bran, a stern, albino boy of the mountains, proved to be the Pendragon, son of King Arthur, brought by his mother "Gwen" forward in time to escape Arthur's anger at her disloyalty. *The Grey King* is a strong, atmospheric story, more unified than the final book, which ties up loose ends in a plausible but scattered manner. In *Silver on the Tree* (1977), human society was becoming ever more corrupted. The Dark was preparing its greatest attack. Will brought back from the drowned Lost Land the crystal sword that might win the battle. Good Farmer John Rowlands had always been wary of the chill dedication of the Old Ones of the Light, but when Rowlands learned his dear wife was a spy for the Dark, though heartbroken, he refused to rescue her, and helped Bran complete the victory. He told her, "I DO NOT BELIEVE ANY POWER CAN POSSESS THE MIND OF A MAN OR WOMAN. I THINK OUR CHOICES ARE OUR OWN, AND YOU ARE NOT POSSESSED. YOU MUST BE ALLIED TO THE DARK BE-CAUSE YOU HAVE CHOSEN TO BE." Although *Silver on the Tree* has too much going on, with its many Arthurian and Celtic details, it is a fitting culmination to Cooper's earnest and suspenseful series.

৯৫ ৯৫

Besides Lewis, Tolkien, and Cooper, dozens of writers have com-bined myth, legend, and fairy-tale elements of Celtic, British, and Norse origin to produce more or less successful fictions. (Since I am not discussing retellings, I pass over T. H. White's Arthurian *The Once and Future King* (1938–1958), a work that is uneven but wonderful.) Today's compelling mystery is why a fantasy series should reach beyond its normal readership and grab the interest of a huge mass audience. The Harry Potter books have been received with manic enthusiasm perhaps because they uniquely combine several kinds of appeal. A fantasy universe can provide risk-free practice in making sense of a complicated, threatening world: our "civilized" world has stretched so far, so thin, that we see holes in its texture; at the same time, its threads are tightly tangled to-gether. J. K. Rowling's books, written in a clear, accessible, though not elegant, style, are very inviting and unintimidating to the reader, and also very complex in their intertwining of different worlds and moods. Readers can be mightily scared by parts of the fictional world but comforted by other parts. And they are wel-comed; no reader is made to feel stupid. There are 1,819 pages so far, in *Harry Potter and the Sorcerer's Stone* (1997), *Harry Potter and the Chamber of Secrets* (1999), *Harry Potter and the Prisoner of Azkaban* (1999), and *Harry Potter and the Goblet of Fire* (2000), following the adventures of Harry and his friends Ron and Hermione.

These books provide a safe, closed world in Hogwarts School of Witchcraft and Wizardry: a type of setting familiar from "realistic" school stories and also thrillingly unfamiliar in its magical aspects. Outside Hogwarts, there are two loose, out-of-control worlds—the dreary, obtuse land of nonmagic people, called Muggles, surrounding Hogwarts's delightful domain; and the dark realm of evil wizardry. The Hogwarts setting is reassuring, clearly structured, and hierarchical. Dull Muggledom can often be circumvented, and evil powers can sometimes be defeated, but neither of those worlds can be destroyed; they must coexist with good wizardry. So the Potter books take you to a safe, magically powerful place with stable borders, also to a numbing adult world of banality—and also to a large, shapeless place of supreme horror over and below and around the small safe place. Earlier boarding-school books stayed totally within a school's smug boundaries, but such complete provincialism doesn't work today; even children won't buy it. At the other extreme, many recent fantasy books are set totally in a large, complex, fierce universe—Ursula K. Le Guin's Earthsea, for instance. Apparently, what most children want now is to combine a happy, empowering version of normality (jolly magical homework and sports and gossip) with occasional jolts of the horrible, serious menace that they know really exists. Rowling has hinted that the proportion of menace will grow larger in the later books.

Rules, schedules, and traditions nurtured Hogwarts students, while innumerable delights opened before them. SHELVES OF THE MOST SUCCULENT-LOOKING SWEETS. CREAMY CHUNKS OF NOUGAT, SHIMMERING PINK SQUARES OF COCONUT ICE, FAT, HONEY-COLORED TOFFEES. . . . THERE WERE A HUNDRED AND FORTY-TWO STAIRCASES AT HOGWARTS: WIDE, SWEEPING ONES; NARROW, RICKETY ONES; SOME THAT LED SOMEWHERE DIFFERENT ON A FRIDAY; SOME WITH A VANISHING STEP HALFWAY UP THAT YOU HAD TO REMEMBER TO JUMP. Playing Quidditch (a bit like soccer, with four balls), children swooped through the air on broomsticks. Benign magic was all around: NEVILLE CAUSED A SLIGHT DIVERSION BY TURNING INTO A LARGE CANARY.

Evil magic too was all around, though vigilance kept it (mostly) from entering Hogwarts. Magicless Muggle society was hovering on the edges. After dismal years of living with his beastly Dursley relatives, who made him sleep in a cupboard beneath the stairs and who kept the magic skills of Mrs. Dursley's sister (Harry's late mother) a dreadful secret, Harry Potter on his eleventh birthday was invited to study at the Hogwarts School, to develop the magical talents he didn't know he had. He also didn't know he was famous among wizards: although Harry's parents, when he was a baby, had been killed by the murderous lord of all dark magic, Voldemort had been unable to kill Harry. The curse had rebounded and virtually destroyed the dark lord, leaving Harry unharmed except for a lightning-shaped scar on his forehead. In the first four books, we learn who Voldemort was, how he regained his human body and his powers, and who his spies were inside Hogwarts walls.

Rowling's books contain no parallel worlds, only overlapping, parallel societies ignoring or accepting or menacing each other; Harry Potter linked all the groups. His years with the nastiest sort of Muggles were horrid, but at least he learned how Muggles lived. (Most wizards ignored or despised Muggle society; some found it fascinating.) Harry's character, though not subtle, is appealing. Average looking, with glasses and floppy hair, and average in his studies, he was a modest, friendly boy, a stunning Quidditch player, and a brave, stubborn fighter against the dark lord who made him an orphan. Readers find him easy to identify with.

In the first book, Harry, helped by stalwart Ron and clever, bossy Hermione, broke through a half dozen enchantments in the Hogwarts dungeons to seize the sorcerer's stone (which produced the elixir of eternal life) just as Voldemort arrived to capture it for himself. Lacking his own body, the spirit of Voldemort had invaded that of a feeble teacher who always wore a turban: now, under the turban, WHERE THERE SHOULD HAVE BEEN A BACK TO QUIRRELL'S HEAD, THERE WAS A FACE. IT WAS CHALK WHITE WITH GLARING RED EYES AND SLITS FOR NOSTRILS, LIKE A SNAKE. The second book describes attacks and threats in the school against those half-Muggle wizards called "Mudbloods" by some bigots. Harry himself was suspected, until he entered the secret chamber through plumbing pipes and defeated Tom Riddle, the half-Muggle Hogwarts student from fifty years earlier who had become Voldemort. In the third and fourth books, Harry survived attacks by terrifying creatures such as the dementors, who GLORY IN DECAY AND DESPAIR, DRAIN PEACE, HOPE, AND HAPPINESS OUT OF THE AIR. GET TOO NEAR A DEMENTOR AND EVERY GOOD FEELING, EVERY HAPPY MEMORY WILL BE SUCKED OUT OF YOU. Voldemort, still lacking human form, managed to kidnap Harry and use his blood in a ritual that restored the wizard's body. With courage and magical skills, Harry escaped alive, but Voldemort had risen again and would collect his old followers to war against decent wizardry—in the next three books.

Harry and his friends knew disguised traitors were living at Hogwarts. The dark lord did more than murder and torture; he stirred up all sorts of vileness. Besides fighting him, Harry's job was to unmask the spies; counter the growing prejudice against "impure," part-Muggle wizards; navigate schoolwork and adolescence; come to terms with his lost parents and his foul relatives; and discover what kind of person he really was. Rowling accomplishes a great deal in these books—to cover all that and still give us moments like the quarreling students who ended up with leeks sprouting out their ears, and the wizard who was told to wear trousers instead of robes in front of Muggles but refused: "I'M NOT PUTTING THEM ON," SAID OLD ARCHIE IN INDIGNATION. "I LIKE A HEALTHY BREEZE 'ROUND MY PRIVATES, THANKS." The Harry Potter stories are loved because they're fun. They are delightful, but they are only one fine series among many. They may sell more copies than any other series, but that doesn't mean they are better.

Today's Classics

When we read about ordinary characters taking on huge dangers, we identify with their desperate vulnerability. One of the satisfactions in the Lewis–Tolkien–Cooper–Rowling kind of fantasy, though, is the knowledge that you are playing for a large, important team, even though you fear the opposing team may turn out to be more powerful. Lewis's children became Kings and Queens of Narnia; Frodo's team included whole races and ages of good creatures; Will Stanton was backed by the Old Ones; and all good wizards were rooting for Harry Potter. But starting in the 1960s, even more in the 1970s, many of the fantasy heroes were lonelier, the bands of comrades smaller, and their advisers more remote, though the evil they fought was as huge as ever.

A generation of excellent writers now considered classics—including Madeleine L'Engle, John Christopher, Virginia Hamilton, and Ursula Le Guin—created fantasy worlds with new, even starker, themes and settings (along with many traditional motifs). L'Engle, Christopher, and Hamilton wrote the science fiction type of fantasy; their created worlds extrapolate from our own modern society. Le Guin, like Lewis and Tolkien before her, invented a whole secondary world of the preindustrial, medieval sort, with geography, history, social structure, and magical practices elaborately worked out: though the technique is familiar, her world is stunningly original.

❧ ❧

Madeleine L'Engle's *A Wrinkle in Time* (1962), *A Wind in the Door* (1973), and *A Swiftly Tilting Planet* (1978) mix scientific notions, lyrical style, and Christianity, a mixture that works surprisingly well. Plain, angry Meg Murry and her precocious little brother, Charles Wallace, had smart, loving parents, both Nobel winners in physics. When their father didn't return from a scientific government mission, Meg and Charles Wallace, with Meg's friend Calvin, were summoned to rescue him from the far planet where he was imprisoned. The guardian angels who summoned them sometimes took the form of three goofy, cozy witches, sometimes of centaurs or invisible voices. By tessering (traveling through a fifth-dimension "wrinkle in time"), the witches carried the children first to another planet where they could glimpse the evil touching Earth: "DID IT JUST COME?" MEG ASKED IN AGONY, UNABLE TO TAKE HER EYES FROM THE SICKNESS OF THE SHADOW WHICH DARKENED THE BEAUTY OF THE EARTH. MRS. WHATSIT SIGHED. "NO, MEG. IT HASN'T JUST COME. THAT IS WHY YOUR PLANET IS SUCH A TROUBLED ONE." On the planet Camazotz, where the ruler, a disembodied brain, required absolute uniformity (a boy bouncing his ball out of sync with his peers' bouncing was reprogrammed by torture), Meg, using stubbornness and love, rescued Mr. Murray from his glass cell and Charles Wallace from the brainwashed trance the ruler imposed on him.

In *A Wind in the Door,* the cosmic war expanded. With Proginoskes, the angelic creature now guiding them, Meg saw the damage spreading in the sky: A SOUND, A VIOLENT, SILENT, ELECTRICAL REPORT, WHICH MADE HER PRESS HER HANDS IN PAIN AGAINST HER EARS. ACROSS THE SKY, A CRACK SHIVERED, SLIVERED, BECAME A LINE OF NOTHINGNESS. Proginoskes, a being of many wings and eyes, explained that Echthroi, fallen angels, were trying to destroy the universe by Xing its citizens—un-Naming them, snuffing their identities with hate. He himself was a Namer, whose job was to know the name of each star in the heavens. "IF SOMEONE KNOWS WHO HE IS, HE DOESN'T NEED TO HATE. WHEN EVERYONE IS TRULY NAMED, THEN THE ECHTHROI WILL BE VANQUISHED." Distant stars were being hurt, and also the tiniest particles within the human body. Charles Wallace became deathly ill; within his cellular mitochondria, tiny farandolae were ceasing to function, persuaded by Echthroi to stop their rhythmic development. Proginoskes led the children inside Charles Wallace's body, where they restored the cell to health. Every cell and every star was connected, in a dance of harmony and wisdom.

As the first two books go into far planets and infinitesimal cells, *A Swiftly Tilting Planet* travels through time. During a comfortable Thanksgiving reunion, Mr. Murray, a government consultant, was telephoned by his friend, the U.S. president, and told that the bloody South American dictator called Mad Dog Branzillo had threatened nuclear attack in twenty-four hours. Again, heavenly powers sent an agent—this time the unicorn Gaudior—to enlist the Murrays' help. Charles Wallace, now fifteen, rode Gaudior into past centuries in their own New England village and entered Within several characters, merging so he shared their senses and thoughts. He became the young Welsh Madoc, who journeyed to the New World and wed a woman of the local tribe but was murdered by his own brother; then he became various descendants of that Welshman, involved in fraternal struggles. He finally managed to change history so that a baby was born in a South American colony to a good rather than an evil descendant. Thus, back at the family Thanksgiving, Charles Wallace learned that the peaceful Patagonian ruler El Zarco had made a friendly call to the U.S. president—no Mad Dog Branzillo had ever been born. L'Engle takes big risks, with her wild plots and environmental-poetic-biblical-uplifting style, but the books are fascinating, full of joy and conviction.

꿍 꿍

L'Engle describes heavenly creatures and space travel; John Christopher's Tripods trilogy stays on earth, though his tyrannical race of Masters came from another planet. *The White Mountains* (1967) tells how three boys escaped the compulsory Capping of thirteen-year-olds, in which a metal mesh implanted in the skull made the victim worship and obey giant metal Tripods that stalked the countryside on three long legs, occasionally swallowing or smashing people. A Vagrant wearing a false Cap, so no one could tell his brain was not controlled, recruited Will, telling him how to get from England to a secret rebel camp in the Alps.

In *The City of Gold and Lead* (1967), Will got into the Tripods' city as a Capped slave, barely survived the heavy gravity and poisonous air, and returned to the rebels with crucial information. The Tripods were vehicles controlled by Masters—stern, green aliens who expressed admiration of Earth's interesting creatures in museum exhibits of beautiful dead human females. Their long-term plan was to cover Earth with their own kind of air, thus destroying all life. The third book, *The Pool of Fire* (1968), tells of the rebels' ingenious triumph over the Masters, which released humanity from slavery. But quarrels among leaders started anew: clearly, humankind had not learned to avoid war. Christopher's books do exactly what they set out to do. His style is clean and fast, details are well worked out, plots exciting, and characters developed with some subtlety.

꿍 꿍

The best books by Virginia Hamilton are probably those that are not fantastic but poetic, such as *The Planet of Junior Brown*. Still, her sci-fi Justice trilogy—*Justice and Her Brothers* (1978), *Dustland* (1980), *The Gathering* (1981)—tells a gripping story, hard to comprehend but easy to sink into, in a style both intimate and vast. Though her appeal is not for a mass audience, she is a splendid writer.

Four normal-seeming African American children in a comfortable Ohio community discovered their linked, supersensory powers, which formed "the unit." IT WAS THOMAS, THE MAGICIAN. IT WAS DORIAN, THE HEALER. IT WAS JUSTICE, WHO WAS THE WATCHER AND THE BALANCE FOR THE UNIT'S STRENGTH. AND IT WAS LEVI, BROTHER OF JUSTICE AND IDENTICAL BROTHER OF THOMAS. LEVI SUFFERED FOR THEM ALL. The unit, leaving their real bodies behind, traveled to the far-future land called Dustland and to the domed city of Sona. There they learned that humanity had turned Earth into a desert. A few seers (descended from mutants like these children) had escaped with healthy people to another planet, leaving the weak and deformed to be governed by sentient, self-reproducing machines.

Life was discouraging for residents of the hyperorganized Sona society and for the few beasts and human children who escaped into stark Dustland, where they developed hunting skills and rituals of interdependence. Colossus, the ruling machine, had almost broken down, but now, repairing itself, was trying to reclaim the Earth and nurture its inhabitants. A part of Justice's power—she being the strongest of the unit—was needed by Colossus: she sent her Watcher self splitting off, to help Dustland and Sona, and became once more a normal child. Or almost normal, as she knew her powers would swell again until she would once more be called to use them.

The eerie texture of Hamilton's writing draws you into these worlds. Her version of ordinary childhood life is itself mysterious, and her dry world of Dustland is overwhelming: deep dunes of dust, varied by rocks; days divided into Graylight and Nolight; storms of mammoth dustwaves. These books are bleak, but hopeful in a scary way. If Madeleine L'Engle's writing is warm, Virginia Hamilton's is both ice cold and burning hot.

ଵଛ ଛଵ

Ursula K. Le Guin is one of the very best. Her Earthsea trilogy was aimed at a young adult market; in each book, a different boy or girl grows wiser and freer by facing some enormous challenge. Adults too find the series enthralling, as the wizard Ged painfully carves out his self and protects his people. In precise language, dignified but not fancy, Le Guin presents the Earthsea archipelago, its heroic legends and its magic lore, along with scenes of everyday life. Le Guin's style and narrative structures show a fine sense of balance, and indeed the theme of balance in the universe is central to the series.

In *The Wizard of Earthsea* (1968), Ged, a poor village boy with a gift for magic, was trained by Mage Ogion, then sent to wizards' school on Roke Island. Arrogant and defensive, he quarreled with his classmates. Playing with a spell to call up dead spirits, he created a terrible crack in the night: A RIPPING OPEN OF THE FABRIC OF THE WORLD. AND THROUGH THAT BRIGHT MISSHAPEN BREACH CLAMBERED SOMETHING LIKE A CLOT OF BLACK SHADOW, QUICK AND HIDEOUS, AND IT LEAPED STRAIGHT OUT AT GED'S FACE. The shadowy thing was now in the world, hiding, searching for years to find Ged. When Ged crossed the stone wall into the dry land of death (only a Mage could do so and return), trying to save a dying child, the shadow was crouching there, waiting. He fled before it across lonely seas and lands—until Ogion told him his only hope was to turn and pursue it, and master it by finding its true name. Finally, Ged faced the writhing, monstrous thing, gave it its name—Ged— AND TOOK HOLD OF HIS SHADOW, THE BLACK SELF THAT REACHED OUT TO HIM, merging with it. Scarred, acknowledging his own dark shadow, he was whole.

In *The Tombs of Atuan* (1971), a six-year-old Kargad girl was chosen to be priestess of the Nameless Ones because she was born the day the old priestess died. A ceremony in the stone temple took her name away and made her the Eaten One, who would live— dressed in black, loved only by a eunuch servant—there and in underground caverns and corridors of the Nameless Ones. *"YOU ARE ARHA. THERE IS NOTHING LEFT. IT WAS ALL EATEN."* "IT WAS ALL EATEN," THE GIRL REPEATED. By fifteen she had learned the labyrinth under the stones. One day a thief appeared in the labyrinth—the Mage Ged, hoping to reclaim for his people (enemies of the Kargads), from the treasure chamber, a sacred ring that would bring peace to the Inner Lands. Arha locked him in the labyrinth, watched him through spyholes, then softened and brought him food. He told her of life outside and gave her her true name, Tenar, which she had forgotten. Together they escaped, to bring the ring to the Havnor princes. It's a great, claustrophobic story, though Tenar's passivity is distressing.

Years later, in *The Farthest Shore* (1972), Arran, teenage prince of Enlad, came to Roke to report trouble in his father's realm: sorcerers' spells had stopped working; harvests had failed; lambs were born deformed. Ged, now Archmage, having heard such news from elsewhere, set off with Arran in a small boat to see for himself. On every island they found despair and madness. In the far South Reach they rested with the Children of the Open Seas, a peaceable tribe who lived on great floating rafts, happily weaving, fishing, and tending babies. But even there the plague of emptiness appeared, at the Long Dance ceremony: "I DO NOT KNOW THE WORDS," THE CHANTER SAID, AND HIS VOICE ROSE HIGH AS IF IN TERROR. "I CANNOT SING. THERE ARE NO MORE SONGS."

Helped by ancient dragons, Ged and Arran discovered that Cob, a twisted Mage seeking immortality, had made a gap in the stone wall separating the dry land of death from the living. They pursued Cob into the dry land, where no wind blew and no water flowed. The dead stood quietly in doorways. Ged and Arran captured and destroyed Cob, but closing the gap in the wall took all Ged's powers: he was alive but no more a Mage. The great dragon flew them to Havnor, where Arran was recognized as the true heir to the king, and the world's balance was restored.

Le Guin has done something unusual, perhaps unique: in 1990, eighteen years after the third Earthsea book, she published a fourth, reflecting a matured perspective less heroic and deliberately more respectful of women, and in 2000 a fifth. Both of these have the same high quality as the trilogy. *Tehanu*, which starts where *The Farthest Shore* leaves off, just after Arran became King Lebannen in Havnar, focuses on Tenar. For twenty-five years after escaping the Tombs she had lived on Ged's native island of Gont with his old teacher Ogion, then as a farmer's wife, then a widow. Now she nursed Ged back to health when the dragon Kalessin carried him to her, barely alive after his battle in the dry land of death. Proud Ged had to fight despair and humiliation, having lost his powers as a Mage. Tenar's task was to weave a life of many strands and strengths, overcoming fears, helping Ged, protecting her adopted daughter Tehanu, who had been raped, deliberately burned and disfigured. All three moved from paralysis to action: Tenar and Ged challenged a corrupt local Mage until he bound them with a curse; Tehanu, the abused child with a crippled hand and half her face burned away, rescued them by summoning Kalessin to help, crying out instinctively in the Old Speech—thus showing she was one of the few humans who were kin to the wise, free dragons.

In *The Other Wind*, angry dragons were destroying fields and towns. King Lebannen, with Tenar, Tehanu now grown up, and other helpers, confronted the dragons and learned their complaint. Once a single race, humans and dragons long ago agreed that dragons (creatures wanting to let go and fly) would live in certain lands; humankind (wanting to keep things and settle) would live in others. But humans, wanting their souls to live after death, had walled off, for the dead, part of the dragon's terrain, creating the silent dry land. Realizing the dead would rather enter the natural cycle of decay and rebirth, Tehanu and King Lebannen journeyed to the dry land and destroyed the wall, so the dead streamed out and dissolved into sun and wind. The dragons flew off to the far west, among them a newly transformed dragon: Tehanu, now healed and golden. Tenar returned to Gont, to her love, Ged, who had never regained his magic powers. He was happily watering the cabbages, and glad to see her. These two were atypical heroes in some ways, fine heroes nonetheless.

New Mythologies

By the 1980s, scores of ho-hum fantasy series appeared, with familiar motifs from Tolkien and other classics. The familiar mythologies can't be used up, and any time new life is breathed into them in new versions readers must be grateful; but they don't need more feeble Arthurian or Norse tales in the sword-and-sorcery mode. Some fantasy writers of the past few decades—notably Robin McKinley, Patricia Wrightson, and William Nicholson—have done much better than that by basing their stories on fresh, vigorous myths and legends.

The setting of McKinley's *The Blue Sword* (1982) resembles a nineteenth-century Middle Eastern country under the British. After a tomboy childhood back Home, Harry Crewe was orphaned and joined her brother at his military station on the Daria peninsula. Disliking confined colonial life in the governor's residence, Harry gazed with longing at the desert and hills beyond, where the stern people of the old Damar kingdom still rode magnificent horses and, it was said, practiced magic. McKinley makes her story seem inevitable rather than farfetched: Corlath, king of the Damar Hillfolk, kidnapped Harry because he saw she had *kelar*, the magic gift possessed only by Damarian heroes. Harry was treated respectfully by the tribe, especially when she had *kelar* visions of forthcoming battles against the cruel, half-human Northerners. Trained by one of Corlath's officers, she won a tournament of warriors and was made a King's Rider. She learned that her mother had Damarian blood: the Lady Aerin, legendary hero of the Hillfolk, was Harry's ancestor and spoke to her in visions. Harry realized she herself was a bridge between colonial Homelanders and Damarian Hillfolk.

Corlath gave Harry the magic sword of Aerin: his people needed a *damalur-sol* again, a lady hero. But when the foul Northerners attacked, she quarreled with Corlath (he had refused to send troops to defend a small pass and warn the Homelander base nearby). Disobeying King Corlath, Harry and some followers rode to the town, gathered troops, and headed for the pass. She was right: the Northern general was there with huge armies ready to pour into Damar. With the magic sword of Aerin and her *kelar* powers, she started an avalanche and destroyed the enemy. Corlath forgave her disobedience and married her.

After *The Blue Sword*, McKinley went back several centuries to tell, in *The Hero and the Crown* (1984), the story of Lady Aerin— how a clumsy, endearing princess stubbornly turned herself into a dragonfighter, then became an immortal warrior and consort of the hero King Tor in Damar's Golden Age. There are bloody battles in the best warrior tradition, which are stirring even if you don't much like that sort of thing. Aerin was the woman who has everything: she saved her country, married the king, and when her triumphant human life was done, went to live forever with her other lover, a thousand-year-old Mage who looked like a handsome young man. These books are exhilarating, and elegantly written as well.

ℛ❧ ❧ℛ

Patricia Wrightson found material for her Wirrun series in a very old mythology, but one that is new to most Westerners. Earth-spirits of the Australian Aborigines crept, flew, swam, and lumbered through her stories, great white bird spirits, headless women, little gray spidery spirits—friendly or hostile or, mostly, neutral to humankind. Urban Happy Folk on the coasts didn't know the spirits; rough, farmer Inlanders knew them a little. Only the native People truly coexisted with earth-things and saw when they dangerously disturbed the harmony of the land.

In *The Ice Is Coming* (1977), Wirrun, a boy of the People who had finished school and was working in a service station, went on a camping trip and worried about the odd patches of ice he saw, in summer. Newspapers reported many ice sightings and futilely suggested THAT THE FROSTS WERE CAUSED BY RAYS FROM A NEIGHBOURING PLANET, OR BY A CRACK IN THE FIELD OF GRAVITY, OR BY VESTED INTERESTS, AND THAT IN ANY CASE IT WAS TIME THEY WERE STOPPED. The People, however, could tell that earth-spirits were involved. Returning to his campsite to investigate, Wirrun met the hero-spirit Ko-in, who chose him as defender of the land because he had noticed and cared. A little ball of quartz gave Wirrun magic powers, so he was able to spread the word that Ninya ice-spirits had left their own caves, planning to conquer the whole land by covering it with ice. THEY LIKE THEIR CAVERNS ARE PURE AND SPARKLING WHITE. THEIR EYEBROWS AND BEARDS ARE NEEDLES OF ICE, AND FROST FALLS FROM THEM AS THEY MOVE.

Wirrun trailed the underground progress of the Ninyas, who surfaced here and there to spread ice and build ice prisons for killing small spirits. He sent for men of the People who lived in the Ninyas' usual territory, to come and sing the creatures back home, but it would take time for the men to arrive. The ice-spirits' first goal was to find and destroy the Eldest Nargun, so he would not use against them his power to call up fire. Narguns were ancient spirits that looked like rocks; sometimes you could make out a BLUNT MUZZLE, EMPTY EYES, AND STUMPY LIMBS. The Ninyas were defeated by a communal effort—a village of the People, a few Inlanders, various Earth-spirits, and the Nargun. But Wirrun knew the decisions were his. THE MEN COULD TRAVEL AFTER HIM AS FAST AS THEY MIGHT, BUT HE MUST FIND THEIR PATH; AND TO DO THAT HE MUST WALK THE LAND IN ITS QUIET PLACES AND TRUST TO IT.

In Wrightson's trilogy, the enemy was not Evil but something that disturbs the natural balance of the land and its various inhabitants. The ice people were simply sent back where they belonged. *The Dark Bright Water* (1978) describes a Yunggamurra waterspirit who was washed away from her sisters and lost in a maze of underground rivers. Yunggamurra were beautiful sirens who splashed and played and drowned careless men. The lost girl's crying disrupted the land: troublesome spirits left their dwellings and streams dried up. Her seductive song haunted Wirrun, back at work in the city: ARE YOU NOT COMING? / SINGS THE BRIGHT WATER; / THE DARK-FLOWING WATER / LIKE WASHES AND RIPPLES OF DARK-FLOATING HAIR.

Because the water was drying up, a messenger from the People came to ask for help from Wirrun, now known as the hero Ice-Hunter. Though dreading the pull of the siren song in his head, Wirrun and his friend Ularra quit their jobs and headed inland. When they found the Yunggamurra in her underground pool, she drowned Ularra in the game she and her sisters always played, and Wirrun dragged her out into the sunlight. She told him of her torment underground. "ALONE IN THE DARK, A LONG TIME." THE BIRD-SWEET VOICE WAS COOL AND INDIFFERENT BUT HE HAD SEEN THE SPIRIT QUIVER. HE FELT A QUICK UNEXPECTED PANG. LOVELY AND LOATHSOME, DELICATE AND ENDURING, GALLANT AND TERRIBLE. These stories stress acceptance: all creatures only behave as they must. Wirrun turned the Yunggamurra human in a ceremony of smoke and fire; he named her Murra, dressed her in a shirt, and loved her—though they knew her sisters would come to claim her. Wrightson's writing is earthy and lovely, though the linear, unrelieved shape of the stories makes them a bit soporific. Except for *The Nargun and the Stars* (1973), a terrific story about a younger boy, her work is hardly known in the United States. It should be known and admired.

❧❧ ❧❧

Garth Nix has created an intriguing world in *Sabriel* (1995) and *Lirael* (2001). A guarded wall separated Ancelstierre to the south, an ordinary, technological nation, from the Old Kingdom, where machinery would not work because of magic oozing everywhere. A Charter and its Mages controlled the use of magic there. Sabriel, though schooled in Ancelstierre, was daughter to the Abhorsen, the Mage who could enter the underworld's river of Death, with its seven Gates and Precincts, and fight with those who tried to come back and harm the upper world. Sabriel's and Luriel's adventures are exciting, fast-paced, and well designed. Nix is good with striking motifs and images, like the Abhorson's set of dangerous magic bells, or the Paperwings—vehicles that RESEMBLED A CANOE WITH HAWK-WINGS AND A TAIL; you flew them by whistling. But his writing can become tiresome and teeter on the edge of cliché, with perhaps too much tired, "strange, inexorable powers" sort of language: SABRIEL COULD ONLY STARE IN TERROR AS THE THING'S FOUR-TALONED HAND SLOWLY OPENED AND REACHED OUT FOR HER. There is a fine line between the dramatic and the melodramatic, the wrought and the overwrought. It would be interesting to compare specific passages—battles with supernatural creatures, for instance—in various fantasy writers to see why some seem artificial and others compel belief. Many fantasy writers are a lot worse than Nix, and he is very readable; but he's not in the top rank.

Cynthia Voigt unquestionably *is* in the top rank, but her invented feudal world, the Kingdom, does not belong in this discussion because it is not strictly a fantasy land; there is no supernatural. Her *Jackaroo*, *On Fortune's* Wheel, *The Wings of a Falcon*, and *Elske* (1985–99) are splendid, complex adventures about young heroes. Diana Wynne Jones, on the other hand, is magical through and through. Jones's *Dalemark Quartet* (1975, 1977, 1979, 1993) covers a vast sweep of time and shifting groups of characters. *Cart and Cwidder* introduces the tumultuous politics of North and South Dalemark, through the story of Clennan, the jolly musician who performed with his family all over the repressive state of South Dalemark, and who was in fact a messenger for Southern rebels and Northern allies. Clennan's children are densely drawn, appealing characters, carrying on boldly after their father was killed. The youngest, Moril, could play the magic heirloom cwidder; in an attack, he saved his people by playing until the hills walked, crushing the enemy.

Drowned Ammet describes a different part of South Dalemark, but the same period. The Earl of Holand by the sea was a tyrant. Tough, surly Mitt, whose fisherman father had died fighting for the rebels, had to flee the city and found himself sailing north in a small boat with two disillusioned grandchildren of the earl, who were running away. In *The Spellcoats*, the best of the four books, Jones tells of Dalemark's prehistory, when the people were close to the Undying, their gods; each family cherished small figures of them. Tanaqui narrates the story: she and her blond siblings were scapegoated by the villagers, declared Heathen enemies who caused cattle to die. They escaped down the river into eerie adventures and battled a sorcerer; her brother Hern became king, and one of the Undying. Thick rugcoats were worn in the cold climate, and Tanaqui wove the story of the clan and the Undying into her magic Spellcoats—a beautiful intertwining of art, history, and religion.

The Crown of Dalemark pulls everything together: it returns to the medieval period of the first two books, and also includes sections set in Dalemark in a time that resembles our own present. Now the children from *Cart and Cwidder* and *Drowned Ammet* became friends and allies, and Maewen from the future joined them, all seeking to bring peace to North and South and restore the throne by finding the hidden Crown once worn by the great King Hern. Hern had been ruler in the Golden Age of Dalemark and was Tanaqui's brother in *Spellcoats*. Young Mitt was revealed as heir to the Crown. When Maewen returned to her home in future Dalemark, she knew from history books that Mitt had been a great king and the land had flourished. The quartet, though as intricate as a Spellcoat, rewards careful reading and rereading. Jones stretches her stories almost to the breaking point; sometimes they sag, but they do hold up.

&? &?

My personal choices for best recent fantasy series would be Philip Pullman and William Nicholson, Pullman being more sophisticated and brilliant, while Nicholson is more fun and accessible. The voice of Nicholson's narrator is wry, sweet but not saccharine. Like Le Guin, Nicholson creates one large world with a wealth of vividly different places, peoples, and events, and provides the right tone and language for each scene. His screenwriting experience (*Shadowlands*, *Gladiator*) is reflected in the immediacy and shapeliness of his stories. The city of Aramanth, in *The Wind Singer* (2000), had a strict "merit" system, with each family assigned a certain level of privilege and housing on the basis of annual exams. But the Hath family was rebellious. Hanno, the father, loved learning but failed exams. Ira, the mother, who was descended from the revered prophet of the Manth people, refused to be bullied. She constantly created scenes and cried out "O unhappy people!"

The Hath twins were very close but very different, Kestrel being outspoken and stubborn, her brother Bowman thoughtful and empathetic. Kestrel insulted a cruel teacher and was sent for Special Training, which meant transformation into one of the Old Children: shriveled, cackling, white-haired children who would never again misbehave. She cleverly escaped; encountered the reclusive emperor, who said she must go on a quest; and left the city with her brother and a pathetic hanger-on from school named Mumpo. The quest was to find the Morah—the spirit-lord who controlled Aramanth—and steal the silver piece that would make the Wind Singer tower sing again and free the city. First they journeyed through the underground domain of the happy round mudpeople (an inspired creation), helping to harvest the delicious mudnuts from the mudfields, and visiting the warm haven where piles of muddy babies were lovingly cared for.

Harrowing events followed, however. Horrible Old Children, pursuing the three comrades, caught Mumpo and made him one of them by stroking him. Kestrel and Bowman managed to steal the silver voice of the Wind Singer. But the Morah, in the form of an old lady, let loose her army of murderous Zars: thousands of beautiful, blank teenagers in white uniforms with gold braid, marching flawlessly as they shouted "Kill! Kill!" With Kestrel's determination and Bowman's ability to hear the thoughts of all living things, the twins cured Mumpo of his spell, struggled back to Aramanth, and slipped the silver piece into the Wind Singer just ahead of the attacking Zars. The people were saved. They would no longer have crushing exams and ratings; they would no longer wear only the proper color for their level.

In *Slaves of the Mastery* (2001), as some Aramanth people were leaving to seek the Homeland promised by the prophet Ira Manth, they were attacked from a new quarter. Soldiers captured a hundred or so and marched them to the beautiful, orderly city of the Mastery to be slaves, burning relatives of any who disobeyed. Kestrel became slave to a silly veiled princess, whose face had been seen by no one except her parents and her maid since she was seven. Princess Sisi had no hope of avoiding the forced royal marriage planned for her, but Kestrel's strength and common sense educated the princess; the two contrived a way out. The Master of the land seemed invulnerable. He had created everything in his world, magnificently. For the royal wedding he composed and conducted exquisite music that filled the streets. He gloried in CONDUCTING HIS MULTIPLE ORCHESTRAS AND CHOIRS, SINGING THE GREAT

ANTHEM AS IT ROLLED OUT OVER HIS CITY BELOW. WITH THE SWEEP OF HIS ARM HE CAUSED A HUNDRED SINGERS TO BURST INTO SONG FIVE STREETS AWAY. HE STABBED A FINGER, AND TRUMPETS SOUNDED FROM THE FLOWER MARKET. But young Bowman had been training his magic powers and defeated the Master; and Kestrel got Princess Sisi away from her tyrannical fiancé. Sisi proudly abandoned her veil, even though another rejected suitor scarred her face and destroyed her beauty; she joined the Aramanth people, who were now free to hunt for their Homeland.

Firesong (2002) tells how this group followed the twins' mother Ira, descendant of the prophet, into hardship and horror, seeking the beautiful land. The prophecy promised a time of cruelty—then the wind on fire—before the time of peace. Indeed, the world was in turmoil, with bandits and murderers; but the Singer people were gathering, ready to sing the firesong that would destroy the Morah's power once more. When the Aramanth pilgrims found their beautiful land, it was at the base of a massive precipice with no way down. But the travelers had survived worse. One asked his friend, "AND NOTHING TO BE DONE, EH?" "OH, I DON'T KNOW ABOUT THAT. THINGS DON'T STAY THE SAME, SIR. EVENTS, THAT'S THE THING. THEY DO KEEP HAPPENING. I SAY WE WAIT FOR EVENTS." And events do keep happening in Nicholson's stories, events involving sacrifice and loss and triumph and quiet happiness. *The Wind on Fire* trilogy is a remarkable work, tender and exciting. It will make quite a movie.

Worlds Beyond

The great created worlds of heroic fantasy generally exist in isolation. They may alternate several levels of existence, like the dry land of the dead in Le Guin; they may allow various races or species to coexist, as in Tolkien and Wrightson; they may allow movement backward or forward in time, as in Jones's Dalemark books; they may combine several subworlds, like the Muggles and Wizards in Rowling. Even so, most stay in a single world or planet. C. S. Lewis, Madeleine L'Engle, and Virginia Hamilton are among the exceptions, sending their characters from a primary place to other worlds. In recent years more fantasy writers have started to do this, incorporating science fiction motifs and new scientific ideas about parallel worlds. Diane Duane, Diana Wynne Jones in some of her books, and Philip Pullman are the most interesting of these.

The difference between science fiction and fantasy doesn't seem important, except that the extreme kinds of sci fi, which focus more on technology and science than on people, may not be to everyone's taste. (Of course, fantasy is not to everyone's taste either.) Diane Duane, a respected writer of science fiction, including *Star Trek* episodes, has written a wild children's series that races from a recognizable modern suburb, to a hideous alternate Manhattan, to planets in other solar systems. In *So You Want to Be a Wizard* (1983), a thirteen-year-old Long Island girl, Nita Callahan, and boy, Kit Rodriguez, stumbled upon a manual for wizards. After they recited the solemn oath to preserve life and growth, their names appeared in the book's Directory of U.S. wizards as novices, along with Area Wizards, Advisories, and Seniors. The manual included a useful list of alternate earths, a mission statement, and a historical summary: When life arose, it brought many Powers to manage it. Some invented planets, light, gravity, and so on. One, the Lone Power, introduced death; cast out by the others, he continued working for destruction and entropy. Wizards evolved, to fight entropy and slow the death of the Universe.

After practicing spells and learning to talk to trees, Nita and Kit faced their probationary Ordeal. Crossing through the Worldgate next to Grand Central Station's heliport, they walked into a desolate, vicious New York City, where the Lone One ruled and crazed hydrants swallowed pigeons. Along with Fred, a friendly spark of light who was really a white hole they had called into the world by mistake (and who occasionally emitted objects like a vacuum cleaner and a cactus), they wandered the streets, fought in a battle of cars bashing each other, and located the book that would defeat the Lone One for a while.

In *Deep Wizardry* (1985), a wonderfully strange underwater story, Nita and Kit turned into whales to help stop earthquakes in the ocean floor caused by the Lone One. Kit almost got trapped forever in his whale form. Nita, who unwittingly agreed to play the role of sacrificed one in the ceremony that reenacted the binding of the Lone One, barely escaped death by shark. In *High Wizardry* (1990), Nita's little sister Dairene, a genius and computer freak, entered wizardry with a bang: following a computer version of the wizard manual, she wandered the galaxies and ended up on a flat planet made of silicon inhabited by a one-celled organism: "ONE BIG SEMICONDUCTOR CHIP! IT'S *ALIVE!*" Through her laptop, she gave the planet instructions that turned it into a vast computer, then created hundreds of little computer creatures and poured into them the contents of her own experience. Helped by Nita and Kit, she prevented the Lone One from taking over there and, with her technological and magical strength, changed his darkness back into light.

Duane's style, somewhat uncomfortably, combines a slangy informality aimed at kids with a liking for scientific concepts and jargon. Nonetheless, the wizardry books are worth reading. There are funny moments, like the time Kit and Nita sneaked into the Madison Avenue office of the Lone One. THE THING SITTING IN A SECRETARY'S SWIVEL CHAIR AND TYPING WAS DARK GREEN AND WARTY. IT HAD LIMBS WITH TENTACLES AND CLAWS, ALL KNOTTED TOGETHER UNDER A BIG EGGPLANT-SHAPED HEAD. EVERY FEW SECONDS IT MADE A MISTAKE AND WENT FUMBLING OVER THE TOP OF ITS MESSY DESK FOR A BOTTLE OF CORRECTING FLUID. The Lone One himself, archenemy of the good, talked on the phone in an inner office: "—LOOK, MIKE, I'VE HAD ABOUT ENOUGH OF THIS SILLINESS. THE BRIGHT POWERS GOT MIFFED BECAUSE I WANTED TO WORK ON PROJECTS OF MY OWN INSTEAD OF FOLLOWING-THE-LEADER LIKE YOU DO, WORKING FROM THEIR BLUE-PRINTS." There are touching moments, too, like Dairene's scenes with the baby computers, her children; and complicated ideas expressed in simple form. Nita came to realize what wizardry was: KEEPING TERRIBLE THINGS FROM HAPPENING, EVEN WHEN IT HURT. NOT JUST POWER, OR DELIGHT IN BEING ABLE TO MAKE STRANGE THINGS HAPPEN. THOSE WERE THE SIDE EFFECTS—NOT THE PURPOSE.

❦ ❦

Diana Wynne Jones is a generous writer. Her books can be over-loaded, though, like a delicious but too elaborate buffet. Her *Howl's Moving Castle* (1986), which many people love, may be too self-consciously clever for others. She shows a lighter touch in the Chrestomanci books, which tell of a universe comprising many sets of worlds. In prehistory, the original world split: two worlds emerged, each with one of the possible outcomes; those multiplied. *Charmed Life* (1977) introduces Chrestomanci, the handsome En-chanter whose job was to make sure witches didn't cause trouble in his world (teeming with magic) or in other worlds. Chresto-manci took two orphans to live with his family on their grand es-tate. Little Cat Chant was a modest chap, bullied by his sister. Gwendolen, proud of her witchery skills, resented Chrestomanci's strict discipline. She enraged the household with pranks—moving all the trees right up against the house, for instance, or causing stained-glass window saints to cavort about and do naughty things during church services. Finally, she ran away to another world, taking a similar girl's identity and causing a ripple of switched identities all through that set of worlds. It seems that Cat had the true magic power, as yet undeveloped, and Gwendolen had been tapping it to increase her own powers; but Cat would be trained as the next Chrestomanci.

The other book in Volume 1 of the *Chronicles of Chrestomanci* is *The Lives of Christopher Chant* (1988), about Cat's mentor, as a child. Uncle Ralph discovered that young Christopher had the unusual gift of traveling to other worlds in his dreams while retain-ing his body and his strength. Greedy Ralph tricked him into smuggling dangerous, illegal magical products back into their home world. Christopher was sickened to realize that the odd, salty-smelling bundles he had brought back were pieces of the friendly mermaids he had played with. The wizards defeated Uncle Ralph, but Christopher lost seven of his nine lives in these adven-tures; he would have to be careful.

In *Witch Week* (Volume 2, 1982), the children at Larwood House boarding school were witch-orphans, living in a world that resembled our modern world, but was overmagicked and still burned witches at the stake. When class 6B received a note saying SOMEONE IN THIS CLASS IS A WITCH, everyone panicked. They started accusing each other, at the same time casting spells. (Most were indeed witches.) Someone filled the classroom with birds, for instance. The authorities were on the track of the child witches, but a desperate student summoned Chrestomanci from his home world. He declared this a unique situation: the Larwood House world had imperfectly split off from its twin, so it had too much magic and the twin world had none at all. And he scolded the children for irresponsible magic: a spell that made all Simon's remarks come true could have destroyed the world—"SIMON COULD HAVE CHANCED TO SAY SOMETHING LIKE 'TWO AND TWO ARE FIVE.' IF HE HAD, EVERYTHING TO DO WITH NUMBERS WOULD HAVE FALLEN APART—THE EARTH, THE SUN IN THE SKY, THE CELLS IN BODIES." The children agreed to merge their world with its magicless twin; their magic would disappear, but each had skills that would build nonmagic talents in this new world.

Jones gives us marvelous imaginative riffs: Cat worried that his kind witch neighbor would bake him her gingerbread men: AS A RULE, GINGERBREAD MEN WERE FUN. THEY LEAPED UP OFF THE PLATE AND RAN WHEN YOU TRIED TO EAT THEM, SO THAT WHEN YOU CAUGHT THEM YOU FELT QUITE JUSTIFIED IN EATING THEM. IT WAS A FAIR FIGHT, AND SOME GOT AWAY. BUT MRS. SHARP'S GINGERBREAD MEN NEVER DID THAT. THEY SIMPLY LAY, FEEBLY WAVING THEIR ARMS, AND CAT NEVER HAD THE HEART TO EAT THEM. Jones's Chrestomanci books do have great charm, but *The Spellcoats* and Jones's other Dalemark books have soul.

☙ ☙

In Philip Pullman's *His Dark Materials* trilogy, there are subtle ideas, intense emotions, fierce energy. A dozen groups of characters from at least six parallel worlds talk and talk about the political-religious controversies tearing the universe apart. What does a ten-year-old Harry Potter fan make of all this? Many children find Pullman irresistible—his hurtling adventures and hot-blooded characters. Adults also love his elegance, seriousness, and elaborate plots. In the mid-twentieth century, Tolkien told stories that moved straight ahead: sometimes the road split into several branches, but we always knew where everybody was and wanted to be. Now at the turn of the new century, with Pullman, we know we're going somewhere exciting, but the trip is confusing. We lunge, breathless, from one plot path to another, hoping all paths will join eventually—and they do. Pullman's structure is right for his universe, where many worlds connect in complicated ways. Tolkien trudges; Pullman swirls. Both are high masters of their art.

The Golden Compass (1995) tells of eleven-year-old Lyra who lived as the ward of dons in Jordan College, Oxford, in a world like our own but different in details. SHE WAS A COARSE AND GREEDY LITTLE SAVAGE, FOR THE MOST PART. WHAT SHE LIKED BEST WAS CLAMBERING OVER THE COLLEGE ROOFS WITH ROGER, THE KITCHEN BOY, TO SPIT PLUM STONES ON THE HEADS OF PASSING SCHOLARS. In her world, every human had a daemon—an external soul in the shape of a talking animal, who comforted, encouraged, sometimes argued with its human. A child's daemon could change shape at will, becoming any kind of animal; at puberty, the daemon settled, becoming an animal appropriate to that person, perhaps a dog, snake, or bird. Someone told of once seeing a woman with no daemon: IT WAS AS IF HE'D SAID, "SHE HAD NO HEAD." THE VERY THOUGHT WAS REPUGNANT. So Lyra explored Oxford always with her dear daemon, Pantalaimon, close by.

The great power in this world was the Magisterium of the church, a dour church descended from Pope John Calvin, with factions fighting for power. The church's Oblation Board had a novel approach, based on the recent discovery that invisible particles called Dust, found everywhere in the air, did not settle on children until puberty. Dust particles seemed to contain intelligence; they fell on adults, representing knowledge and experience. They were Original Sin. The fanatic head of the Oblation Board, Mrs. Coulter, led a movement to prevent children from acquiring dust, by severing the child from its daemon with a sort of guillotine—a process hideously painful, heartbreaking, and often fatal.

Mrs. Coulter, who took Lyra to live with her and proved to be her mother, was beautiful and smart. But when Lyra overheard the truth about the Oblation Board—that they were the Gobblers who kidnapped children, to have their daemons severed in an Arctic laboratory—she ran away to the safety of her rough but kind Gyptian friends, who lived on river barges. The Gyptians formed an army to journey to the Arctic and rescue kidnapped children. They were helped by a clan of good witches and a massive armored bear, who became Lyra's friend and defender. Lyra was captured and almost severed, but escaped; she and her friend Roger went farther north to search for her father, the brilliant Lord Asriel, who was conducting mysterious experiments with Dust. She didn't know she was leading her friend into danger. Using energy released by severing poor Roger, Lord Asriel created a bridge through the Northern Lights into another world. Lyra followed, alone except for her daemon.

The Subtle Knife (1997) introduces Will Parry, a boy of Oxford—not in Lyra's Oxford, but in the world we know. Will's explorer father had vanished years earlier. His mother was a sweet madwoman, convinced men were watching her. Will protected her; when he realized there really were threatening men, he trapped the burglars searching his father's papers and accidentally killed one. Fleeing, he stumbled upon a window in the bushes, a space leading into the world next door. On the other side lay Cittàgazze, an elegant seaside city deserted by its inhabitants except for packs of children, because Specters devoured adults, feeding on their souls. There Will met Lyra, who had also wandered into Cittàgazze. At first appalled to see a daemonless boy, she decided Will, and others in his world, had internal daemons, souls, instead. Joining forces, they struggled toward their goals: Will became bearer of the magic knife of the Cittàgazze Guild—sharp enough to cut anything, even windows between worlds. Lyra, who had heard hints that she had a strange destiny involving Dust, sought out Mary Malone, a scientist in Will's Oxford, hoping she could explain the phenomenon. The particles of dark matter Malone studied were clearly the same as Dust; they were attracted to human consciousness.

The worlds were being damaged—Arctic ice melting, animals behaving erratically—because Lord Asriel's explosion, which opened a new world, had disrupted magnetic fields. Asriel was collecting an army from all worlds, to fight the Magisterium and end its repression. When Will tracked down his explorer father, John Parry urged him to keep the powerful knife and join in the coming battles: "THERE ARE TWO GREAT POWERS, FIGHTING SINCE TIME BEGAN. EVERY INCREASE IN HUMAN FREEDOM HAS BEEN FOUGHT OVER FEROCIOUSLY BETWEEN THOSE WHO WANT US TO KNOW MORE AND BE WISER AND STRONGER, AND THOSE WHO WANT US TO OBEY AND BE HUMBLE." In *The Amber Spyglass* (2000), an angel explained that the Authority, thought to be the creator, was really only an angel: "THE FIRST ANGEL, BUT FORMED OF DUST AS WE ARE, AND DUST IS ONLY A NAME FOR WHAT HAPPENS WHEN MATTER BEGINS TO UNDERSTAND ITSELF. IT SEEKS TO KNOW MORE ABOUT ITSELF, AND DUST IS FORMED." Rebel angels, tall beautiful creatures made of light, had fought the Authority and Magisterium for ages; they supported Asriel's efforts to destroy the Kingdom of Heaven and set up a Republic of Heaven, with free citizens.

Mary Malone, the scientist, hiding from church-sponsored thugs, escaped to a startling world where creatures had evolved on a diamond-shaped plan rather than a central spine. Intelligent, kind Mulefa beasts had a leg on each side, one in front, and one in back. Pullman describes in lovely detail the peaceful, productive Mulefa society. They too knew about Dust: their ecology depended on it to fertilize special trees, and the trees were dying because Dust was leaking away.

Instead of traveling to Lord Asriel's fortress, Lyra insisted that she and Will must go to the land of the dead and apologize to Roger for leading him to death in the Arctic. These scenes are very moving, first when Lyra, suffering wretchedly, had to part with her daemon on the bank of the oily river of Death; then when she and Will decided they must free the sad, whispering dead standing around bleakly for all eternity. As Will cut an opening into a living world, she explained to them, "ALL THE PARTICLES THAT MAKE YOU UP WILL LOOSEN AND FLOAT APART, INTO THE AIR AND THE WIND AND THE TREES AND THE EARTH AND ALL THE LIVING THINGS. YOU'LL BE OUT IN THE OPEN, PART OF EVERYTHING ALIVE AGAIN." Joyfully, the ghosts drifted into the beautiful Mulefa world. Lyra, reunited with her daemon and resting in a flowering grove, now fulfilled the prophecy she didn't know about: the new Eve, once more bringing the gift of Dust and knowledge to humanity, realized she and Will loved each other. LYRA TOOK ONE OF THOSE LITTLE RED FRUITS. WITH A FAST-BEATING HEART, SHE TURNED TO HIM AND SAID, "WILL." AND SHE LIFTED THE FRUIT GENTLY TO HIS MOUTH. Their union attracted the flow of Dust and healed its sickness, while Lord Asriel and a remorseful Mrs. Coulter were killed destroying the power of the Magisterium. Lyra and Will had only a few days together: people could not stay healthy in another world for more than a short time, so, miserably, they had to separate. The intricate pattern of this remarkable series was complete: a rich pattern barely hinted at here.

Tales of Joy and Pain

I did a lot of flying in the 1940s: with Mary Poppins on a peppermint stick, with Peter Pan, with the Little Lame Prince escaping his prison tower on a magic cloak. It gave me a fine, clear view of many worlds. In 1960, I journeyed through Middle-earth for the first time: just out of college, on a trip through Europe, I refused to look at Rome until I finished the last page of *The Return of the King*. In 1972, I read *The Lord of the Rings* again, at a time when I had three babies under four years old and a husband with pneumonia, and had just moved to a drafty farmhouse in February. I wasn't seeking escape, but sense and coherence. Those paperback copies of Tolkien still show me coherence, and joy. So does my childhood copy of *Mary Poppins*, with the chocolate-chip-cookie smudges on its pages. In *The Language of the Night*, Ursula K. Le Guin says, "Maturity is not an outgrowing, but a growing up: an adult is not a dead child, but a child who survived" (p. 44). She also says, "I doubt that the imagination can be suppressed. If you truly eradicated it in a child, he would grow up to be an eggplant" (p. 42).

That's why we need exploration in *Harold and the Purple Crayon*; liberation in *Harry Potter*; creation in Nesbit's *The Magic*

City, where Philip visited the toy city he had built, now grown large and stately. In Michael Ende's *The Neverending Story* (1983), Bastian entered the book he was reading and helped protect the land of Fantastica from the horrible spreading Nothingness. When he returned, the old bookseller, who had traveled there once himself, told him: "THERE ARE PEOPLE WHO CAN NEVER GO TO FANTASTICA, AND OTHERS WHO CAN, BUT WHO STAY THERE FOREVER. AND THERE ARE A FEW WHO GO TO FANTASTICA AND COME BACK. LIKE YOU. AND THEY MAKE BOTH WORLDS WELL AGAIN."

Admittedly, those who dwell forever in the land of fantasy are unhealthy. But those who never go there are like the pleasant citizens in *The Giver*: who were bred to see no colors; who knew no strong emotions; who had no knowledge of other times or places; who never questioned authority. Jerome Bruner (in *Actual Minds, Possible Worlds*) claims that, to keep the world from chaos, people must understand

> that many worlds are possible, that meaning and reality are created and not discovered. The function of literature is to open us to the hypothetical, to the range of possible worlds that a text can refer to. Literature subjunctivizes, makes strange, renders the obvious less so, the unknowable less so as well. Literature is an instrument of freedom, lightness, imagination, and yes, reason. It is our only hope against the long gray night. (p. 159)

Our world, our experience, must include Dorothy and Babar and Frodo and Lyra, and new child-heroes who are somewhere being created.

❧❧ ❧❧

Along with lightness and freedom and joy, of course, the realm of fantasy includes pain; fantasy does not conquer or ignore the long gray night. There's a moving novel for adults (not a fantasy) that explores suffering, imagination, and children's stories, and embodies many of the themes I have discussed here: Peter Rushforth's *Kindergarten* (1980), winner of the British Hawthornden Prize, has a terrible resonance in the twenty-first century. On Christmas

Eve in England, 1978, three sons of a school headmaster prepared to celebrate with their grandmother Lilli. A famous illustrator in prewar Germany, Lilli lost her family in concentration camps; now she was recovering from a stroke. The boys' mother had been killed by terrorists in an airport months earlier; their father was away raising money for victims' families. The boys watched news reports of a terrorist group holding children hostage in a Berlin school.

This small, loving family was surrounded by a world of sorrow—the pathless forest in which Hansel and Gretel were abandoned. Fifteen-year-old Cornelius felt IN THE DARKNESS AND COLD AIR, AS IF HE WERE AT THE EDGE OF THE EARTH, FACING OUT AT UNMAPPED AND DESOLATE REGIONS STRETCHING ENDLESSLY AWAY. He had been reading heartbreaking letters from the 1930s, found in a school cupboard: Jewish parents were trying to arrange for their children to escape from Germany to the school. Cornelius's misery—for his family and for the world—was incurable, but he and his brothers and grandmother responded to chaos by shaping it with stories, songs, and ceremonies.

Theirs had been a home of art and celebrations; just before the mother was killed, they had an evening of Victorian music and readings. Now the household was a fabric torn but knit together by jokes, concerts, Dungeons-and-Dragons games, and quotations from *Winnie-the-Pooh* and other children's books. The Jewish grandmother created an elaborate "German Christmas Eve." After her stroke, Cornelius had helped her find her way back to health through maps, puzzles, and games of Twenty Questions. She was able to fight against the long gray night by returning to her painting. *Kindergarten* includes, first, a horrible version of *Hansel and Gretel* in which the witch made the children take off their clothes and walk naked into the oven; then at the end, another, healing, version saved them from the oven and reunited them with their father. This family held onto the meaning of their suffering yet moved through it—by means of story, the saving, shaping creation of the imagination.

Those fantasy books that describe harmonious worlds will always be read and cherished. The other kind will continue to describe the horrors inside cruel, pathless forests, and they will also continue to show the way out, the way for survivors to avoid despair. As in Ursula K. Le Guin's *Tehanu*, intolerable facts can be framed and faced: the suffering of the little girl raped and burned by her father and his friends; the grief of the great mage Ged, so badly wounded saving Earthsea from destruction that he lost all his powers. Intolerable truth can be examined, understood, and partly transcended.

Older children and adults can contemplate Frodo's excruciating ordeal in *The Lord of the Rings* and Lyra's aching loss at the end of *The Amber Spyglass*. Younger children can experience the initial disgust of Wilbur, the pig in *Charlotte's Web*, at learning his spider friend lived on the blood of her prey, as well as his sadness later at learning she would die alone at the fairgrounds. "OH, CHARLOTTE," HE SAID. "TO THINK THAT WHEN I FIRST MET YOU I THOUGHT YOU WERE CRUEL AND BLOODTHIRSTY! WHY DID YOU DO ALL THIS FOR ME?"

"YOU HAVE BEEN MY FRIEND," REPLIED CHARLOTTE. "I WOVE MY WEBS FOR YOU BECAUSE I LIKED YOU. AFTER ALL, WHAT'S A LIFE, ANYWAY? WE'RE BORN, WE LIVE A LITTLE WHILE, WE DIE. A SPIDER'S LIFE CAN'T HELP BEING SOMETHING OF A MESS, WITH ALL THIS TRAPPING AND EATING FLIES. BY HELPING YOU, PERHAPS I WAS TRYING TO LIFT UP MY LIFE A TRIFLE. HEAVEN KNOWS ANYONE'S LIFE CAN STAND A LITTLE OF THAT." Back in the barn, when Charlotte had first promised to save Wilbur from being slaughtered, she had comforted him with a lullaby:

SLEEP, SLEEP, MY LOVE, MY ONLY,
DEEP, DEEP, IN THE DUNG AND THE DARK;
BE NOT AFRAID AND BE NOT LONELY!
THIS IS THE HOUR WHEN FROGS AND THRUSHES
PRAISE THE WORLD FROM THE WOODS AND THE RUSHES.
REST FROM CARE, MY ONE AND ONLY,
DEEP IN THE DUNG AND THE DARK!

Readers of fantasy journey deep into the dung and the dark. There they will find the warmth of friendship and the powerful consolation of understanding.

BIBLIOGRAPHY

Secondary Works Cited

Ariès, Philippe. *Centuries of Childhood: A Social History of Family Life.* New York: Vintage Books, 1967.

Bettelheim, Bruno. *The Uses of Enchantment: The Meaning and Importance of Fairy Tales.* New York: Vintage Books, 1977.

Bruner, Jerome. *Actual Minds, Possible Worlds.* Cambridge, MA: Harvard University Press, 1986.

Cox, Harvey. *The Feast of Fools: A Theological Essay On Festivity and Fantasy.* Cambridge, MA: Harvard University Press, 1969.

Cox, Maureen. *The Child's Point of View.* New York: St. Martin's Press, 1986.

Csikszentmihalyi, Mihaly. *Flow: The Psychology of Optimal Experience.* New York: Harper & Row, 1990.

Dillard, Annie. *Living by Fiction.* New York: Harper & Row, 1982.

Driver, Tom F. *Liberating Rites.* Boulder, CO: Westview Press, 1997.

Egoff, Sheila, G. T. Stubbs, and L. F. Ashley, eds. *Only Connect: Readings on Children's Literature.* Toronto: Oxford University Press, 1969.

Egoff, Sheila. *Worlds Within: Children's Fantasy from the Middle Ages to Today.* Chicago: American Library Association, 1988.

Frye, Northrop. *Anatomy of Criticism: Four Essays.* New York: Atheneum, 1957.

Hentoff, Nat (interviewing Maurice Sendak). "Among the Wild Things." *Only Connect.* Egoff, Stubbs, and Ashley, eds. Toronto: Oxford University Press, 1969.

Huizinga, Johan. *Homo Ludens: A Study of the Play Element in Culture.* Boston: Beacon Press, 1955.

Kramer, Deirdre A. "Conceptualizing Wisdom: Affect-Cognition." *Wisdom.* Robert Sternberg, ed. Cambridge: Cambridge University Press, 1990.

Landsberg, Michelle. *Reading for the Love of It: Best Books for Young Readers.* New York: Prentice Hall, 1987.

Langer, Susanne K. *Feeling and Form: A Theory of Art.* New York: Scribner's, 1953.

———. *Philosophy in a New Key.* New York: Mentor Books, 1942.

Le Guin, Ursula K. *The Language of the Night: Essays on Fantasy and Science Fiction.* New York: Perigee Books, 1979.

Lewis, C. S. "On Three Ways of Writing for Children." *Only Connect.* Egoff, Stubbs, and Ashley, eds. Toronto: Oxford University Press, 1969.

Lynn, Ruth Nadelman. *Fantasy Literature for Children and Young Adults—An Annotated Bibliography.* New Providence, NJ: RR Bowker, 4th ed., 1995.

Manlove, C. N. *The Impulse of Fantasy Literature.* Kent, OH: Kent State University Press, 1983.

Moore, Thomas. *The Re-Enchantment of Everyday Life.* New York: HarperCollins, 1996.

Reilly, R. J. "Tolkien and the Fairy Story." *Tolkien and the Critics.* Isaacs, Neil D. and Rose A. Zimbardo, eds. Notre Dame, IN: University of Notre Dame Press, 1968.

Singer, Dorothy G. and Jerome L. *The House of Make-Believe: Children's Play and the Developing Imagination.* Cambridge, MA: Harvard University Press, 1990.

Sternberg, Robert, ed. *Wisdom: Its Nature, Origins, and Development.* Cambridge: Cambridge University Press, 1990.

Storr, Anthony. "The Child and the Book." *Only Connect.* Egoff, Stubbs, and Ashley, eds. Toronto: Oxford University Press, 1969.

Tolkien, J. R. R. "Children and Fairy Stories." *Only Connect.* Egoff, Stubbs, and Ashley, ed. Toronto: Oxford University Press, 1969.

Turner, Victor. *The Ritual Process.* Harmondsworth, England: Penguin Books, 1969.

Vygotsky, L. S. *The Vygotsky Reader.* R. Van der Veer and J. Valsiner, eds. Oxford: Blackwell, 1994.

Winnicott, D. W. *Playing and Reality.* New York: Basic Books, 1971.

Yolen, Jane. *Touch Magic.* Little Rock, AR: August House Publishers, expanded ed., 2000.

Children's Books

Since these books appear in many different editions, this list does not include publication information for specific editions. Only the year of first publication is mentioned here.

Aiken, Joan. *The Wolves of Willoughby Chase.* 1962.
Black Hearts in Battersea. 1964.
Alexander, Lloyd. *Chronicles of Prydain:*
The Book of Three. 1964.
The Black Cauldron. 1965.
The Castle of Llyr. 1966.
Taran Wanderer. 1967.
The High King. 1968.
Applegate, K. A. Animorphs books:
The Invasion. 1996.
The Visitor. 1996.
The Encounter. 1996.
The Secret. 1997.
The Departure. 1998.
Babbitt, Natalie. The *Search for Delicious.* 1969.
Tuck Everlasting. 1975.
Banks, Lynne Reid. *The Indian in the Cupboard.* 1980.
Barrie, James M. *Peter Pan.* 1911.
Baum, L. Frank. Oz books:
The Wonderful Wizard of Oz. 1900.
The Land of Oz. 1904.
Ozma of Oz. 1907.
The Road to Oz. 1909.
The Emerald City of Oz. 1910.
Bellairs, John. *The House with a Clock in its Walls.* 1973.
The Figure in the Shadows. 1975.
Billingsley, Franny. *Well Wished.* 1997.
The Folk Keeper. 1999.
Bond, Nancy. *A String in the Harp.* 1976.
Boston, L. M. Green Knowe books:
The Children of Green Knowe. 1954.
The Treasure of Green Knowe. 1958.
A Stranger at Green Knowe. 1961.
An Enemy at Green Knowe. 1964.

Brittain, Bill. *The Wish Giver.* 1983.
Brooks, Walter R. *Freddy the Detective.* 1932.
    Freddy Goes Camping. 1948.
Brown, Margaret Wise. *Goodnight Moon.* 1947.
Brunhoff, Jean de. *The Story of Babar.* 1933.
    Babar the King. 1935.
Cameron, Eleanor. *The Court of the Stone Children.* 1973.
Carroll, Lewis. *Alice's Adventures in Wonderland.* 1865.
    Through the Looking-Glass. 1871.
Cassedy, Sylvia. *Behind the Attic Wall.* 1983.
Christopher, John. Tripods series:
    The White Mountains. 1967.
    The City of Gold and Lead. 1967.
    The Pool of Fire. 1968.
    When the Tripods Came. 1988.
Clarke, Pauline. *The Return of the Twelves.* 1962.
Colfer, Eoin. *Artemis Fowl.* 2001.
Cooper, Susan. *The Dark Is Rising* series:
    Over Sea, Under Stone. 1965.
    The Dark Is Rising. 1973.
    Greenwitch. 1974.
    The Grey King. 1975.
    Silver on the Tree. 1977.
Dahl, Roald. *Charlie and the Chocolate Factory.* 1964.
    James and the Giant Peach. 1961.
    The BFG. 1982.
Dickinson, Peter. *Eva.* 1988.
Duane, Diane. *So You Want to Be a Wizard.* 1983.
    Deep Wizardry. 1985.
    High Wizardry. 1990.
Eager, Edward. *Half Magic.* 1954.
    Knight's Castle. 1956.
    Magic By the Lake. 1957.
    The Time Garden. 1958.
    Seven-Day Magic. 1962.
Ende, Michael. *The Never-Ending Story.* 1983.
Farmer, Nancy. *The Ear, the Eye and the Arm.* 1994.
Farmer, Penelope. *Charlotte Sometimes.* 1969.
    A Castle of Bone. 1972.

Garner, Alan. *Elidor*. 1965.
　　The Owl Service. 1967.
Goudge, Elizabeth. *The Little White Horse*. 1946.
　　Linnets and Valerians. 1964.
Grahame, Kenneth. *The Wind in the Willows*. 1908.
Hamilton, Virginia. *The Justice Cycle*:
　　Justice and Her Brothers. 1978.
　　Dustland. 1980.
　　The Gathering. 1981.
　　Sweet Whispers, Brother Rush. 1982.
Hoban, Russell. *The Mouse and His Child*. 1967.
Ibbotson, Eva. *The Secret of Platform 13*. 1994.
　　Island of the Aunts. 1999.
Jansson, Tove. *Moomintroll Madness*. 1948.
Johnson, Crockett. *Harold and the Purple Crayon*. 1955.
Jones, Diana Wynne. *The Dalemark Quartet*:
　　Cart and Cwidder. 1975.
　　Drowned Ammet. 1977.
　　The Spellcoats. 1979.
　　The Crown of Dalemark. 1993.
　　The Chronicles of Chrestomanci:
　　Charmed Life. 1977.
　　The Magicians of Caprona. 1980.
　　Witch Week. 1982.
　　The Lives of Christopher Chant. 1988.
Juster, Norton. *The Phantom Tollbooth*. 1961.
Kendall, Carol. *The Gammage Cup*. 1959.
Langton, Jane. *The Fledgling*. 1980.
Le Guin, Ursula K. Earthsea books:
　　A Wizard of Earthsea. 1968.
　　The Tombs of Atuan. 1971.
　　The Farthest Shore. 1972.
　　Tehanu. 1990.
　　The Other Wind. 2000.
L'Engle, Madeleine. *Wrinkle in Time* trilogy:
　　A Wrinkle in Time. 1962.
　　A Wind in the Door. 1973.
　　A Swiftly Tilting Planet. 1978.
Lewis, C. S. Narnia books:
　　The Lion, the Witch, and the Wardrobe. 1950.

Prince Caspian. 1951.
The Voyage of the Dawn Treader. 1952.
The Silver Chair. 1953.
The Horse and his Boy. 1954.
The Magician's Nephew. 1955.
The Last Battle. 1956.
Lindgren, Astrid. *Pippi Longstocking.* 1950.
Lindsay, Norman. *The Magic Pudding.* 1918.
Lively, Penelope. *The House in Norham Gardens.* 1974.
Lowry, Lois. *The Giver.* 1993.
Mayne, William. *Earthfasts.* 1966.
  A Game of Dark. 1971.
McCaffrey, Anne. Harper Hall books:
  Dragonsong. 1976.
  Dragonsinger. 1977.
  Dragondrums. 1979.
McKinley, Robin. *The Blue Sword.* 1982.
  The Hero and the Crown. 1984.
McLerran, Alice. *Roxaboxen.* 1991.
Milne, A. A. *Winnie-the-Pooh.* 1926.
Mulock, Dinah. *The Little Lame Prince.* 1874.
Nesbit, E. *Five Children and It.* 1902.
  The Phoenix and the Carpet. 1904.
  The Story of the Amulet. 1906.
  The Enchanted Castle. 1907.
  The Magic City. 1910.
Nicholson, William. *The Wind on Fire trilogy:*
  The Wind Singer. 2000.
  Slaves of the Mastery. 2001.
  Firesong. 2002.
Nix, Garth. *Sabriel.* 1995.
  Lirael. 2001.
Norton, Mary. *The Borrowers.* 1953.
  The Borrowers Afield. 1955.
  Bed-Knob and Broomstick. 1957.
O'Brien, Robert C. *Z Is for Zachariah.* 1974.
Park, Ruth. *Playing Beatie Bow.* 1980.
Paton Walsh, Jill. *A Chance Child.* 1978.
  The Green Book. 1982.

Pearce, Philippa. *Tom's Midnight Garden*. 1958.
Pierce, Tamora. *Song of the Lioness* series:
　Alanna. 1983.
　In the Hands of the Goddess. 1984.
　The Woman Who Rides Like a Man. 1986.
　Lioness Rampant. 1988.
　The Immortals series:
　Wild Magic. 1992.
　Wolf-Speaker. 1994.
　Emperor Mage. 1995.
　The Realms of the Gods. 1996.
　Circle of Magic series:
　Sandry's Book. 1997.
Pilkey, Dav. *The Adventures of Captain Underpants*. 1997.
　Captain Underpants and the Invasion of the Incredibly Naughty Cafeteria Ladies from Outer Space. 1999.
Pinkwater, Daniel. *Lizard Music*. 1976.
　Alan Mendelsohn, the Boy From Mars. 1979.
　The Magic Moscow. 1980.
　Slaves of Spiegel. 1982.
Potter, Beatrix. *The Tale of Peter Rabbit*. 1902.
　The Roly-Poly Pudding. 1908.
　The Tale of Jemima Puddle-Duck. 1908.
　The Tale of Mr. Tod. 1912.
Pullman, Philip. *His Dark Materials* trilogy:
　The Golden Compass. 1995.
　The Subtle Knife. 1997.
　The Amber Spyglass. 2000.
Rowling, J. K. Harry Potter books:
　Harry Potter and the Sorcerer's Stone. 1997.
　Harry Potter and the Chamber of Secrets. 1999.
　Harry Potter and the Prisoner of Azkaban. 1999.
　Harry Potter and the Goblet of Fire. 2000.
Sachar, Louis. *Sideways Stories from Wayside School*. 1978.
　Holes. 1998.
Saint-Exupéry, Antoine de. *The Little Prince*. 1943.
Sauer, Julia L. *Fog Magic*. 1943.
Sendak, Maurice. *Where the Wild Things Are*. 1963.
　In The Night Kitchen. 1970.
　Outside Over There. 1981.

Seuss, Dr. *And to Think that I Saw It on Mulberry Street.* 1937.
Snicket, Lemony. *A Series of Unfortunate Events* books:
   The Bad Beginning. 1999.
   The Reptile Room. 1999.
   The Wide Window. 2000.
Steig, William. *Sylvester and the Magic Pebble.* 1969.
   Dominic. 1972.
   The Amazing Bone. 1976.
Tolkien, J. R. R. *The Hobbit.* 1937.
   The Lord of the Rings trilogy:
   The Fellowship of the Ring. 1954.
   The Two Towers. 1954.
   The Return of the King. 1955.
Travers, P. L. *Mary Poppins.* 1934.
Voigt, Cynthia. *Building Blocks.* 1984.
   The Kingdom books:
   Jackaroo. 1985.
   On Fortune's Wheel. 1990.
   The Wings of a Falcon. 1993.
   Elske. 1999.
Westall, Robert. *The Wind Eye.* 1977.
White, E. B. *Charlotte's Web.* 1952.
White, T. H. *The Sword in the Stone.* 1938.
   Mistress Masham's Repose. 1946.
Willard, Nancy. *Voyage to Cythera.* 1974.
Wrede, Patricia. *Enchanted Forest* trilogy:
   Dealing with Dragons. 1990.
   Searching for Dragons. 1990.
   Calling on Dragons. 1993.
Wrightson, Patricia. *The Book of Wirrun* trilogy:
   The Ice Is Coming. 1977.
   The Dark Bright Water. 1978.
   Behind the Wind. 1981.
Yolen, Jane. Pit Dragon series:
   Dragon's Blood. 1982.
   Heart's Blood. 1984.
   A Sending of Dragons. 1987.
   The Devil's Arithmetic. 1988.

INDEX